THE
WORLD'S
MONEY

INTERNATIONAL BANKING
FROM BRETTON WOODS
TO THE BRINK OF INSOLVENCY

MICHAEL MOFFITT

A TOUCHSTONE BOOK
Published by Simon & Schuster, Inc.
New York

Designed by Irving Perkins Associates

Manufactured in the United States of America

10 9 8 7 6 5 4 3 2 1

10 9 8 7 6 5 4 3 2 1 Pbk.

Library of Congress Cataloging in Publication Data
Moffitt, Michael.
    The world's money.
    Includes bibliographical references and index.
    1. International finance. I. Title.
HG3881.M575   1983   332'.042   83-402
ISBN 0-671-44682-7
ISBN 0-671-50596-3 Pbk.

ACKNOWLEDGMENTS

Like most books, this book reflects the ideas and insights of many people. I would like to thank a few of them here.

Harry Magdoff first suggested that I take up this subject and taught me the vital lesson that no theory can substitute for an honest inquiry into the facts. Among academic economists, Robert Triffin remains the premier student of the political economy of international money. Richard Weinert answered my technical questions from his vantage point as a banker; as a student of the subject, he contributed important insights of his own. Cary Reich's superb portraits of individual bankers for *Institutional Investor* taught me the importance of people in the world of finance. The late Charles Coombs, formerly of the Federal Reserve Bank of New York and First Chicago, taught me how foreign currency markets work. His book *The Arena of International Finance* is one of the leading works in the field. Former Representative Henry Reuss, C. Fred Bergsten and Edward Bernstein gave me important insights on the key events of 1971–73. The latter also provided background information on the Bretton Woods meetings. Alger Hiss provided extensive background on Roosevelt's foreign policy and how it helped shape the postwar world.

Over the years, I have enjoyed many conversations on banking and finance with knowledgeable friends, including Herman Starobin, Stanley Weiss, Professor Edward S. Herman, Jane D'Arista, Dr. Odeh Aburdene, David Moore, Jack Blum, Michael Manley, and Norman Girvan. Among others whose works on financial affairs I have particularly enjoyed are Hyman Minsky, Albert M. Wojnilower, "Adam Smith," Paul Erdman, Charles Kindleberger,

5

Joan Spero, M. S. Mendelsohn and, of course, John Maynard Keynes.

Many bankers I interviewed may disagee with the conclusions of this book, yet a number of them contributed immeasurably to my understanding of international finance. They include Lord Eric Roll, Robert Roosa, Geoffrey Bell, Michael von Clemm, Irving Friedman, John Heimann, Ann Parker Mills and David Edwards. Trevor Adamson was gracious and helpful.

My visits to foreign exchange trading rooms at Manufacturers Hanover, Bank of America, National Westminister and Irving Trust were particularly helpful, as were my conversations with traders in these and other banks who requested anonymity. The writings and speeches of the Federal Reserve's Henry Wallich are particularly informative. For observers of international banking, Morgan Guaranty's monthly *World Financial Markets* and American Express International Bank's *Amex Bank Review* are essential. The same can be said of the two leading magazines in the field, Padric Fallon's *Euromoney* and Gilbert Kaplan's *Institutional Investor*. At the International Monetary Fund, E. Walter Robichek, Azizalli Mohammed and M. Narasimham were forthcoming.

The most important help I received was from personal friends and colleagues without whom this book might never have been written. Conversations with Stanley Weiss and Eliot Stein, Jr., convinced me that international money is the most interesting and important subject around. Dan Morgan initially had more faith in my ability to write this book than I did. Esther Newberg and Alice Mayhew believed in this project from the beginning, as did Richard Barnet. It would not have been possible without them. The same is true of the support I received from Peter and Cora Weiss, Judy and Albert Ruben, Edward and Paula Echeverria, David Moore, and Dr. Harold Kaufman. Paul Sweezy renewed old contacts on my behalf. At Simon & Schuster, David Masello provided helpful editorial suggestions and Phoebe Rentschler was generally helpful.

Richard Barnet, Ronald Müller, Orlando Letelier and Marcus Raskin gave me a start in Washington, which is all anyone has a right to ask. Robert Schwartz did the same in New York. Ash Ellefson taught me things that continue to be helpful.

My former colleagues at the Institute for Policy Studies who gave me support and encouragement include the director Robert Borosage, and also Isabel Letelier, Alyce Wiley, Mark Hertsgaard, Peter Kornbluh, Leah Goldman, Olivia Warren, Rachel Fershko, James Cox and Doris Porter. On a project on the international monetary system and the Third World, I worked closely with Ismail Sabri Abdalla, Howard Wachtel, Gary Jefferson, Carol Grigsby, Charles Hale, Pierre Moeller, Richard Kohl, Sven Hamrell, Marc Nerfin and Lynn Kitzmiller.

Financial support was generously provided by the Samuel Rubin Foundation and the Institute for Policy Studies.

Maria Enrico and Susan Chromiak typed most of the manuscript and made helpful suggestions along the way.

Finally, none of this would have been possible without the unselfish generosity of my mother and father.

Needless to say, all are absolved of the ways I made use of their help.

FOR KATHERINE

CONTENTS

CHAPTER 1

FROM BRETTON WOODS TO CAMP DAVID

On July 1, 1944, more than 700 delegates from 44 countries arrived at the Mount Washington Hotel in Bretton Woods, New Hampshire, to take part in the most comprehensive international economic negotiations in history. The Allied nations, haunted by three decades of depression, financial ruin and world war, gathered at Bretton Woods to draft a blueprint for a postwar economic order. The United States and Britain viewed the task of building a viable postwar economy with such urgency that they started to lay the groundwork for Bretton Woods even before the tide of war had turned against the Nazis.

The Bretton Woods conference, which lasted for more than three weeks, displaced many well-to-do vacationers from the mountain resort. The proceedings were dominated by two intellectual giants dedicated to a liberal and internationalist postwar economic order. The chief British representative was John Maynard Keynes, the most influential economic thinker of the twentieth century, who served as chairman. Keynes' opposite number was Harry Dexter White, the chief technical adviser to U.S. Treasury Secretary Henry Morgenthau. White was an admirer of the more eminent Keynes, yet at Bretton Woods, backed by the reality of American power, White emerged as the dominant figure. Though they disagreed on specifics, White and Keynes provided the intellectual capital for the two new institutions created at Bretton Woods, the International Monetary Fund (IMF) and the International Bank for Reconstruction and Development (World Bank). The IMF and World Bank were designed to be central institutions in a world free of war and destructive economic nationalism. As Lord Eric Roll, the distinguished economic historian and chairman of London's prestigious merchant bank, S. G. Warburg & Co., observes, "Seldom can there have been concentrated for the ordering of human affairs so comprehensive a combination of economic and political vision, of administrative and technical expertise, of idealism and interest."

After marathon discussions, the Bretton Woods accords were adopted late in the evening of July 22. The agreements provided the institutional setting for the greatest economic boom in history. In the next 25 years, more steel, autos, ships and consumer goods would be produced than had ever been manufactured previously. No serious depression or financial panic occurred. In Western industrial countries, personal income grew substantially, creating mass consumer societies that were a far cry from the spectacle of desperate men selling apples on steet corners. The United States benefited disproportionately from the Bretton Woods arrangements and became the wealthiest nation in the history of the world. Europe and Japan would recover from wartime devastation to challenge U.S. industrial supremacy within a generation. Even some Third World countries, such as Brazil, would take advantage of the open world economy created at Bretton Woods to become industrial powers.

Neither Keynes nor White lived to see the fruits of his labors. Keynes died in April 1946 after an exhausting trip to the United States for the inaugural meeting of the IMF. Two years later, in August of 1948, White appeared before the House Un-American Activities Committee where he was accused of being part of a Soviet spy network. By that time, as a result of charges leveled against him by Whittaker Chambers and Elizabeth Bentley, White had been forced out of his post as chief U.S. representative to the IMF. During the hearings, White informed the committee of his chronic heart trouble and requested a short break every hour. The committee, noting his weekend volleyball games on the mall near the Treasury Department as evidence of good health, denied the request. Three days after his appearance, on a weekend vacation in New Hampshire, White died of a heart attack.

I

The agenda of the Bretton Woods Conference was essentially dictated by two key developments in the international economy. The first was that the United States had become the dominant global power. The United States emerged from the Second World War with an economy that was fundamentally strong and poised for takeoff. The war mobilization, rather than the New Deal, cured the Great Depression. During the war, extensive government planning facilitated a rapid expansion of industrial production and created millions of jobs. The United States, which had become a creditor nation during the First World War, had become *the* creditor by the time of the Second. United States loans to the Allies financed the war effort. After the war, only the United States had the means to finance global economic reconstruction. The United States had the power of money and also the Bomb.

Bretton Woods was also a response to the manifest failures of global economic management during the crisis-ridden 1920s and 1930s. The recovery from the First World War and depression of 1920–21 was largely confined to the United States, and even that turned out to be precarious. Germany and Austria both experienced hyper-inflations during the 1920s that rendered their currencies worthless. Later, the German preoccupation with fighting inflation led to high unemployment and low wages, both grist for Hitler's mill. In Britain, a nostalgic attachment to laissez-faire and obsession with maintaining a high value for the pound led to high unemployment and economic stagnation. After the American stock market crash of October 1929 and the European financial crisis of 1931, the international economy wound down in a spiral of falling prices, falling production, bankruptcies and rising unemployment. The collapse was fueled by protectionism and other forms of economic nationalism. The United States went protectionist with the Hawley-Smoot tariff of 1930 and this led to retaliatory measures abroad. World trade contracted violently, further disrupting production. Total world exports fell from $33 billion in 1928 to $13 billion four years later.

To a great extent, the mission of Bretton Woods was to create an international environment in which the United States could act as an engine for global recovery. In 1931, Keynes had declared that "the world will never be prosperous without a trade recovery in the United States." While influential figures on both sides of the Atlantic voiced fears that a new depression would follow the war, there was general agreement that the U.S. economy would be stronger than others. If prosperity did not spread beyond American shores, White and Keynes concurred, the world might drift into another depression and trade war, and perhaps a new world war.

The problems of accommodating American hegemony and fashioning effective means of global economic management were deeply interrelated. From the middle of the nineteenth century, there was a striking correlation between relative international economic stability and the existence of a hegemonic global power. Prior to the end of the Napoleonic Wars, there was no integrated global economy to speak of, only competing mercantilist blocs. Thus, there was no sense of global economic management, particularly in finance. As Charles Coombs, formerly the top international monetary affairs expert at the New York Federal Reserve Bank, has written, international finance "resembled a merciless battlefield of national rivalries with no rules of the game save the devil take hindmost." To some extent, international economic anarchy was tempered by the arrival of what Eric Roll calls "Aequilibrium Britannicum" after 1815. For nearly a century, the anatomy of international commerce was essentially determined by British hegemony in industry, shipping and finance. Britain's economic supremacy reshaped global commerce more or less on the principles of free trade. As Professor Robert Skidelsky observes:

> ... the world market of the free traders was thus brought into being by British military and naval power to serve the needs of the world's workshop and carrier. And, of course, Britain inherited thereby primary responsibility for international order.

Aequilibrium Britannicum was held together by Britain's willingness to maintain open markets and grant other countries access to the financial resources of the City of London. Nineteenth-century Britain was the prototype of a hegemonic power. She was the dominant industrial and military power and also the world's banker. Britain was primarily responsible for guaranteeing international monetary stability. The world's banker must let its domestic currency function as international money and encourage a free flow of funds through its financial system. "The way to remain an international banker," Keynes once told the House of Lords, "is to allow checks to be drawn upon you." Since money is a store of value, the world's banker must maintain the integrity of its currency. In the years before the First World War, Britain did this by linking the pound sterling with gold. In addition to performing clearinghouse functions, the world's banker must provide long-term investment capital to finance economic growth abroad. Finally, the dominant power must be prepared to act as an international "lender of last resort" to prevent depressions and banking failures from destroying the fabric of the international financial system. For all these reasons, as the economic historian J. B. Condliffe writes, the City of London became the financial center "not only of Britain and of the British Empire overseas but of the whole trading world. It conducted an immense and varied volume of financial transactions by organizing methods that made funds investable yet available. A small investor could buy a parcel of shares, place his money on deposit with a bank, buy shares in an investment trust, or deposit what cash he had in a savings bank or building society. Insurance companies or foreign banks could place their temporary surpluses in the market for use by specialist brokers or discount houses. A foreign government or national bank might keep its reserves almost immediately available and yet earning interest in the short-term market. . . . Many foreign central banks operated their monetary systems by keeping at least part of their reserves in interest-earning short-term assets in London, where gold could always be bought. Some of the British dominions went further and frankly operated what had been called a sterling exchange standard."

The coming of the First World War marked the formal end of British hegemony. During the war Britain pulled the legs out from under the old system by effectively suspending the link between the pound sterling and gold. Meanwhile, the United States became a leading creditor. As a result of the war, the locus of world economic power shifted dramatically. Britain never recovered its preeminent position. In the 1920s, the strength of the U.S. recovery plus the emergence of U.S. corporations and banks as major foreign investors made the United States the dominant power in the world economy. Yet the new realities of American power were not translated tangibly into new international institutions capable of filling the vacuum left by the decline of British power. Neither the Genoa conference of 1922 nor the London World Economic Conference of 1933 proved capable of establishing international economic and monetary cooperation. After the financial traumas of the late 1920s, the major economies turned inward and the world economy that had flourished for a century under the British disintegrated into competing economic blocs.

The emergence of the United States as the dominant economic power was not matched by American willingness to perform the functions Britain had a century before. When the economy turned down in 1929, the United States made no real effort to stop the dramatic fall in prices and production, which was the essential cause of the depression. Instead, its policies contributed to spreading the crisis. As the world's largest market, the United States and its economy determined prosperity abroad. The United States did not open its market to foreign produce. It did not supply other countries with enough credit to avert a dramatic contraction of economic activity. Apparently more concerned about the possibility of inflation than the reality of depression, the Federal Reserve clung to financial orthodoxy and refused to stimulate the economy with easy money. In the rest of the world, these policies produced what became known as the "dollar shortage." The rest of the world needed to earn dollars through exports or borrow them in New York in order to maintain economic activity. Thus the world's biggest economy, mired in depression, spread depression and deflation everywhere else. Edward M. Bernstein, one of Harry White's cadre of assistants and later research director of the IMF, argues that when the United States failed to adopt policies designed to counteract the depression, there was no one else around to fill the void:

. . . The United States, which could have taken leadership in cooperative action, was unaware of the dangers of worldwide deflation and it was more concerned about the domestic economy than about the world economy. . . . Furthermore, there was no consensus among the great trading countries on the policies called for by the great depression. Finally, there were no institutional arrangements for mobilizing the resources that would have been necessary for international action to halt the deflation.

The lesson is, as Charles Kindleberger writes in *The World in Depression*, ". . . for the world economy to be stabilized, there has to be a stabilizer, one stabilizer." By then, Kindleberger argues, Britain was too weak to act as a stabilizer and the United States was unwilling. When prices and production collapsed, a farsighted hegemonic power should have kept its markets open and loaned funds abroad to prevent financial rot from spreading. The United States was either unwilling or unable to see that the health of the domestic economy was bound up intimately with the health of the international economy.

By the early 1940s, however, Franklin Roosevelt's foreign policy advisers were convinced that the United States could not afford more of the kind of isolationism that followed the Versailles treaty of 1919. Roosevelt, who had been in Wilson's Navy Department, knew the United States had no choice but to take the lead in organizing the postwar economy. The administration began planning for the transition long before the war was over. Like most New Deal initiatives, the postwar planning process was a pragmatic blend of liberal idealism and the calculated self-interest of a great power. Despite the claims of Roosevelt's conservative critics, the New Dealers were not anticapitalist. Like Britain before it, the United States desired an open world economy with few fetters on trade and financial flows. The State and Treasury departments, though they competed vigorously for turf, concurred that the aim of the postwar planning process was to create, in Treasury Secretary Henry Morgenthau's words, "a world in which international trade can be carried on by businessmen on business principles." For the New Dealers, one important lesson of the depression years was that the market did not always work by itself; it had to be encouraged by government policy.

Drafts of different plans for postwar economic organization had shuttled back and forth between Washington and London since 1942. But at Bretton Woods the decisive factor was not the intellectual merits of the White plan versus the Keynes plan, but the reality of American power. In return for underwriting the transition to postwar recovery, the U.S. Treasury demanded to call the shots on how the funds of the new Bretton Woods agency would be used. White may have been a left-leaning idealist, but he was tough where U.S. interests were concerned. Keynes and the British were negotiating from a position of fundamental weakness, White realized this and made sure the United States "dictated the essential terms of the Bretton Woods arrangements."

The main purpose of the Bretton Woods agreements was to provide a stable monetary climate to facilitate a resumption of international trade. The aim was to establish new trading rules the major trading countries could live with and entrust a new international agency with the authority to enforce them. This was the responsibility of the International Monetary Fund. In the 1930s, countries often resorted to protectionism and currency depreciation in order to gain advantages over their trading partners. At Bretton Woods, the IMF was charged with policing the trade and monetary practices of member countries.*

In the monetary area, the Bretton Woods accords sought to achieve both stability and flexibility. In the nineteenth and early twentieth centuries, most major nations tied their currencies to gold. Under the gold standard, which was the darling of the London financial establishment, the volume of currency in circulation was limited by the nation's gold supply. Keynes had long argued that the gold standard contributed to unemployment and depression because monetary policy was hamstrung by the limited global supply of gold. Gold, he wrote, "is and always has been, an extraordinarily scarce commodity. A modern liner could convey across the Atlantic in a single voyage all the gold which has been dredged or mined in several thousand years." For Keynes, this meant that the real economy was held hostage to the vagaries of gold production. Governments that were on the gold standard were unable to expand money

---

* In the trade area, the IMF was supplemented in 1947 by the signing of the General Agreement on Tariffs and Trade.

supplies to counter business downturns or pursue other social goals, such as expanding services to the poor. At bottom it was a gimmick to control government spending. Keynes attacked the gold standard as "part of the apparatus of conservatism" and ridiculed bankers who considered it the "sole prophylactic against the plague of fiat moneys." Long before Keynes' brilliant polemics against the gold standard, William Jennings Bryan ran for president on a silver or bi-metallist platform.* He attacked the gold standard as the handmaiden of Wall Street bankers. In the United States, the issue effectively died when he lost the 1896 election.

In the international arena, the gold standard made it difficult for a nation to live for very long with a trade deficit. In the nineteenth and early twentieth centuries, when countries exported gold to settle trade deficits, governments were forced to decrease the money supply. This led quickly to depression and high unemployment. Bankers approved of this arrangement because it ensured financial integrity. Once governments became concerned about unemployment, the gold standard had to go. FDR took the United States off the gold standard in 1933 and it has never been reinstituted, despite some tendencies in this direction among Ronald Reagan's advisers.

The Bretton Woods solution to the monetary muddle was a compromise between the adoption of a full paper standard and a return to the gold standard. White generally shared the Keynesian critique of the gold standard, but he had to mollify the powerful New York bankers who were staunchly progold. His solution was to make the U.S. dollar a coequal of gold. The use of gold in international commerce had been declining for a long time, but to bolster the dollar's credibility, Treasury pledged to redeem foreign dollar holdings in gold at the 1934 price of $35 per ounce. As a store of value, gold and the dollar were considered equals. To enhance monetary stability, the Bretton Woods accords established fixed exchange rates between currencies. To prevent the reemergence of monetary warfare, countries had to secure IMF approval to change the values of their currencies. In the event of a "fundamental disequilibrium" in a na-

---

* William Jennings Bryan was the Democratic presidential candidate in 1896 who was defeated by William McKinley. His principal issue was monetizing silver, which he advocated to break Wall Street's power in the economy and strengthen farmers and other debtors.

tion's balance of payments, IMF terminology for chronic trade deficits or surpluses, governments could change the values of their currencies.

A novel feature of the Bretton Woods arrangements was that they provided automatic access to credit to allow countries time to adjust to economic difficulties. Before Bretton Woods, countries had to rely on private bank credits, which were notoriously unstable, and emergency government loans. Keynes, well aware that Britain would be a debtor after the war, fought hard for an IMF that would provide large overdraft facilities to its members. Representing a debtor, he wanted automatic access to international credit with few strings attached to the use of overdrafts. This would give a country breathing space to adjust to economic difficulties without throwing the economy into a depression. "Keynes' essential concern," wrote leading monetary scholars Fred Hirsch and Peter Oppenheimer, "was to create an international safeguard for full employment policies." The United States steadfastly refused to create the $20 billion monetary fund Keynes wanted. As a creditor, the United States also wanted tough conditions attached to the use of IMF money. To avoid embarrassing Keynes, Treasury did not push the issues of what kind of conditions would be attached to IMF drawings. The issue was left vague in the final draft of the accords. Since White and Keynes expected to be top officials of the Fund or the World Bank, they apparently decided to hammer it out at some later date. As a result, Keynes could go home and tell Parliament that use of Fund credit would not bring foreign intervention into domestic economic policy making in Britain. He said it was the exact opposite of the gold standard. White, for his part, wrote in *Foreign Affairs* six months after the meeting that the IMF would not simply dole out money to debtor countries. The Fund, he asserted, would force countries to take measures that under the gold standard would have happened automatically.

II

Despite the painful lessons of the 1930s, congressional approval of the Bretton Woods accords was by no means automatic. At times, the agreement seemed destined to share the fate of the League of Nations. Isolationist sentiments ran deep in Congress. Initially, Wall Street was adamantly opposed to the agreements, particularly U.S. membership in the IMF. New York bankers were repelled by the thought that the U.S. government would bankroll an international institution that would undermine their monopoly over the international credit business. They despised the Keynesian concept of automatic overdrafts and believed it would sanction fiscal irresponsibility. In general, they were suspicious of FDR's global economic planners. Conservatives were enraged that the Soviet Union would be participating in the Bretton Woods organizations. As Jews, Morgenthau and White were both susceptible to conservative charges that they had "foreign" interests at heart.

To counter the technical and political criticisms of the Bretton Woods accords, Treasury mounted a major campaign to drum up support for the agreements. They argued that the Bretton Woods institutions were essential to the restoration of economic confidence and were thus in the interests of American business. Morgenthau warned that failure to ratify Bretton Woods could lead to a new series of catastrophes like those of the 1930s. In the January 1945 issue of *Foreign Affairs,* he wrote:

> . . . One important reason for the sharp decline in international trade in the 1930s and the spread of depression from country to country was the growth of the twin evils of international economic aggression and monetary disorder. . . . It is necessary only to recall the use of exchange controls, competitive currency depreciation, multiple clearing practices, blocked balances, bilateral clearing arrangements and the host of other restrictive and discriminatory devices to find the causes for the inadequate recovery in international trade in the decade before the war.

Preventing the use of these "restrictive and discriminatory devices," he argued, would be the responsibility of the IMF. Writing in the same issue, White asserted that the IMF would enforce global financial discipline, not undermine it.

Morgenthau and White also believed that economic cooperation enhanced the prospects for peace. They were confirmed partisans of what would later become known as détente. They argued that encouraging the Soviet Union to participate in the postwar organizations would give them a stake in economic cooperation and thus advance the cause of world peace. As Morgenthau wrote:

> The United States is as indubitably a capitalist country as Russia is a socialist one. Yet both agree not only on the desirability of promoting monetary stability and international investments but on the means required to realize these ends. . . . I am firmly convinced that capitalist and socialist societies can coexist, as long as neither resorts to destructive practices and as long as both abide by the rules of international economic fair play.

In the end, Treasury's hard sell prevailed. The bankers, weakened politically and economically by the depression, finally accepted the agreement because they really had no alternative. On more than one occasion, Treasury threatened to revive Roosevelt's campaign against the "economic royalists" if the bankers blocked the accords. To ensure passage, however, Treasury agreed to a compromise that created a National Advisory Council on International Monetary and Financial Problems, chaired by the Treasury secretary and including, among others, the secretary of state and the chairman of the Federal Reserve Board. The U.S. representatives to the Bank and the Fund would be required to consult with the National Advisory Council before voting on important issues. Through their contacts at State and the Federal Reserve, the bankers would be able to keep track of White, who had wide support as the first U.S. executive director of the Fund.*

Despite the objections of the bankers, the Bretton Woods agreements easily passed both houses of Congress. In April 1946, the Bank and the Fund set up shop with an inaugural meeting in Savannah, Georgia. Despite Keynes' protests, the United States wanted both institutions located in Washington, where the State and Treasury departments could look after them. The United States, which provided the bulk of the funding for the Bretton Woods institutions, bargained hard to insure that real power over

---

* In retrospect, it is ironic that the bankers directed most of their ire at the Fund, which turned out to be much more conservative than the World Bank. Three decades later, the IMF was bailing out New York banks from precarious loans they had made all over the globe.

decision making in both would be vested with the Executive Board, in which the U.S executive director had a veto, rather than in the hands of international civil servants. The voting power on the boards of both was apportioned so that the U.S. executive director could veto any major policy measure, a privilege the United States still retains.

One important source of U.S. power in the Fund was the fact that White, the first U.S. executive director to the IMF, stacked the Fund staff with his cadre of economists from Treasury, including Frank Coe, Edward Bernstein and Irving Friedman. Given the vague wording of many key Bretton Woods resolutions, control over the staff was a crucial element in shaping the policies of the new institution.

The Fund was destined to be the key institution in the Bretton Woods order, but the final accords also created the less controversial International Bank for Reconstruction and Development. Though congressmen complained about foreign "give-away" programs, there was general agreement that large-scale reconstruction aid would be necessary to rebuild Europe. The Bank was designed to facilitate reconstruction by lending to devastated areas to rebuild roads, bridges and other essential infrastructure. To ensure good behavior by the borrowers, countries that wanted to borrow from the World Bank had to join the IMF first. Like the Fund, the bank was indelibly an American institution. The United States put up most of the seed money, and the Bank's financial survival depended on the success of its bond issues on Wall Street. The best way to ensure a favorable reception was to put men in charge of the Bank whom Wall Street knew and trusted. Accordingly, bankers Eugene Meyer, Eugene Black and Wall Street lawyer John McCloy were its first presidents.

III

Like Aequilibrium Britannicum before it, Aequilibrium Americanum depended upon the political, economic and military power of the United States. After the war, the U.S. dollar was the only currency generally acceptable in international commerce. Wall Street became the world's preeminent market for raising long-term capital. Once reconstruction took root, the United States became the biggest market for the world's output. The substantial U.S. military presence in Europe and Asia provided allies with protection against the "Soviet threat" and homegrown radical movements that threatened U.S.-backed regimes.

Despite their positive features, the Bretton Woods arrangements were still defective in important respects. It is an exaggeration to say that they effectively bridged the transition to the postwar recovery. Keynes had been right. The IMF and World Bank were too small to do what they were supposed to do: provide the huge sums needed to finance the European recovery. By early 1947 the recovery in Europe was faltering and the Fund and Bank were proving inadequate to do much about it. The main problem was the old "dollar shortage" which had helped strangle the world economy during the two world wars. The United States had a disproportionate share of the world's productive capacity and more modest import needs than many of its trading partners. The problem intensified immediately after World War II. In 1946 and 1947, the United States ran a large trade surplus while the rest of the world used its meager gold and foreign currency holdings to purchase U.S. products. If this pattern had persisted, Europe would have been bankrupt in no time. With Europe unable to buy U.S. products, the United States would have had to cut back production and would have sunk into recession. Once a new recession had begun, no one could estimate how bad it might become.

Like the Anglo-American loan that kept Britain from bankruptcy in 1946, the problem of financing reconstruction on the Continent was destined to be solved outside the World Bank-IMF complex. What saved the shaky postwar recovery was not the Bretton Woods arrangement, but the cold war. This resulted in the Marshall Plan. In 1945 it would have been inconceivable for Congress to approve a large give-away program to finance the rebuilding of Europe. But that changed with rising United States-Soviet tensions. As Professor Fred Block points out:

The Marshall Plan became possible only in the worsening international political climate of 1947. Without the intensification of the Cold War, it would have been impossible to contemplate sending such a massive aid program to Congress.

Basically, Truman presented the Marshall Plan as essential to preventing Communist domination of Europe. He exploited the challenges to U.S.-backed regimes in Greece and Turkey to raise the specter of Soviet belligerence in Europe and thereby justify a massive new aid program for America's allies. In June 1947 Secretary of State George Marshall announced the European recovery program in his commencement address at Harvard.

During the short life of the Marshall Plan, the United States shipped more resources abroad than the World Bank and the IMF were worth. From mid-1948 to 1952, the Marshall Plan provided over $12 billion in loans and grants to Europe and Japan. By contrast, during the same period, the IMF and World Bank expended less than $3 billion combined. As Thomas Balogh, the noted British economist, has written:

> The dollar shortage . . . was resolved by a new element in the international political situation . . . the growing antagonism of the two giant states which were left dominant, each in its own sphere, after the conflict which shattered the strengths of Europe. It took $84,000 millions of grants and loans . . . or 15 times the original dollar component of the IMF and 6½ times the total maximum lending power of the Bank; and military expenditures and supply grants abroad of an average of well over $5,000 millions per annum since 1952 to restore balance.

The Marshall Plan proved to be the starting point for the European recovery. In *The World After Keynes,* Eric Roll points out that as a result of the Marshall Plan,

> . . . productive capacity and output had been greatly increased, standards of living were improved, barriers to trade within Europe were considerably reduced, and conditions created for a major step forward in the liberalization of trade between Europe and the rest of the world. Balance of payments positions were made much healthier, internal financial stability was restored in large measure, and, in general, an environment was created in which the higher hopes that had inspired the Bretton Woods Agreements no longer seemed utterly impossible of fulfillment.

Once the Marshall Plan got rolling, the Bretton Woods monetary system began to operate. The system's most important achievement was establishing the dollar as the world's key currency. International trade and investment are impossible without international money. By the end of the war the only currency that could perform that function was the dollar. The gold-dollar system was clearly superior to the classical gold standard because, unlike gold, dollars could be created to expand world trade. Dollars flowed out of the United States in ever larger amounts to finance military bases, aid programs, overseas investments by U.S. corporations and foreign bank loans. The dollar was considered "as good as gold" by businessmen and governments. When the Soviet Union bought and sold on the world market, it used dollars. Most countries used dollars for their foreign currency reserves.

The United States created new international money through balance of payments deficits. The balance of payments, briefly defined, is the difference between what a country buys from abroad in any given year and what it sells.* If a country sells more abroad than it buys, it has a balance of payments surplus. When the reverse is true, it runs a deficit. U.S. balance of payments deficits became a regular feature of the postwar economy. Robert Solomon, formerly the Federal Reserve's top international economist, calculates that out of the $8.5 billion increase in international money during the 1950s, U.S. balance of payments deficits provided about $7 billion.

These deficits averaged $1.1 billion per year from 1949 through 1959. By definition, the reserves of the rest of the world increased by the same amount. . . . Thus the United States took on one major role of the world central bank, fulfilling a function left unspecified in the Bretton Woods agreement: the United States created international money by expanding its liquid liabilities to the rest of the world.

Just as the adoption of Keynesian policy techniques in the major industrialized countries hastened the recovery from war and de-

---

* The balance of payments is normally divided into the current account and capital account. The current account consists of merchandise trade and services (including repatriated profits from multinational corporations' overseas operations). The capital account measures flows of loans and capital.

pression, the United States stimulated the world economy by spending more abroad than it took in. Success was not long in coming. In John Kenneth Galbraith's words:

> By the mid-50s . . . the European economies had been fully restored and more. Exports were again in a reasonable relationship to imports. . . . A sensible substitute for the gold standard seemed to have been found. Presently, as with the gold standard before the two wars, the basic arrangements—fully convertible currencies among the major industrialized countries, occasional difficulties bridged by borrowing from the IMF, occasional major adjustments—were taken for granted. Thus, as before 1914, although now with a somewhat diminished role for gold, international monetary arrangements seemed, on the whole, to have been solved.

Until the late 1950s, the Bretton Woods monetary system worked reasonably well. While economists generally celebrated the end of the dollar shortage, Professor Robert Triffin of Yale saw storm clouds approaching. In compelling testimony before the Congressional Joint Economic Committee in 1959, Triffin argued that the Bretton Woods system was congenitally weak. The mechanism responsible for its success, chronic U.S. balance of payments deficits, carried the seeds of the system's destruction. The essence of what became known as the Triffin Dilemma was that the U.S. balance of payments deficit could not serve indefinitely as a source of new international money while the United States maintained the link between the dollar and gold. If the hemorrhage of dollars stopped, the old dollar shortage would reappear and strangle world trade. Alternatively, a steady flow of dollars out of the United States would create an excess of dollars abroad, prompting foreign governments to cash in their dollars for gold. Treasury's gold stock would shrink, undermining confidence in the ability of the United States to maintain the gold pledge, thus leading to an international monetary crisis.

The second horn of the Triffin Dilemma eventually wrecked the Bretton Woods system. As early as 1960, the amount of gold owned by the U.S. Treasury was less than the supply of dollars held abroad. The dollar shortage had turned into a dollar glut. During the 1960 presidential campaign, speculation in gold broke out when rumors circulated that the growing imbalance between dollars and gold would force the United States to suspend gold sales or devalue the dollar by raising the price of gold. In October, speculation on the London gold market pushed the price of gold over $40. Once elected, President Kennedy hastened to reassure the world's financiers that the United States would adhere to the Bretton Woods gold pledge.

As the 1960s wore on, the situation grew steadily worse. The U.S. gold supply continued to shrink while foreign dollar holdings soared. The root of the problem was the large and growing U.S. deficits. In the first half of the 1960s, U.S. balance of payments deficits averaged $742 million per year. From 1965 to 1969, they ballooned to $3 billion annually. The U.S. balance of payments veered out of control for two main reasons, both related to the decline of U.S. power. First, by the mid-1960s, Europe and Japan had reemerged as formidable economic competitors and challenged U.S. industrial supremacy. West Germany and Japan were competing effectively in autos, steel, machinery, and other markets. They won customers away from U.S. firms in world markets and their imports became increasingly attractive to American consumers. The U.S. surplus in trade and service industries declined from over $9 billion in 1964 to about $3.4 billion in 1969.

The second major cause was Vietnam. Arguably the most destructive event in postwar U.S. economic history, the Vietnam War added billions to the U.S. deficit. Since the Second World War, the United States had run a big enough surplus in trade and profits on foreign investment to cover the bulk of military and other government spending abroad. In the 1950s, when the United States had a big trade surplus, the costs of managing an informal global empire were negligible. As U.S. industrial supremacy declined, however, pressure mounted on the United States to reduce foreign expenditures in other areas, such as military spending. Vietnam made this impossible.

A related consequence of Vietnam was rising inflation. In the first half of the 1960s, inflation in the United States averaged a modest 1.5 percent per year. What changed that was Lyndon Johnson's fateful decision to try to finance both the war and domestic social programs without raising taxes. The war was never popular, and raising taxes to pay for it would have increased opposition. Instead, the president financed the war by using a well-worn technique—printing money. The federal government ran large budget deficits and the administration leaned on the Federal Reserve to print enough money to keep interest rates down, leading to some classic confrontations between Johnson and Fed Chairman William McChesney Martin. Robert Lekachman, liberal professor of economics at the City University of New York, describes the results of Johnson's policies this way:

> Vietnam expenditures were piled on top of consumer and business spending already close to full-employment levels. Johnson's political calculation set in motion a classic demand-pull inflation, a typical pursuit of too few goods by too many dollars. In short order, unions began to disregard the wage guideline and prices, long quiescent, began to rise. . . . By refusing to ask his constituents to choose between guns and butter, Lyndon Johnson compelled the Federal Reserve to print enough money to finance both.

Inflation shot up from 1.9 percent in 1965 to 4.7 percent in 1968. The war and declining U.S. industrial supremacy fed on each other. Growing domestic inflation priced many U.S. manufactured products out of the market. The penetration of the U.S. market by imports was especially pronounced in automobiles, machinery and textiles. The balance of payments continued to deteriorate.

The Vietnam War dealt the Bretton Woods system a blow from which it never recovered. As the overhang grew, periodic speculative flare-ups besieged the dollar. Foreign governments cashed in unwanted dollars for gold at the Treasury Department. The gold stock dwindled; the Bretton Woods gold pledge was basically dead. As time went on, it became clear that the system had become a handmaiden of U.S. policy. The United States could run constant balance of payments deficits because the dollar served as the world's currency. To finance them, the United States printed dollars—which are essentially IOUs—virtually without regard for sound money management. As Harry Magdoff, a leading critic of the Bretton Woods order, points out, it was as if you had a printing press in your basement to cover all the checks you wanted to write. Ironically, at Bretton Woods, the United States had opposed automatic international overdrafts. In fact, the role of the dollar in the

Bretton Woods system gave the United States unlimited access to international credit.

When the United States refused to remedy its balance of payments deficits, the Bretton Woods monetary order became a growing liability for the Europeans and Japanese. Inflation in the United States reduced the purchasing power of the dollar and thus the value of Europe's foreign currency holdings, mainly dollars. Since they were obliged to maintain relatively fixed exchange rates, when speculators sold dollars, the Europeans and Japanese were forced to intervene in the markets to absorb the dollars. To buy dollars, they had to print more marks, yen and francs. To the extent that this resulted in overly expansionary monetary policies, the dollar overhang became a device for exporting American inflation to Europe.* The irony was that the excess dollars were invested in Treasury securities, helping to finance the U.S. government's budget deficit. As early as 1965, de Gaulle condemned the "exorbitant privilege" the Bretton Woods system conferred on the United States and called for a return to an international gold standard. Unable to elicit much interest in that, de Gaulle led the raid on the U.S. gold stock.

Even before de Gaulle's brazen attacks, it became clear that the Bretton Woods monetary system was on a collision course with changing economic realities. This prompted JFK's top international money man, Treasury Under Secretary Robert V. Roosa, now a partner at Brown Brothers Harriman, to assemble a multilateral life support system for the dollar. Beginning in 1961, Roosa, assisted by an obscure young economist named Paul Volcker, launched a coordinated effort among the Allies that would prolong the life of the Bretton Woods system for a decade. First, Treasury and the New York Federal Bank persuaded foreign monetary authorities to establish a gold pool to hold the gold price at $35. When speculators sold dollars and bought gold, the gold pool sold the yellow metal to satisfy increased demand. When the speculative demand subsided, the gold pool replenished its hoard. Second, Treasury sold "Roosa

---

* One study published by the Federal Reserve Bank of Boston argues that excess money creation in Germany in the late 1950s and 1960s resulted from foreign currency transactions (buying dollars) rather than deliberate action to stimulate the German economy. *Monetary Policy in Twelve Industrial Countries.*

bonds," denominated in foreign currencies, which allowed foreign governments to reduce their dollar holdings. The Roosa bonds also substituted for gold transfers. In early 1962, Treasury also authorized the New York Fed to initiate foreign currency "swap lines" with foreign central banks. At the New York Fed, foreign exchange expert Charles Coombs and his traders used the foreign currencies to buy dollars and relieve the dollar glut.

Later, under President Johnson, the United States endorsed an IMF plan to create a new international currency known as Special Drawing Rights or "paper gold." SDRs were descendants of an international currency unit known as "bancor" which Keynes had proposed in the early 1940s as the basis for the postwar monetary order. In 1968, the industrialized countries authorized the IMF to create SDRs to supplement the dollar and gold as international money. The hope of Triffin and other SDR advocates was that SDRs would eventually replace the dollar as the world's key international currency unit, thus relieving the key source of pressure on the monetary system. After four years of negotiations, the SDR scheme that finally emerged was considerably more modest. The SDR became a mere addition to the stock of international money, not a replacement for the dollar or gold.

The quantity of SDRs remained small relative to the global supply of dollars. Over the period 1970–72, about $9.5 billion worth of SDRs were created, compared to more than $40 billion in foreign hands. Although the creation of SDRs legitimized the concept of an international currency, they were no solution to the problems of the Bretton Woods system. As S. M. Mendelsohn of *The Banker* writes in *Money on the Move,* the SDR was "too late, too small and too timid in its conception to save the system." This suited bankers because, since the time of Keynes, they viewed this sort of thing as a scheme to flood the world with funny money. To allay the bankers' fears, the new SDRs were allocated according to an old biblical principle: "to them that hath shall be given." Most of the new SDRs were allocated to the five countries that controlled the IMF's purse strings: the United States, Britain, France, West Germany and Japan. Of this, the bulk went to the U.S. Treasury.

While Roosa's efforts were an outstanding display of financial statesmanship, ultimately none of his innovations proved capable of treating the essential defects of the Bretton Woods system.* They treated only symptoms. Even when Treasury resorted to direct controls on capital flows out of the United States in 1968, the underlying situation continued to deteriorate. When there was no improvement in the U.S. balance of payments, the dollar overhang bulged until it defied management. There were simply too many dollars in the world's money markets. Money markets function like any market. When the supply of any commodity regularly exceeds demand, the price falls. Despite periodic European currency revaluations, the dollar remained artificially high because of the IMF's fixed rate system. Like the pound before it, the dollar was destined to be devalued. The only question was when.

IV

On Friday, August 13, 1971, William Safire, the *New York Times* columnist who was formerly a speechwriter for Richard Nixon, was seated next to Herbert Stein, chairman of Nixon's Council of Economic Advisers, in a helicopter bound for Camp David. That day, Treasury Secretary John Connally, who had flown to Texas for the weekend, turned around and came back to join the president, Connally's deputy Paul Volcker, Federal Reserve Chairman Arthur Burns and others at the presidential retreat in Maryland's Catoctin Mountains. On the way to Camp David, Stein told Safire that "this could be the most important weekend in the history of economics since March 4, 1933," when FDR closed the banks and took the United States off the gold standard.

The events which led up to the historic weekend in August 1971 were in motion long before Richard Nixon entered the White House. Nixon did not create the dollar problem. Like the Vietnam War, he inherited it from his predecessors. The roots of the dollar

* In 1966, after he left government service, Roosa told Fred Hirsch of *The Economist* that European complaints were not unreasonable. As Roosa put it, "the uses that we, at least in the United States, made of our reserve currency position were in some measure abuses.... Our own deficits were running too large for too long.... I would say that much of the European criticism has a grain of truth in it."

problem, the war and declining U.S. competitiveness, were not solved by the election. Despite reduced American casualties, the war continued to be a major drain on the U.S. balance of payments. Meanwhile, the U.S. trade surplus deteriorated. In 1971, for the first time in decades, the U.S. trade balance would actually be in the red. Unlike the Roosa days, however, Nixon's economic advisers sought to turn adversity into a strategic advantage. If a devaluation of the dollar was inevitable, Nixon and Connally concluded, why accept it as a humiliating defeat, when it could be presented as a triumph of American power. As National Security Adviser Henry Kissinger saw it, "we were strong in monetary affairs; our partners were increasingly powerful commercially." Under Nixon, the United States sought to exploit the central role of the dollar in the world economy to nullify growing European and Japanese economic strength. This was blunt dollar diplomacy.

The international monetary situation had stabilized briefly in 1969 and 1970, leading to a false sense of optimism about the future of the Bretton Woods arrangements. In reality, stability was a by-product of the U.S. recession. President Johnson's belated 1968 tax increase and tight money, engineered by Federal Reserve Chairman William McChesney Martin, slowed the economy down in 1969 and produced a recession in 1970. This reduced U.S. demand for imports and improved the trade balance by about $2 billion in 1970. More importantly, high interest rates in the United States attracted sizable flows of dollars from abroad, reducing the pressure of the dollar overhang.

By 1971, however, Nixon had had enough of recession and high interest rates. Although thought by many to be a traditional conservative, Nixon quickly embraced Keynes to end the 1970 recession. He turned out to be an even bigger spender than Lyndon Johnson. Charles Coombs, a traditional Republican who, from the foreign exchange desk at the New York Fed, observed Nixon's conversion, recalled that Nixon got a good deal of help from his newly appointed Federal Reserve chairman, Arthur Burns, also thought to be a conservative. In his book, *The Arena of International Finance,* Coombs writes that when Burns was sworn in in 1970, Nixon beseeched him, "Dr. Burns, please give us some money," which he did. Easy money and bigger budget deficits were on the way. That

meant more inflation in the United States and a worsening competitive position for U.S. products. As Coombs wrote:

> . . . the budget deficit ballooned out to $23 billion in fiscal 1971 from the
> surplus of $3 billion registered in 1969. Meanwhile the price-wage spiral
> gained momentum as the administration rejected any form of incomes
> policies. Thus the competitive strength of the U.S. in world markets
> continued to erode.

While Nixon shocked many Republicans when he declared himself
a Keynesian in 1971, he was only confirming something that was already established in practice.

The outcome of the Nixon-Burns policies was identical to that of
Johnson's guns and butter policies. As interest rates declined, dollars flowed out of the United States, the trade surplus evaporated
and the balance of payments deteriorated. At a time when Europe's
and Japan's appetites for dollars were waning, Nixon's policies were
forcing them to accumulate even more. The size of the dollar overhang swelled from less than $50 billion in 1970 to more than $67
billion in 1971. Most of the dollars eventually wound up in the
vaults of European central banks. The dollar holdings of foreign
governments soared from less than $24 billion in 1970 to over $50
billion in 1971.

The big difference between Nixon and Johnson, however, was
how they dealt with the dollar problem. In the Roosa years, the
quid pro quo Europe demanded for accumulating dollars was cooperative intervention in the currency markets to maintain fixed exchange rates. Under Nixon, there was no pretense of cooperation
with the Allies. Nixon and Connally adopted an explicit policy of
"benign neglect" toward the dollar. The mechanisms that Roosa
put in place to contain the dollar crisis were dismantled. When
Arthur Burns, a statistician who had little experience with international finance, took over at the Fed, he froze Coombs and the New
York Fed staff out of all but the most mundane policy discussions.
Behind this pronounced shift in U.S. policy was a conviction that
the Bretton Woods monetary arrangements had become a serious liability for the United States. Nixon and Connally blamed the U.S.
payments deficit on the Bretton Woods fixed exchange rate system.
In those days, the gospel in Washington was that, despite periodic

revaluations of the German mark, the U.S. deficit resulted from an artificially overvalued dollar. The traditional solution to this problem would have been a dollar devaluation. But if the world's banker devalued, particularly in the midst of a losing war effort, it might have been interpreted as a sign of weakness. Therefore, the political challenge was to turn the dollar problem into a bargaining chip. A group of advisers around Nixon, including Connally, Labor Secretary George Shultz, and leading monetarist economist Milton Friedman of the University of Chicago, convinced the president that the dollar problem was a club the United States could brandish to get trade concessions out of Europe and Japan. One of these advisers, Professor Hedrick Houthakker of Harvard, later explained the administration's dollar policy in the *Wall Street Journal:*

> [It] was aimed at forcing a depreciation of our overvalued dollar. At that time, there was no possibility of devaluating the dollar unilaterally, since several countries had made it clear they would devalue by an equal amount, thus nullifying our move. These countries, therefore, *had to be persuaded by a continuing accumulation of inconvertible dollar balances.*

Coombs, who had been dealing with the Europeans on these issues for a decade, doubted the Europeans were ever rigidly opposed to a dollar devaluation. As an alternative to the growing chaos in the monetary system in the spring of 1971, Coombs suggested that the administration approach the Allies and negotiate a series of bilateral devaluations. Before Connally had arrived in Washington, Paul Volcker tried to initiate multilateral discussions on the subject. But Volcker served under a weak Treasury secretary, Chicago banker David Kennedy, and the discussions never got off the ground. Once Connally took over, Volcker, sensing which way the wind was blowing, contented himself with just keeping lines of communication with the Allies open. When Pierre-Paul Schweitzer, the French managing director of the IMF, suggested that the United States devalue the dollar by 8 percent, Connally would not hear of it.

The Nixon administration's account of the dollar problem was also highly selective. The overvalued dollar did hurt some U.S. exports, but it had also been a boon to U.S. multinational companies operating abroad. For U.S. multinationals, foreign investment and overseas production are much more important than exports. When the multinationals changed their overvalued dollars for local currencies, they were able to buy foreign plants, equipment and labor at a substantial discount. Moreover, the international role of the dollar was an integral part of the entire Bretton Woods arrangement which financed years of domestic prosperity in the United States. So the image Nixon created of the United States struggling to remain solvent in a hostile trade and exchange rate regime was not altogether accurate.

Nixon and Connally were using aggressive nationalistic economic policies to try to restore a world that could not be restored. Much of the U.S. deficit was rooted in overseas military and aid expenditures that the United States could no longer afford, except within the framework of the dollar-based system. As for declining American competitiveness, the problem was real, but devaluation was not a simple panacea. The United States had such a huge lead in technology and productivity at the end of the Second World War, other nations were bound to close the gap sooner or later. In some markets, such as automobiles, price is not the key determinant of consumer behavior. If people believe Toyotas and Hondas are superior to Fords and Chryslers, they may be willing to pay higher prices for them. It would probably take a massive price rise to change their minds. Finally, by the 1970s, some U.S. industries, such as steel, were so senile that no currency devaluation could restore the U.S. competitive position.

As the effects of the Nixon budget deficits and the Fed's easy money filtered through the economy in early 1971, the U.S. trade picture deteriorated rapidly while inflation rose. Unemployment hovered at politically unacceptable levels. Sensing that Nixon would eventually be forced to devalue, speculators attacked the dollar with unprecedented enthusiasm. In May, European central banks battled the speculators as long as they could and then closed their currency markets. By that time, it was clear, in Edward Bernstein's words, that "the dollar [was] the problem of the international monetary system." It was also clear that Connally was looking for a way to change the Bretton Woods rules.

His opportunity came in the second week of August when the

British asked Volcker to reactivate the Fed's swap lines to cover hundreds of millions of dollars they had absorbed in recent weeks. Connally told Nixon something rather different: that the British wanted gold, perhaps as much as $3 billion, which would have drained more than one-quarter of the remaining U.S. gold stock. (Nixon repeats this version in his *Memoirs.*) Coombs has called Connally's story "a travesty of the facts," arguing that no Bank of England official in his right mind would have asked for $3 billion in gold. Treasury would have said no and immediately closed the gold window. But as Coombs put it, "all Connally had to hear was that some limey wanted gold" and his mind was made up. What mattered to him was that the Europeans had betrayed the United States by refusing to accept the dollar as the universal currency and they had to be punished for it.

At Camp David, Connally dominated the discussions. Kissinger was not there and Arthur Burns argued only meekly for a more diplomatic approach. Connally's toughness and decisiveness impressed Nixon. He was easily persuaded that drastic initiatives were called for. On August 15, Nixon went on television to announce what amounted to a unilateral renunciation of the Bretton Woods accords. (Neither the IMF's managing director or the head of the New York Federal Reserve Bank, who had to face chaotic currency markets the next morning, knew what was going on. Connally did invite M. Schweitzer to his office to watch Nixon on television.) The package was called the New Economic Policy (NEP).

First, Nixon renounced the gold pledge of Bretton Woods by closing the U.S. gold window. Henceforth, foreign governments would be prohibited from cashing in their dollars for gold at the Treasury Department. Second, Nixon imposed a 10 percent surcharge on imports to reduce pressure on American jobs and the balance of payments. The domestic component was comprehensive wage and price controls. Two weeks earlier, Nixon had denounced controls as a dreaded "Galbraith scheme . . . supported by many of our Democratic Senators." The president's conversion to Keynesianism had been hasty.

Despite the wave of foreign criticism that greeted the NEP, some of the dire predictions of Connally's critics did not materialize. An abrupt turn toward economic nationalism by the United States did not result in a 1930s-style trade war. The world economy, for all its problems, did not fall apart. The Europeans and Japanese protested the import surcharge vigorously, but they were either unwilling or unable to do anything about it. The power of the dollar was real. For this reason, Nixon's NEP was a tremendous success. Nixon successfully shifted the blame for unemployment and a sluggish domestic economy to the Europeans and Japanese. When he closed the gold window, Nixon appeared a tough fighter for American interests. Domestically, the controls slowed inflation without engineering a recession in the midst of the 1972 election campaign. Professor Robert Z. Aliber of the University of Chicago observes that after the master strategy of August 15, Nixon's reelection tactics, which ended in part in Watergate, were probably unnecessary.

In the long run, the significance of Nixon's unilateral abrogation of the Bretton Woods principles was that it effectively purged gold from the international monetary system. It would take the IMF years to "ratify" the U.S. decision, but that was only a formality. Gold, after having been demoted to a coequal with the dollar at Bretton Woods, was now out of the picture. In the process, the dollar's chief competitor had been eliminated. When the international money markets reopened for business after the "Nixon Shokku," as the Japanese called it, the world was completely dependent on the U.S. dollar. It was also dependent on the dollar's alter ego: the American banks.

THE GLOBAL
MONEY MARKET

Grappling with chronic balance of payments problems and the fortunes of the world's principal currency preoccupied American economic policy makers from the early 1960s. The principal architect of what *The Banker*'s M. S. Mendelsohn calls the "financial reenactment of Custer's last stand" was Robert V. Roosa, now a partner at the prestigious investment bank, Brown Brothers Harriman. Sitting in Brown Brothers' cavernous offices at 59 Wall Street, the portly, bespectacled Roosa admits that many of his tactics were stopgap measures and that some of them had perverse effects.

The perverse developments began with a July 1963 initiative called the interest equalization tax (IET). Roosa's IET was designed to reduce foreign borrowing in the United States by levying a punitive tax on such borrowings. Since the end of the Second World War, New York had become the world's preeminent capital market. U.S. multinational corporations, international organizations, foreign corporations and governments employed Wall Street's financial resources. This was the essence of America's role as the world's banker. However, it also contributed to a hemorrhage of capital that worsened the U.S. balance of payments.

The IET was a tax levied on U.S. investors who purchased foreign bonds issued in the United States. The purpose was to plug the leakage of capital by making it more expensive for foreign entities to borrow in New York. Roosa hoped the IET and a series of measures that followed would improve the U.S. balance of payments by slowing the outflow of dollars. Instead, they ignited the greatest banking exodus in history, effectively exporting the American banking system. Wall Street quickly discovered that dollars were fungible. What the banks couldn't do from New York, they could do from London.

I

One of the main victims of the Great Depression and the Second World War had been the international banking system. A rash of bank failures, defaults and violent contractions in international trade and investment had shattered confidence in international lending. Banking across national borders ground to a halt in the early 1930s and really did not resume until after the Second World War. As monetary scholars Fred Hirsch and Peter Oppenheimer have pointed out, "The machinery of private international finance spent twenty years in cold storage."

The establishment of the Bretton Woods monetary system had restored confidence in international trade and investment. The accords established a new set of rules governing trade, finance and exchange rates that formed the basis of the postwar world economy. With a secure financial framework in place, multinational business blossomed. U.S.-based multinationals went abroad to produce automobiles, mine copper and grow bananas. Foreign investment quickly became essential to the health of America's biggest corporations. Multinationals revolutionized economic life by creating what Richard Barnet and Ronald Müller have termed a global shopping center.

The practical business requirements of running a global shopping center eventually led U.S. banks to create history's first global money market. With global markets for raw materials, labor and technology, it stood to reason that money had to be managed globally. The postwar revolution in communications technology was crucial to this undertaking. Ultramodern communications and information technology soon bound banks together in a single global financial market. Technology has linked financial institutions, savers, borrowers and lenders from more than a hundred countries. Today, banks can flash up-to-date information on interest rates, exchange rates and market conditions around the world instantly.

Walls that used to separate national financial markets from one another have crumbled. According to New York's Citibank:

> . . . the postwar revolution in information processing and communication has an impact similar to the drastic decline in transport costs—both for overland and ocean carriers—in the 19th century. With the development of rail networks and steamship services, prices for goods increasingly came to be set in international markets and the influence of local and national conditions began to weaken. Similarly, in the contemporary financial arena, international credit flows have tended to disintegrate the regulatory and monopolistic barriers that once delineated national financial markets.

Citibank's chairman, Walter Wriston, banking's preeminent globalist, puts it best when he says, "Mankind now has a completely integrated international financial and informational marketplace capable of moving money and ideas to any place on this earth in minutes."

Despite the boom in multinationals' overseas activities, banks lagged behind the corporations by a decade or so. Eventually, however, banks were forced to emulate corporations by establishing a global money market to serve the worldwide corporate network that was already in place. "Business is going to create those capital markets that suit it best," according to Wilson Gay, treasurer of Dow Chemical Company. "The thing we've said for a long time is that we're moving toward international capital markets." Joseph Abely, chief financial officer of R. J. Reynolds, puts it this way: "Having banks that are structured to operate around the world in much the same way this company does is crucial." Banks initially went abroad to keep up with their multinational corporate clients. An ARAMCO executive in Riyadh, who needs money management advice on Monday morning, cannot wait seven hours until Chase Manhattan or Citibank opens for business in New York. If ARAMCO has excess cash on hand or bills to pay in a currency it does not have, prompt advice on interest rates, exchange rate trends and money market conditions is essential. In a world where interest rates and exchange rates change instantly, slack money management can mean lost profits. "The more money you make overseas," warns New York's Chemical Bank, "the more money you may be losing." Not surprisingly, banks stress their global reach when pursuing corporate business. "When you want Dollars, Yen, Guilders or Deutschmarks or any other currency fast," states a glossy Chase Manhattan ad, "you need a bank that will instantly track down the best buy. Not just in London, New York, Frankfurt or Paris. But in Tokyo, Zurich, Bahrain. Now as never before, time is money. In the race against time, the Chase is on."

There is nothing new about overseas branching or lending by U.S. banks. Six U.S. banks had branches abroad by the time of the First World War, and by the early 1930s there were nine banks with a total of 132 branches and foreign offices. International banking contracted markedly during the depression. After World War II, the foreign expansion of U.S. banks resumed. The globalization push took place in two distinct stages. In the 1950s, only a handful of U.S. banks had foreign branches and only the three biggest, Chase Manhattan, Bank of America and Citibank (the First National City) had worldwide networks of branches. (First National City, in fact, had dozens of branches around the world for much of the century.) Between 1950 and 1965, the number of banks with global operations increased gradually. In 1950, the seven U.S. banks operating abroad had 95 foreign branches. By 1965, 13 U.S. banks had 211 branches overseas with nearly $9 billion in assets, up from $3.5 billion five years earlier.

The most popular site for locating overseas branches was London. London's tradition as an international financial center made the City a natural place to begin a foreign branch network. London branches are the crème de la crème of international branches. Of the 211 foreign branches U.S. banks had in 1965, only 17 were in London. But these 17 branches had assets of $4.4 billion, or about half of the total assets of overseas branches of U.S. banks. In the branch hierarchy, London was followed by branches in other European cities and rapidly growing Third World corporate outposts, such as Mexico City, Rio or Buenos Aires. However, these did only a fraction of London's business.

Despite the growing network of U.S. bank branches abroad, international banking in the mid-1960s was still a highly elite club. It was run mainly by the big New York, Chicago and San Francisco bankers to the *Fortune* 500. "Most banks," says Richard S. Weinert, managing director of New York's Leslie, Weinert, & Co., "regarded international departments as exotic." In the mid-1960s, Chase, Bank of America and Citibank had over 80 percent of the total foreign branches of all U.S. banks. Global business was still marginal for most banks.

What changed that was the series of measures that Robert Roosa launched in 1963 to stem the flow of capital out of the United States. The greatest international banking boom in history began when the U.S. government imposed various restrictions on foreign loans by U.S. banks. The first step was the interest equalization tax. As noted above, the IET raised the costs for foreign borrowers to issue bonds on Wall Street. The IET was highly effective. In 1963, according to data from Morgan Guaranty Trust Company, about 72 percent of all international bonds were issued in the U.S. In 1964 the percentage dropped to 55 percent and by 1968 it had declined to 28 percent. While the IET was understandable in light of Roosa's objective, it posed a real threat to the future of the international economy. The United States was the world's banker and the rest of the world needed dollars to sustain the postwar recovery.

One banker took the challenge posed by the IET personally. He was Siegmund Warburg, scion of the legendary German banking family, which opened its first bank in the sixteenth century in the Prussian town of Warburg, also the inspiration for the family's surname. Warburg fled the growing anti-Semitism of Germany in 1933, and though he never intended to become a banker, opened S.G. Warburg & Co. in London in 1946. The iconoclastic Warburg quickly showed how a small, resourceful merchant bank (roughly the equivalent of an American investment bank) could compete successfully with London's banking giants. The secret of success, says Warburg's distinguished chairman, Eric Roll, is that the bank is managed by a small group of men who seem more like good friends than banking colleagues. When Siegmund Warburg got wind of the news that the United States was about to take steps that would adversely affect the New York bond market, he discussed the implications of U.S. policy with European central bankers. He resolved not to "let the international capital market die," instead deciding to "open an international capital market and do it from

London." The day before the IET was announced, S.G. Warburg issued $15 million in bonds in London on behalf of Autostrada, the Italian government highway agency. This was a seminal event in the birth of the Eurodollar bond market. Eurobonds are bonds denominated in U.S. dollars but issued outside the United States. The IET did not affect bonds issued abroad, and the Autostrada bonds showed that a dollar bond market could flourish in London beyond the reach of the U.S. government.

Siegmund Warburg did not invent the Eurodollar market. The Eurodollar, a U.S. dollar circulating outside the United States, was created soon after the Second World War. Oddly enough, it began as a result of dollar dealing in western Europe by the Soviet Union and China. Like nearly everyone else, the Russians conducted international transactions in dollars. They wanted their dollars to circulate without fear of confiscation by the U.S. government, so they invested them in banks in London and Paris, rather than in New York. In his authoritative *Money on the Move,* M. S. Mendelsohn of *The Banker* points out that:

> The origins of the modern Eurocurrencies market go back to 1949 when the new Chinese government began disguising its dollar earnings by placing them with the Russian-owned Banque Commerciale pour l'Europe du Nord in Paris. This happened even before Peking's identifiable dollar balances in the United States were blocked under American legislation forbidding trade with the enemy, following the outbreak of the Korean War in 1950. Soon after, the Russian bank in Paris and the Moscow Narodny Bank began disguising their dollar balances too, for fear that they might be similarly blocked.
>
> The disguise and safeguarding of Communist countries' dollar balances took the form of placing them with banks in Western Europe rather than directly in New York. . . . Hence, the origin of what was at first known as the European market for dollar deposits. In the jargon, such deposits soon became known as Eurodollars. . . .

The Euromarket thus began as a kind of dollar market in exile where America's adversaries could traffic in dollars without fear of political intervention.*

---

* The illusion that Eurobanking was immune from politics ended on November 14, 1979, when Jimmy Carter froze the assets of the government of Iran in both the domestic and foreign branches of U.S. banks.

Still, the Euromarket was not a significant force in international banking until the U.S. government started slapping controls on capital exports. The IET was only the beginning. Although the IET mainly affected investment banks, it chased a sizable amount of banking business out of New York, which set a precedent for commercial banks as well.* As the U.S. balance of payments deteriorated, the United States beefed up its capital controls. As one measure failed to correct the problem, another was soon added. In 1964, the IET was amended to include short-term loans to certain foreign borrowers. In 1965 the Johnson administration supplemented the IET with two additional mechanisms—the Voluntary Foreign Credit Restraint Program (VFCR) and new rules governing corporate foreign investment issued by the Office for Foreign Direct Investment (OFDI). Under the VFCR program, banks agreed to "voluntary ceilings on their loans to foreign entities." According to OFDI guidelines, corporations were supposed to improve their balance of money flows with their foreign subsidiaries, sending less abroad and repatriating more. Since the new regulations did not apply to the foreign branches of commercial banks, U.S. banks continued to finance the foreign activities of their corporate clients. They just did their lending from London. More banks set up foreign branches so that they could compete on an equal footing with the giants that already had them. The volume of international dollar banking grew. As Andrew Brimmer, a former member of the Board of Governors of the Federal Reserve System points out:

> The introduction of the VFCR program was a major stimulus to the growth of foreign branches of U.S. banks. At the end of 1964, only eleven banks had established branches abroad—although in combination they were operating from 181 locations. By the end of September 1974, there were 129 banks with a total of 737 foreign branches. By lending from their foreign branches, and therefore outside the VFCR, U.S. commercial banks could assist their customers to comply with the restraints on financing foreign investment with U.S. source funds.

* The Glass-Steagall Act of 1933 separated commercial banking from investment banking in the United States. Henceforth commercial banks like Chase dominated the deposit and loan business while investment banks like Morgan Stanley dominated the bond market, securities underwriting and mergers and acquisitions.

The new wave of expansion that took place in response to the VFCR and other government regulations was different from the first wave of expansion in important respects. First of all, many more banks went global after 1965. The new wave of bank expansion included smaller banks from California and America's industrial heartland, whose international business was almost nonexistent before 1965. The greatest outward thrust came after LBJ made the OFDI rules mandatory in 1968. Companies shifted more borrowing abroad and the banks followed. That year, 26 U.S. banks had 375 foreign branches with $23 billion in assets. Two years later, 79 American banks had 536 branches abroad with over $52 billion of assets.

Two novel kinds of overseas bank operations characterized international bank expansion in the late 1960s and 1970s. The first was the multinational consortium bank, a new bank created by several established parent banks. Multinational consortia of U.S. and foreign banks often combined the lending muscle of the big American banks with the savvy and experience of European financial institutions. For big U.S. banks like Chase and Manufacturers Hanover, forming consortia with established European banks positioned them to take advantage of the personnel and market skills of its partners. (For smaller American banks it was a way to break into the international money game.) Many of the European banks were a fraction of the size of behemoths like Citibank, but their familiarity with European markets and customs were useful to the Americans, especially in the underwriting and placing of bonds. For the Europeans, faced with a veritable invasion by the U.S. banks, it was a case of joining rather than fighting. Intra-European consortia could also compete more effectively with the Americans. The first consortium bank, Midland and International Bank, Ltd., or MAIBL, as its placard on Throgmorton Street still reads, started in 1964 by Britain's Midland Bank, the Toronto Dominion Bank and the Commercial Bank of Australia, Ltd., was formed for this reason. Later on, Chase joined Germany's Westdeutsche Landesbank, London's National Westminster, Mitsubishi and others to form the Orion Banking Group.* Manufacturers Hanover, anxious to partic-

* Royal Bank of Canada bought Orion in May 1981, and it is now called Orion Royal.

ipate in London's booming Eurobond market, but prohibited by Glass-Steagall from engaging in investment banking in the United States, hooked up with N. M. Rothschild in 1968 to form Manufacturers Hanover Ltd. By the early 1970s, about 60 multinational bank consortia had been formed and business grew rapidly. Consortium banks were able to obtain business on the reputations of the parent banks while the parent was not compelled to put up a lot of its capital to underwrite a large increase in lending.

The second new kind of overseas operation established by U.S. banks in the late 1960s and early 1970s was the shell branch. A shell branch is not really a bank at all, but a device to get around U.S. government regulations. Between 1968 and early 1972, shell branches of U.S. banks mushroomed in Caribbean tax havens, especially the Bahamas and Grand Cayman islands. In 1968, according to the Federal Reserve, there were only three branches of U.S. banks in the Bahamas and Cayman islands and Panama. (Britain's Barclays and the Royal Bank of Canada were in the Caymans before U.S. banks arrived.) By 1972, there were 94 U.S. bank branches in the two British protectorates, and at the end of 1974, 84 U.S. banks had 90 branches in the Bahamas and 30 banks had another 30 branches in the Caymans. Before 1969, the Bahamas and Caymans did virtually no international banking business. By 1973, they had assets of nearly $24 billion, one-fifth of the total assets of foreign branches of U.S. banks, and this increased to $41 billion by 1975. Shell branches in the Caribbean grew so rapidly that by mid-1979, according to data from the Federal Reserve Bank of Atlanta, U.S. banks had 177 branches in the Bahamas, Caymans and Panama with a total of $120 billion in assets. They cut deeply into London's share of the international banking business: London's share of the overseas assets of U.S. banks peaked at 66 percent in 1969. Ten years later, London's share had fallen to 35 percent, while that of the Bahamas, Caymans and Panama rose to one-third.

The Cayman islands, 500 miles from Miami, with a population of about 15,000, may seem an odd location for an international banking center. Not long ago, according to Richard B. Miller, editor of *Bankers Magazine,* the three islands were virtually on a barter system and without much need for banks. Today, according to Miller, Georgetown, the Caymans' capital,

... has more banks per capita than any city in the world. A few of the banking offices are full-functioning financial institutions, mostly branches of international banks from Canada, the United States and England. These banks have licenses that let them do business on and off the island. The other nearly 320 banks operate offshore and are represented in the Caymans by local banks, trust companies and law and accounting firms.

The shell branches of major U.S. banks are so sparsely furnished they would make a bank in rural Iowa look like the headquarters of J.P. Morgan. No shell branch officer has any real decision-making power. Citibank's Nassau branch, for instance, is run from the "Nassau desk" at 399 Park Avenue. Most shell branches do no local business. In the Bahamas, shell branches are not allowed to have offices on the ground floor, presumably because a local resident might confuse them with a real bank. In the Caymans, you can establish an offshore branch with a minimum of $244,000 in capital and the payment of an annual fee of $6,100 to the government. One other stipulation: at least one of the bank's directors must have some banking expertise. Shell branches are, in Brimmer's words, merely "Eurocurrency market way stations." One lawyer told journalist Anthony Sampson that some of his clients demand special insurance on a business booked in the Bahamas to guard against losses in the event of a Cuban invasion. "I have to explain," he says, "that Castro wouldn't find any Eurodollars in the safe. They're all *really* held in New York or London."

The global network in place, the volume of international banking business exploded. Loans and other international business began to grow much more rapidly than domestic business. U.S. banks' foreign loans, as a percentage of total loans, grew from 3 percent in 1960 to over 15 percent in 1972. In 1965, U.S. banks had about $377 billion in loans on the books of their domestic offices and less than $9 billion in their foreign branches. By 1976, assets on the books of foreign branches had increased more than 20 times to over $219 billion, whereas domestic loans had merely tripled. The rate of increase of international business was so explosive that it soon became the growth industry of the financial world.

Foreign deposits also soared. Before 1965, only Citibank, Bank of America and Chase Manhattan had more than 10 percent of their total deposits overseas. The top ten U.S. banks had only 6 percent of their total deposits from abroad in 1964, but by 1973 about a third of their total deposits came from abroad. Even before Oil Shock I in 1973, Citibank, Chase and Bank of America had 49 percent, 37 percent and 35 percent of their total deposits, respectively, in overseas branches. Half a dozen banks, including First Chicago, Continental Illinois, Mellon Bank, Irving Trust and Security Pacific, which had virtually no foreign deposits in 1964, had more than 20 percent of their total deposits in foreign branches by 1973.

For the big American banks, the boom in international business came along just in time. As far as profits were concerned, the 1970s were dismal years in domestic banking. Inflation, the severe recession of 1974–75 and large real estate losses produced dramatic declines in domestic earnings for some of America's biggest banks. They were saved from potential disaster by foreign profits. From 1970 to 1976, for example, Chase Manhattan, New York's second largest bank, saw its domestic profits plummet from $108 million to $23 million. During the same period, however, Chase's international earnings rose at a steady rate of 17.8 percent per year, from less than $31 million in 1970 to over $108 million in 1976. Chemical Bank, Manufacturers Hanover and Bankers Trust all suffered declines in domestic earnings from 1970 to 1976 as shown in Table I below. Without this large increase in foreign earnings, some of New York's biggest banks could have been on the ropes, facing oceans of red ink and possibly failure, liquidation or forced mergers. Their salvation was large and growing foreign earnings. The top ten U.S. banks registered no growth in their domestic operations, whereas their foreign profits were growing at 33 percent per year.

In less than a decade, America's biggest banks had become acutely dependent on foreign profits. The growth of international earnings outstripped domestic earnings and quickly rose to half or more of banks' total profits. As Andrew Brimmer puts it, "a basic transformation had occurred in the character of U.S. banking." As Table 2, provided by Salomon Brothers' analyst, Thomas Hanley, shows, the ten largest U.S. banks make about half of their total profits abroad. For the biggest three banks, Citibank, Bank of America and Chase, the percentages are even higher.

The frantic pace of globalization by U.S. banks slowed after the

Table 1
TOP 10 U.S. MULTINATIONAL BANKS AFTER TAX EARNINGS
(1970–1976)

| | In millions of dollars | | | | Compound annual rate of change 1970–76 | |
| | Domestic | | International | | | |
	1970	1976	1970	1976	Domestic	International
Citicorp	87.1	112.0	58.0	293.0	4.3%	31.0%
Bank of America Corp.	141.5	201.5	25.0	134.4	6.1	32.4
J.P. Morgan & Co., Inc.	77.1	95.3	25.5	107.4	3.6	27.1
Chase Manhattan Corp.	108.6	23.0	30.7	82.0	−22.8	17.8
Manufacturers Hanover Corp.	76.0	63.1	11.4	80.2	−3.1	38.4
Chemical New York Corp.	70.2	51.7	7.7	41.0	−5.0	32.1
Bankers Trust New York Corp.	46.3	20.7	7.8	36.9	−12.6	29.6
Continental Illinois Corp.	64.4	101.0	−0.1	30.0	7.8	a
First Chicago Corp.	61.0	77.1	1.2	15.8	4.0	53.7
Security Pacific Corp.	57.4	71.0	0.2	5.3	3.6	72.7
TOTAL	789.6	817.3	167.4	826.0	−1.4%	33.4%

SOURCE: Federal Reserve Bank of Boston

Table 2
TEN LARGEST U.S. BANKS:
INTERNATIONAL EARNINGS AS PERCENTAGE OF TOTAL EARNINGS
(1970–1981)

	1970	1971	1972	1973	1974	1975	1976	1977	1978	1979	1980	1981
Citicorp	58.0	43.0	54.0	60.0	62.0	70.6	72.4	82.2	71.9	64.7	62.1	57.1
Chase Manhattan	22.0	29.0	34.0	39.0	47.0	64.5	78.0	64.9	53.3	46.9	49.1	55.7
Bank of America Corp.	15.0	19.0	21.0	24.0	29.0	54.7	46.7	43.0	34.4	37.5	43.9	55.0
Manufacturers Hanover Corp.	13.0	24.0	29.0	36.0	47.2	49.1	59.3	60.2	51.2	48.8	49.1	46.8
J.P. Morgan & Co., Inc.	25.0	28.9	35.0	45.9	45.0	60.2	46.1	47.9	50.8	52.2	57.6	62.7
Chemical N.Y. Corp.	10.0	17.0	14.2	18.5	34.0	41.6	41.1	38.8	42.0	31.7	38.4	34.3
Bankers Trust N.Y. Corp.	14.5	19.1	31.0	40.0	52.0	58.6	60.4	82.8	67.9	51.5	57.5	60.0
First Chicago Corp.	2.0	7.0	11.0	12.0	3.0	34.0	17.0	20.7	16.0	3.5	---	19.7
Continental Illinois Corp.	0.2	3.0	17.0	20.0	4.0	13.4	23.0	16.7	17.8	16.5	28.1	28.1
Security Pacific Corp.	0.4	2.0	5.0	12.0	16.0	12.6	6.9	11.2	16.6	11.0	12.9	25.4
TOTAL	**17.5**	**23.8**	**29.3**	**35.6**	**39.6**	**52.5**	**50.8**	**50.8**	**45.5**	**42.3**	**46.0**	**48.0**

SOURCE: Salomon Brothers
Reprinted with permission

middle of the 1970s, but the slack was taken up by the overseas expansion of foreign banks. The strength of the U.S. economy plus the central role of the dollar initially gave U.S. banks a large competitive advantage over other banks. In the early 1970s, U.S. banks dominated the global banking marketplace. U.S. banks' share of the international loan business peaked at about 45 percent in 1974 and now accounts for less than one-third of the total. The rapid growth of foreign banks in recent years, particularly the Japanese, has pushed some big U.S. banks out of the category of the world's largest banks. While the United States still boasts more than one-quarter of the 500 largest banks in the world, only Citibank and Bank of America are perennially among the top 10 banks. Chase Manhattan generally makes it into the top 20. Germany's Deutsche Bank, France's nationalized giants, Banque National de Paris and Crédit Lyonnais, and Britain's National Westminster are among the most effective international banks. In the international bond market the slippage of U.S. banks is even more pronounced. In 1968, six U.S. banks were among the top 20 international bond issuers. By the early 1980s, only Morgan Stanley, Salomon Brothers and First Boston remained. (First Boston and Switzerland's Crédit Suisse are partners in London's highly effective Crédit Suisse First Boston Ltd., the perennial champion of the Eurobond market.)

The late 1970s witnessed a major move by foreign banks into the U.S. market. Foreign-owned banks were insignificant in the U.S. early in the decade. In 1972, according to data from the Federal Reserve Board, there were 104 foreign bank offices in the U.S. with about $25 billion in assets. By 1980 there were over 340 foreign banking offices controlling more than $170 billion in assets, a six-fold increase. Two hundred and fifty-five foreign banks have offices in the United States, including 80 of the top 100 foreign banks. Foreign bank activity is concentrated in New York, Texas, California and Florida, where the foreigners compete directly with large U.S. commercial banks to finance corporate America. The penetration of foreign banks into the U.S. market has led to some highly publicized and acrimonious takeover battles. The leading example was the bitter struggle by the Hong Kong and Shanghai Bank to acquire Buffalo's Marine Midland. The takeover of Marine Midland, which was opposed by New York State Banking Supervisor Muriel Siebert, who had jurisdiction over the state-chartered Marine Midland, was consummated only after Marine Midland became a "national" bank supervised by the comptroller of the currency. Comptroller John Heimann supported the merger. (No sooner had Hong Kong and Shanghai's ambitious chairman, Michael Sandberg, acquired Marine Midland than he locked horns with the Bank of England in an unsuccessful bid to take over the Royal Bank of Scotland.)

II

Like any other profession, banking has its share of fads. In the late 1960s and early 1970s the biggest fad was going global. Competition presented banks with what Barnet and Müller had called "the Oligopolist's dilemma: If I don't do it others will." The specter of competition forced banks to come up with newer and more creative ways of doing business, particularly in the international arena. But above all, the name of the game was growth. Once banks had expansive foreign branches, the officers who ran them had to generate enough business to justify the costs of going global. The more aggressive banks became, the easier it was to get business. As one old Euromarket hand, European Banking Corporation's Stanislas Yassukovitch observes, "In this business, the most important thing is to be seen doing business." For Eurobankers, the emphasis on growth complemented their career objectives nicely. A rapid increase in lending and borrowing was the way to advance careers and reach the pinnacle of top management.

The history of the Euromarket is the history of the men whose careers were tied to its success. The Euromarket was particularly important for American bankers. Not only did the creation of a dollar market in London give American banks access to European markets, it was personally rewarding. Since the war, American banking had been dominated by stodgy "golf-course bankers," conservative, undistinguished men, many of whom had been burned during the 1930s and had no desire to repeat the experience. Until the advent of the Euromarket, few American bankers had achieved global prominence. Hardly any were in the class of Siegmund Warburg, Lazard Frères's André Meyer or Sweden's Marcus Wallenberg. Not since the days of J.P. Morgan or Bank of

America's A.P. Giannini did any American banker hold exclusive claim to the title of America's premier banker.

This changed with the growth of the Euromarket. By the middle of the 1960s, the golf-course bankers were being edged out by younger men who understood the need to go global. The newer breed consisted of gunslingers who were not excited by the prospects of financing steel plants or tire factories in Pittsburgh or Dayton. Cosmopolitan in their outlook, they convinced top management that the way to make money was to go abroad and that the road to mediocrity was concentrating on domestic business. The men who made names for themselves in American banking in the 1960s and 1970s did so largely in the international arena.

The man destined to inherit Giannini's crown was Citibank's indomitable Walter Wriston. Not since Giannini told a Senate committee in 1929 that global banking "is coming, gentlemen, and you cannot stop it," has American banking produced such a confirmed globalist. After starting out as a $2,800 auditor at the old First National City Bank (henceforth, Citibank) in 1946, Wriston rose steadily to the top of New York's biggest bank where he earns $779,000 today. The 6'4" giant has built the world's most aggressive bank by making loans today and worrying tomorrow about how they will be repaid. The desire to build a global bank free of government regulation runs like a thread through Wriston's career. For Wriston, the Euromarket represented the best of all possible worlds. By dealing dollars from London rather than New York, Citibank retained all the advantages of American economic, political and military power without any of the cumbersome regulations. Of the major American banks, Citibank makes more of its profits abroad than anyone else. From 1977 to 1981 Citibank made 66 percent of its profits abroad. The average for the top ten U.S. banks is 48 percent.

Wriston's first major innovation, however, was not in the international arena but in the domestic market. The problem, as usual, was how to get around government regulations. In the early 1960s, when Wriston was a lowly vice-president, U.S. banks began to lose deposits from their traditional sources; a process known as "disintermediation." For the first decade or so after the Second World War, corporations typically kept large checking accounts with banks. But Federal Reserve Board regulations prohibited banks from paying interest on checking accounts. Gradually, corporations and affluent individuals got smart and began to transfer their funds out of checking accounts and place them in other kinds of financial instruments where they could earn interest, such as Treasury securities. This forced banks to come up with new ways to attract corporate savings and thereby stop the drain of funds. In 1961, Wriston found the solution, and his eventual reward was the chairmanship of New York's biggest bank. Wriston is credited with inventing the negotiable certificate of deposit (CD). To tap corporate savings, banks sell certificates of deposit in denominations of $100,000 or more for 30 to 180 days at competitive interest rates. Wriston's invention allowed banks to bid competitively for corporate funds. They quickly became dependent on funds raised through the sale of CDs. Before federal regulators had a chance to debate the pros and cons, the regulators accepted the CD market as a *fait accompli.*

Soon the pressures to take the new instrument abroad became irresistible. Shortly after Wriston invented the CD, he hired a young Harvard anthropologist named Michael von Clemm. Von Clemm blazed his own trail to the top by proposing that Citibank issue certificates of deposit in London, or Euro-CDs. In 1964 von Clemm had received a telephone call from an official of Bernard Cornfeld's Investor's Overseas Services, then a respectable offshore mutual fund used by European investors to avoid taxes. IOS had $50 million to play with and wondered if Citibank issued certificates of deposit in Eurodollars. The call prompted the aggressive von Clemm to circulate a proposal to create Euro-CDs. At first, top management looked askance at the suggestion. Chairman Stillman Rockefeller was especially skeptical about the new instrument. He is said to have objected on the grounds that offshore deposits could become a vehicle for investing Mafia money via secret Swiss accounts. But von Clemm's persistence paid off, and in May 1966, Citibank issued the first certificates of deposit denominated in Eurodollars.*
A year later, Citibank issued the first three-year Euro-CD which it used to fund a three-year loan to Boeing.

Citibank's partner in the fledgling Euro-CD market was White

---

* At present, according to Salomon Brothers, there are about $100 billion in Euro-CDs.

Weld, Inc., an international investment bank that had operated in Europe for decades. As Cary Reich, editor of *Institutional Investor,* has pointed out, the Euro-CD market got off the ground because von Clemm persuaded his old friend, White Weld's Stanislas Yassukovitch, to make a market in Euro-CDs. The Euro-CD market really took off in the early 1970s when von Clemm, after a stint at the Harvard Business School, returned to London and joined White Weld. The father of the Eurodollar certificate of deposit now jetted around marketing it.

Today, Michael von Clemm, a tall, imposing man who wears a blue necktie with the symbols of the world's major currencies on it, is one of the superstars of the Euromarket. He is the head of London's Crédit Suisse First Boston, Ltd., the classy offspring of the huge Swiss bank and one of America's oldest investment banks. The merger was von Clemm's idea and it turned out to be a major success. The firm, as brash and cocky as its chairman, is perennially the top bank in the big Eurobond market. Under von Clemm, CSFB has not only done a large volume of business, it has been a major innovator. CSFB pioneered the Eurobond market's "bought deals," wherein CSFB as underwriter swallowed huge new bond issues on its own, rather than sharing them through traditional syndications. Recently, CSFB took the lead in issuing the so-called zero-coupon bonds, bonds sold at large discounts from face value which do not pay interest but yield large capital gains at maturity. "Zeroes" offer advantageous tax benefits in countries where governments tax current interest income at higher rates than they tax capital gains.

Von Clemm has also helped liven up London's drab cuisine by opening a string of plush French restaurants. Le Gavroche, he notes proudly, recently became London's first French restaurant to win the Guide Michelin's three-star award for excellence in French cuisine. Success in London has prompted von Clemm to launch plans for a new restaurant venture in Northern France. "It's my dream," von Clemm told *Institutional Investor,* "to be able to eat in a first-class restaurant wherever I am in the world. So if we can spawn enough restaurants, I won't ever get indigestion again."

The birth of the Eurodollar certificate of deposit was as important for Citibank as it was for Michael von Clemm. Citibank's ability to raise funds outside the United States soon came in handy. In line with growing inflation in the United States, interest rates in the United States began to rise. In 1966, as part of its strategy to combat the Vietnam inflation, the Federal Reserve tried to engineer what is known as a "credit crunch"; i.e., a reduction in the supply of credit designed to slow down the economy. For the first nine months of 1966, the Fed tightened monetary policy and this resulted in the highest interest rates in the United States since the 1920s. To limit the supply of bank credit, the Fed invoked something known as Regulation Q and refused to raise the interest ceilings that banks could pay on certificates of deposit. When their CDs matured, the companies did not renew them. As corporations withdrew their deposits, the banks faced a real shortage of funds, which constrained their ability to lend.

Citibank's response was to raise the rates it offered on Euro-CDs in London, where the Fed had no authority over interest rates. Once Citibank and the other major banks who had Euromarket branches in 1966 raised funds in Europe, they transferred the funds to the parent bank in New York for relending to their top corporate clients in the United States. Thus, the Euromarket became an alternative source of funds when U.S. authorities tightened the screws on banks at home, a mechanism used to this day.

For American banks, the initial attraction of the Euromarket was as an alternative source of funds to finance the operations of their major corporate clients. Once established, however, the Euromarket offered vast new opportunities to expand the banks' clientele. In this respect the dramatic increase in oil prices in late 1973 was a crucial development. A persistent misconception about the Euromarket is that dollar recycling began after Oil Shock I in late 1973. In fact, the so-called petrodollar recycling process was only an outgrowth of what was already standard fare in the Euromarket. When a handful of oil-rich countries began to accumulate huge financial surpluses, the proceeds had to be recycled to oil consumers. Otherwise they would have been unable to afford OPEC oil and the world economy would have ground to a halt. OPEC dumped the funds into the Euromarket and the banks did the lending. Many of these loans were not traditional project loans, but went for balance of payments support. In many cases, banks gave countries blank checks to be used as the borrower wished.

Soliciting Euromarket deposits became an art form after Oil Shock I in 1973. When Saudi Arabia, Kuwait, Libya, and a few other countries suddenly had huge cash surpluses to invest, many banks hired professional "Arabists" to visit the Middle East to bid for Arab funds. The U.S. Treasury has estimated that between 1974 and 1980, the OPEC countries placed about $117 billion into the Euromarket and another $11 billion into domestic bank deposits, or about a third of the estimated OPEC investable cash surplus for the period. By contrast, that was more than the whole Euromarket was worth in 1971. Initially, only about a dozen U.S. and European banks attracted deposits from the OPEC countries. Many bankers who made the pilgrimage came away empty-handed. "You have to drink a lot of coffee with them and be very patient," according to one Arabist who made the trip many times for a major U.S. bank. Generally, a banker on his way to Riyadh will telex the Saudi Arabian Monetary Authority (SAMA) ahead of time with an offer, for instance, to pay 13.5 percent on a 90-day certificate of deposit. Upon arrival, bankers have been known to spend days in hotels in Riyadh or Kuwait waiting for a call from SAMA or Kuwait's Ministry of Finance. When a banker manages to get an audience at SAMA, he notes, "You have to spend at least ten minutes saying hello and another ten minutes saying good-bye." Once a banker makes his pitch, it is not uncommon for him to receive an icy stare and be told, "Improve it." One banker quickly learned the tricks of the trade: "You can't go with a thin wallet or a weak heart."

Once a bank gets access to the OPEC cash mountain, the trips to the moneylenders' mecca come with increasing frequency. Trying to keep other banks from poaching on their deposits, Euromarket Arabists are perpetually occupied trying to engineer "rollovers." A few days before a CD matures, a bank holding Arab funds will telex a new offer to Riyadh or Abu Dhabi, hoping to persuade the client to roll over his CDs, i.e., renew them for another 90 or so days. With the enormous sums of money that began to flow to the Middle East after 1973, this ritual became critical to the survival of the international banking system. As of March 1981, Middle Eastern OPEC countries had deposits of nearly $20 billion in the six largest U.S. banks and another $4 billion in the next 15 largest banks. No one knows for sure, but it is widely assumed they had even more in British, Swiss, German and Japanese banks.

After Oil Shock I in late 1973, Eurobanks took prime responsibility for the petrodollar recycling process. Oil Shock I not only did wonders for the Arab oil exporters, it was also a boon for the banks. One of the best recyclers around was Minos Zombanakis. The Greek-born Zombanakis, a kind of poor man's David Rockefeller, received a degree in public administration at Harvard and broke into global banking in the Rome branch of Manufacturers Hanover. In 1968, he went to London to run the new consortium bank, Manufacturers Hanover, Ltd. Even before 1973, Zombanakis soon established himself as a gunslinger by capitalizing on the fledgling syndicated Euroloan business. The syndicated loan market is the primary Euromarket lending mechanism. Banks compete vigorously for "mandates" to manage loans for prized borrowers. Rather than assuming the whole risk of, for example, a $100 million loan to Mexico, the lead bank will telex a hundred others and offer them a piece of the loan. Syndicated loans are priced at the going interest rate, known as LIBOR (London Inter-Bank Offered Rate) plus a margin known as a spread, which is inversely proportional to the perceived creditworthiness of the borrower. (For years, Brazil borrowed at a tiny fraction over LIBOR. Once bankers got wind of Brazil's smoldering debt problems, its spreads quickly soared over 2 percent.)

Zombanakis did not invent the syndicated loan, but he is the one who put real flesh and blood in the market. Zombanakis brought numerous countries to the market who had never borrowed in international money markets before. Jetting around the world, he dropped in on companies and finance ministries drumming up loan business for Manufacturers Hanover, Ltd. In the late 1960s, when the shah of Iran was virtually unknown outside the Middle East, he was introduced to Europe's banking elite by Minos Zombanakis. As one banker told *Institutional Investor*, "Zombanakis almost singlehandedly got Manufacturers to make a loan to Iran when it did not even have enough reserves to cover a month's imports." Loans like these were extremely risky and were sold more on Zombanakis' bravado than on Iran's credit-worthiness. (Once Iran was rolling in oil wealth, the shah did not forget his benefactor. Zombanakis was an honored guest at the 2500th anniversary celebration of the Persian Empire.)

In those days, the watchword of the Euromarket was growth, and bankers like Zombanakis were more concerned about sending out new money than how the loans would ever be repaid. *Institutional Investor*'s Cary Reich estimates that in a little over three years, Zombanakis did $3 billion worth of business. After three years at Manny Hanny, Zombanakis departed to run the international operations of First Boston. Unlike big commercial banks, investment banks seldom put up large amounts of money in syndicated loans, but Zombanakis' knack for matching borrowers and willing lenders generated huge management fees for First Boston. In his first year and a half at First Boston, only mammoth Citibank put together more syndicated loans than Minos Zombanakis.

If his flamboyant style was somewhat unorthodox, Zombanakis' career in London nonetheless symbolized the Euromarket explosion. As petrodollar recycling began in earnest, Zombanakis was active on both sides of the market, gathering money from the Arabs and lending it out to other countries. Banks were scrambling to attract petrodollars and Zombanakis' contacts put him in on the ground floor of the recycling business. Soon Zombanakis was shuttling off to the Middle East, tapping the Saudi Arabian Monetary Agency's billions, investing them and earning fees and commissions for First Boston. Zombanakis arranged the first private borrowing from SAMA by a major U.S. corporation, a $100 million package for AT&T in 1975.

Thanks to Minos Zombanakis, a whole new breed of Third World borrowers joined multinationals and experienced borrowers like Italy and Mexico. Between 1972 and 1974, the size of the Euromarket nearly doubled, from $205 billion to $390 billion. Though the Euromarket's rate of growth slowed after 1974, lending and borrowing raged on. In 1973, the Third World owed private banks about $30 billion. A decade later, they would owe the banks over $300 billion.

Zombanakis is also a prime example of the axiom that a banker is only as good as his last deal. When the biggest fad of the Euromarket was growth, Zombanakis was the hottest thing around. Years later, when bankers began to get nervous about their vast loans to the Third World, Zombanakis was seldom heard from. His failure to adapt to the temper of the times led to quasi exile at an obscure London office of Blythe Dillon's INA Holdings.

Another major new development in Euromarket lending in the early 1970s was a large increase in credits to the Soviet bloc countries. "Before 1970," as the *Wall Street Journal* puts it, "Western loans to Eastern Europe would have fit into a wallet." Scarcely a decade later, according to the Bank for International Settlements, private banks had about $60 billion invested in the Soviet bloc. Western governments extended billions more in trade financing.

Several factors accounted for the rise in Euromarket borrowing by the Soviet bloc. Undoubtedly the most important was the increase in East-West trade that accompanied the easing of cold-war tensions. Following the ouster of Khrushchev in 1964, the Kremlin opened up Russia's foreign trade policy to speed internal technological and industrial development. This coincided with liberalization of western European attitudes concerning East-West trade. Italy's Fiat broke the ice with a 1966 agreement to produce cars in the Soviet Union. The Fiat venture prompted other western European countries to ignore the American commercial embargo against the Soviets and cash in on business in the Soviet bloc. Still, U.S. policy discouraged East-West trade and consequently U.S. firms quickly fell behind in the race to supply a rapidly growing eastern European market, but their interest in those markets was growing. Despite the 1968 Russian invasion of Czechoslovakia, pressure on the U.S. government to change this policy intensified. It finally did with the onset of détente in 1972. Kissinger quickly made U.S. corporations and banks avid partisans of rapprochement with the USSR. No doubt U.S. multinationals' interest in eastern Europe also hastened the movement toward détente. While U.S. exports to the Soviet Union rose briskly after Nixon's 1972 visit, U.S. firms never succeeded in encroaching upon western Europe's share of trade with the COMECON countries. Germany, France and Italy continued to dominate trade with the Soviet bloc.

Increased trade required larger financial flows between East and West. The Soviets were no strangers to the Euromarket. After all, they are credited with launching the market in the late 1940s by dealing in dollars in London and Paris. The prime Soviet banks,

Moscow Narodny and Banque Commercial pour L'Europe du
Nord and eastern European banks, such as Poland's Bank Handlowy, operate in the Euromarkets like any other bank. To finance
their trade with the West, the Soviets and eastern Europeans cashed
in on the Euromarket relationships Moscow had established years
before. Polish, Rumanian and Hungarian banks even joined pre-
dominantly Western bank consortia.

If they needed any added incentives, the banks discovered that
Soviet power east of the Elbe had a silver lining: a Soviet "umbrella" over the foreign debts of eastern Europe. The Soviet default
on czarist bonds was ancient history to the banks. And the USSR,
an industrialized country with huge oil, gas and gold resources, was
perceived to be a first-rate credit risk. One international banker put
it this way:

> Comecon's debt and debt service remain small in relation to the area's
> resources. The community has an untarnished credit record, an impera-
> tive to keep that record and the means to do it. . . . Far more important
> is the Soviet Union's interest in making sure that no Comecon member
> runs into arrears or default, for the sake of the area as a whole, and the
> USSR has the means to avoid such a thing happening.

By 1972, the banks were falling over each other to lend money to
the Soviet bloc. As in the case of bank lending to the Third World,
the intense competition in the Euromarkets was a chief factor in the
increased lending to the East. Thus William McDonough of First
Chicago Bank observed in early 1973, "Socialist countries can now
legitimately claim that they receive offers far beyond their needs for
loans." The lending included short-term trade credits as well as
medium and long-term syndicated loans to support ambitious economic development schemes, such as the Gierek rapid industrialization program in Poland.

European banks were responsible for the bulk of Euromarket
lending to the Soviets and eastern Europe, but the big U.S. banks
soon got into the act. Here David Rockefeller's role as American
banking's senior statesman gave the Chase an advantage over
archrival Citibank. Under Wriston, Citibank had surpassed Chase
in size, and Rockefeller was regularly pilloried in the financial
pages for acting more like a roving ambassador than a banker. The

Chase had suffered one humiliation after another at the hands of Wriston's bank. This time, David's global connections paid off. Rockefeller, who had been going to the Soviet Union for years, went to Russia on the heels of Nixon's summit with Brezhnev. In May 1973, Chase Manhattan became the first U.S. bank with a branch office in Moscow. Following his retirement from the Chase, Rockefeller casually ascribed his success with the Soviets to his role as the greatest living symbol of American capitalism. "The Soviets," he told *Institutional Investor*, "would rather deal with someone they consider to be a real capitalist than somebody they consider to be a parlor pink."

In China, Rockefeller staged a repeat performance. At home with shahs, Latin American generals and Communists, Rockefeller charmed Chou En-lai with a long lecture on the nuts and bolts of the Bretton Woods monetary order. Then he got down to business, persuading Chou to let the Bank of China establish a correspondent relationship with Chase. Two months after the opening of its Moscow branch, Chase had the first correspondent relationship with the Bank of China of any U.S. bank since the Chinese Revolution.

III

From its modest origins, the Euromarket has rapidly become the headquarters of the global financial system. Today, the Euromarket is a huge pool of what *Business Week* calls "stateless money" worth a staggering $2 trillion. Any borrower who is creditworthy can buy overnight Eurodollars, take out seven- to ten-year syndicated loans and the best borrowers can issue long-term Eurobonds. Though London is still its headquarters, the Euromarket has mushroomed in places such as Amsterdam, Tokyo, Zurich, Hong Kong and Bahrain, a tiny island off the coast of Saudi Arabia. The Euromarket has become a 24-hour-a-day financial supermarket which provides banks and other customers with instant access to all the world's major currencies and money markets. "The Geobankers," brags Manufacturers Hanover's London affiliate, "can lead the way for you in Eurocurrency finance worldwide. From London, Hong Kong and New York, the Geobankers provide governments, their agencies and multinational companies with access to the

largest source of funding in the world—the Eurocurrency market."
The Euromarket has transformed the nature of banking. By uni-
fying national financial markets, it has created a single global
money market. Being transnational, the Euromarket is virtually
free of all government regulations. As *Business Week* says:

> Instead of local banks dealing in a single currency in a national market-
> place—as banking used to be—there is now a vast, integrated global
> money and capital system that can send billions of Eurodollars, Euro-
> marks, and other "stateless" currencies hurtling around the world 24
> hours a day.
>
> Huge amounts of these Eurocurrencies have leaked across national
> boundaries and out of government hands, despite increasingly tough
> exchange controls that are specifically aimed at slowing the movement
> of capital from country to country. The money has moved instead into
> the Euromarkets, where there are no controls and where anyone can
> trade or invest in it.

No one knows for sure how large this well of "stateless money" is.
Bank secrecy laws are notorious in Switzerland, Liechtenstein,
Panama and other Euromarket outposts. Eurobankers fight zeal-
ously to prevent government bureaucrats from keeping close track
of how much money is changing hands in the Euromarket. The
British authorities in particular, ever fearful of driving Eurobanking
business out of London, have always helped shield the banks from
greater outside scrutiny. Thus, in gauging the size of the Euromarket, we must rely on various "guesstimates," which indicate, however imprecisely, that the market is huge. According to data published monthly by Morgan Guaranty, at the end of 1981 the "gross"
size of the Euromarket stood at $1.8 trillion. Though such figures
must be used with caution, comparing the size of the Euromarket to
the U.S. money supply provides some perspective on how big the
market is. At the end of 1981, the size of the U.S. basic money supply (M–1), which includes cash and checking accounts, was $442
billion, or less than a quarter of the size of the Euromarket. Needless to say, the Euromarket is much larger than the money supplies
of every other country on earth.

Some money supply purists object to comparing the Euromarket
to M–1 in the United States because they maintain that it is like

comparing apples and oranges. Indeed, they say, taking the broader measures of the U.S. money supply like M–2 ($1.8 trillion) or M–3 ($2.1 trillion) cuts the Euromarket down to size.* Bankers frequently object to the Morgan gross figures because much of what goes on in the Euromarket consists of interbank trading; i.e., bank loans to other banks. Thus, they argue, there is a lot of double counting. Estimates of the size of the interbank market vary, but most agree that the interbank market accounts for between half and two-thirds of the total Euromarket. Subtracting these interbank deposits, Morgan estimates that the "net" Euromarket totals $855 billion. Of this, according to Morgan, $800 billion consists of loans that the Eurobanks have made to corporations, governments and central banks around the world.

No matter how you slice it, $800 billion is a lot of money. Moreover, the Euromarket is growing faster than national money markets. An analysis by the Federal Reserve Bank of New York shows that since 1974, both the gross Euromarket (including interbank transactions) and the net Euromarket (which excludes interbank transactions) have grown about 25 percent per year, more rapidly than any measure of the U.S. money supply. The message of these numbers is that the Euromarket is much more important in global finance than it used to be, and it grows more important with each passing year.

From a practical business standpoint, the significance of the Euromarket is that it allows banks to expand credit faster than they could if the market did not exist. The creation of the Euromarket is a major reason why in recent years international banking has grown faster than world production and international trade. According to Citibank, from 1964 to 1978 international bank lending grew about 25 percent per year, compared to 5.25 percent for world GNP and 7.5 percent for world trade. In the last couple of years, trade and economic growth have contracted, but the growth of the Euromarket has raged on.

Despite its heady debut, the Euromarket was beset by trepidation that U.S. banks would go home and the market would shut down if

* M–2 includes M–1 plus savings deposits and such instruments as money market mutual funds. M–3 includes M–2 plus large denomination time deposits at banks and other financial institutions.

Table 3
GROWTH RATES OF EURODOLLAR DEPOSITS AND
U.S. MONETARY AGGREGATES

	1974	1975	1976	1977	1978	1979	1980	1981 (Jan.-Sept.)
Eurodollar deposits*								
Gross	28.9	38.0	24.3	19.6	24.6	27.4	27.4	20.2 (26.3)
Net	**	21.8	30.9	17.1	24.6	29.1	23.5	22.6 (24.2)
U.S. monetary aggregates***								
M-1	4.4	4.8	6.6	8.0	8.2	7.1	6.5	2.2 (5.9)
M-2	5.6	12.7	14.1	10.9	8.3	8.2	9.0	9.2 (9.8)
M-3	8.5	9.6	12.0	12.4	11.4	9.3	10.3	10.8 (10.5)

* Percentage changes in the outstanding end-of-period levels.
** Not available.
*** Percentage changes in the monthly average levels for the last month of
the period.
SOURCE: Federal Reserve Bank of New York, *Quarterly Review*, Spring
1982.

the United States ended its controls on capital flows. However, even
after Robert Roosa's controls were dismantled by the Nixon administration, the Euromarket kept growing by leaps and bounds.
This is because two key institutional traits of the Euromarket give it
a competitive advantage over national money markets. One is the
lack of any reserve requirements on Euromarket deposits. In 1933,
Congress authorized the Federal Reserve to place legal reserve requirements on U.S. banks. Reserve requirements limit the amount
of credit a bank can extend for every dollar of deposits. The Fed
requires its member banks to keep a certain percentage of their deposits in idle accounts with the Fed. They prevent banks from lending out all their deposits during a speculative boom and then going
belly-up when the speculative bubble bursts and banks are unable
to redeem their liabilities to depositors. By limiting the amount of
loans banks can make, reserve requirements also help influence the
volume of credit in the banking system and thus the overall level of
economic activity. By contrast, Eurobanks can lend out every

Eurodollar they take in. The absence of reserve requirements on Euromarket deposits also allows banks to pay more for deposits and charge less for loans in London than they do in New York. The premiums on deposits and discounts on loans between London and New York are slight, usually a fraction of one percentage point, or 50 to 70 "basis points."* To the layman this may seem insignificant, but spread over billions of dollars of transactions these fractions amount to substantial amounts of money. This, combined with the absence of controls on interest rates, is why the Euromarket outlived U.S. balance of payments controls. As Citibank observes:

> ... the removal of the regulatory handicaps to international banking based in the United States that had nourished the Eurodollar market in its infancy did little to slow offshore banking activity. For the extra costs imposed on banks in the United States by reserve requirements on deposits were sufficient to maintain the competitive edge on offshore banking even without the aid of Regulation Q and balance of payments controls. With an effective Eurodollar system in place, the competitive advantage of not having to maintain legal reserves which earn no interest is sufficient to keep the Euromarket growing.

The rapid growth of the Euromarket has also been fueled by the development of the large interbank market. The interbank market is the mainstay of the Euromarket. According to Morgan's estimates nearly 70 percent of all Euromarket deposits come from other banks. The Bank of England estimates that as much as 80 percent of nonsterling deposits in London are interbank deposits. The importance of the interbank market is reflected in the following table, which shows that the ten largest U.S. banks receive nearly 45 percent of their total foreign deposits from other banks. Some banks, such as New York's Chemical Bank, First Chicago and Continental Illinois, obtain more than half of their foreign deposits from the interbank market.

The large interbank market makes the Euromarket look essentially like a wholesale money market for banks. But the interbank market is only a means to an end: making more loans to corporations, governments and other borrowers. The interbank market is a

---

* One basis point is the equivalent of one one-hundredth of a percentage point.

Table 4

INTERBANK DEPOSITS AS A %
OF TOTAL FOREIGN DEPOSITS

Bank of America	42.4
Citibank	33.5
Chase Manhattan	30.1
Morgan Guaranty	41.4
Manufacturers Hanover	47.9
Chemical Bank	61.6
Continental Illinois	52.1
Bankers Trust	44.1
First Chicago	54.9
Security Pacific	41.3
AVERAGE	**44.9**

SOURCE: Group of 30

clubby arrangement. It was created to enable banks to fund rapidly growing loan portfolios. Except during times of crisis, funds are always available at a price. Psychologically, this is crucial. It allows banks to market loans aggressively because they know they can always obtain the money to fund them. This is possible because most Euroloans carry floating interest rates which are adjusted every six months to reflect changes in LIBOR. In effect, it allows a Eurobank to put a borrower on hold while obtaining the funds to lend him on the other line. The interbank market encourages aggressive lending because banks can make long-term loan commitments that they fund with short-term money taken from the interbank market.

For banks and their customers, the laissez-faire, free-wheeling spirit of the Euromarket seemed like the best of all possible worlds. The Euromarket opened up vast new opportunities to wheel and deal on a global scale. For would-be borrowers, the banks' willingness to lend plus the increasing array of financial instruments they offered encouraged a greater reliance on foreign credit. A generation before, John Maynard Keynes advocated the creation of an international pool of money that borrowers could draw on to temper the harsh winds of economic distress. At Bretton Woods, Keynes had been defeated. But before long his dream became reality. It was called the Euromarket.

CHAPTER 3

THE TRIUMPH OF HAUTE FINANCE

The two developments that dominated the international financial world in the last decade were the decline of the Bretton Woods monetary institutions and the phenomenal growth of the private money markets. Today's international financial system is largely a private system with only marginal official participation.

The transition from a government-dominated monetary system to a market-oriented system was not a smooth one. It was marked by a series of monetary crisis and upheavals that were among the most tumultuous in history. Essentially these were manifestations of a struggle between governments and the private banks for control over the international monetary system. The showdown between governments and the banks came during the currency crises of 1972 and 1973. Despite intensive high-level monetary negotiations, governments were losing influence over events. Exchange rates were out of control. Frantic negotiations and the patchwork solutions they produced were not enlightened initiatives in pursuit of reform but desperate attempts to stave off chaos in the international money markets. The closing of the U.S. gold window in August 1971, the Smithsonian agreement and the second U.S. devaluation had been way stations on the road from the Bretton Woods fixed exchange rates to a regime of floating rates. The midwife in the transition from a government-dominated regime to a market-oriented one was massive speculation against the dollar in the currency markets.

· · ·

In the aftermath of the Nixon August 15, 1971, announcement, relations between the United States, Europe and Japan had grown steadily worse. The Europeans and Japanese were fuming about the import surcharge, but to no avail. Connally refused to budge. Connally's hard line prompted Henry Kissinger, a self-professed economic novice, to force a solution to the monetary problem in order to avoid a deeper rift in the Western alliance. Kissinger supported Connally's attempt to reassert American power, but he thought the feisty Texan had gone too far. Unlike Connally, Kissinger was unwilling to risk a collapse of the alliance just to teach Europe and Japan a lesson.

Two unsolved issues remained on the monetary agenda. The first was the future role of gold in the international monetary system. Though it had virtually no commercial role, gold still functioned as a kind of financial lifeboat for individuals and governments. A more pressing issue was the problem of exchange rates. The U.S. dollar was clearly overvalued and other major currencies undervalued. But no one agreed on how much adjustment in currency values was needed. New exchange rates had to be negotiated that would give the United States some relief from imports but not destroy European and Japanese competitiveness. A related question involved the exchange rate regime. Would exchange rates be fixed or allowed to fluctuate in response to supply and demand? If so, would rates float freely or be managed by governments? Floating exchange rates were an unknown quantity, but fixed rates were clearly not working. Something had to be done.

The way the administration went about resolving the 1971 crisis was puzzling. Perhaps because they knew so little about international economics, Nixon and Kissinger chose to negotiate with the French, the most strident critics of the dollar-based monetary system. A nation of goldbugs, the French had consistently attacked U.S. efforts to place the dollar at the center of the international monetary system. In March 1968, the French opposed a decision by the Group of 10, the caucus of finance ministers of the rich countries, authorizing the IMF to create Special Drawing Rights or "paper gold" as a supplement to the dollar. The French wanted to eliminate the dollar-based system and replace it with one based on gold. But as Paul Fabra, an economics correspondent for *Le Monde* points out, de Gaulle's position was undermined by the student and worker unrest of May 1968. To restore social peace de Gaulle attempted to buy off French workers with large wage increases. The franc plunged. In return for help in supporting the franc, de Gaulle muted his criticism of U.S. policy and dropped his opposition to the SDR. By late 1971, de Gaulle was dead and the United States chose to pursue a settlement to the monetary problem with his successor Georges Pompidou.*

During the second week of December 1971, Nixon, Kissinger and Connally went to the Portuguese Azores to meet with Pompidou and his finance minister, Valéry Giscard d'Estaing. Kissinger negotiated directly with Pompidou, presenting the U.S. position drawn up by Connally and Paul Volcker. The strategy worked. In return for maintaining the concept of fixed exchange rates, as Kissinger puts it, Pompidou "was willing to acquiesce in our going off the limited gold standard." Not that he had much choice, but Pompidou could have been more difficult about the issue than he was. The United States agreed to devalue the dollar by raising the official gold price, which, incidentally, increased the value of the French gold stock. During the negotiations, Pompidou promised that the Allies would realign their currencies to reflect their increasing economic strength.

A week later, the Pompidou-Nixon covenant was ratified at a meeting of the Group of 10 in Washington. Under the Smithsonian Agreement, the dollar was devalued by 8 percent as the official gold price was raised from $35 to $38. The other major currencies were revalued upward by varying amounts. The yen was revalued by nearly 17 percent. Moreover, the Group of 10 agreed to permit their currencies to fluctuate around wider "bands" of 2.25 percent, as opposed to the 1 percent stipulated in the Bretton Woods agreement. The basic idea behind Smithsonian was to allow greater flexibility in currency values without completely jettisoning the concept

---

* Nixon's choice may have been determined by a process of elimination. The pound was weaker than the dollar and so Britain's negotiating position was irrelevant; Kissinger and Nixon disliked German Chancellor Willy Brandt; and Connally felt the same way about the Japanese. If the French agreed to a U.S.-inspired compromise, Kissinger reasoned, the other European countries would follow suit.

of fixed exchange rates. Nixon called the Smithsonian Agreement "the greatest monetary agreement in history."

Within a year, powerful new speculative pressures accumulated that overwhelmed the currency values negotiated at Smithsonian. As Professor Robert Aliber says, the December agreement soon found a place alongside the other odd relics housed in the Smithsonian Institution. The international monetary order was again in shambles. Under the Smithsonian accord, Western countries agreed to maintain new exchange parities for their currencies within bands of 2.25 percent. However, by the middle of 1972, with rumors of new devaluations flying, the pound weakened under speculative pressures. In mid-June, the bears pummeled the pound and in a week the British authorities spent roughly $2.6 billion in the markets defending it. Finally, on June 23, they gave up and let the pound float.

Not long after the pound began to float, speculative pressure on the dollar increased. As 1973 opened, the dollar fell against European currencies and the Swiss National Bank, which had been intervening to support the dollar, decided to stop throwing good money after bad. The Swiss let the franc float. For 1972, the United States ran a balance of payments deficit of about $10 billion. Clearly, the Smithsonian devaluation had not corrected the problem. To the world's money traders this was a familiar story. The U.S. payments deficit would swell the dollar overhang and depress the dollar in the currency markets. Nixon still had a broad domestic backing to continue to fight for U.S. interests abroad. To eliminate that deficit, he would be forced to seek a new devaluation. Moreover, since the Swiss had stopped intervening to support the dollar, could the rest of Europe be far behind?

In early February, massive speculation against the dollar began. Dollars flowed into Europe's money markets. On February 6, the Bundesbank and other central banks bought $1.7 billion to support the dollar. This was, in the words of *The Banker*'s M. S. Mendelsohn, "the most concentrated flight there had ever been out of the dollar.... More than ten billion was switched into other currencies." During February, the Bundesbank and Japan absorbed about $8 billion of that. As the speculation reached a frenzy, Treasury Under Secretary Paul Volcker was dispatched on a globe-trotting mission to inform the Allies of a new dollar devaluation. Volcker's presence in Europe confirmed all the rumors about devaluation and intensified the speculation. Finally, on February 12, the foreign currency markets were closed. When they reopened the next day, the dollar had been devalued by another 10 percent. The second devaluation hardly made a dent in the speculation. The speculators had the dollar on the ropes and they wanted blood. On March 1, barely two weeks after the devaluation, a new wave of dollar selling hit Europe, forcing the Bundesbank and other central banks to spend nearly $4 billion to defend the dollar. Again, on March 2, the markets were closed. For the next two and one-half weeks, according to a study by the U.S. Senate Subcommittee on Multinational Corporations,

> ... the international money markets of the free world were almost all shut. It was the first peacetime suspension of virtually all foreign exchange transactions in virtually all foreign exchange markets. When the markets were reopened the currency alignment which had been agreed on a month earlier, on February 12, was abandoned, and the currencies of the Western world were allowed to float, that is, to change parity.

The move to floating exchange rates was initially viewed as a temporary expedient until order could be restored in the money markets. Yet, speculation continued and quickly ended any hopes of returning to fixed exchange rates. Despite two devaluations, the dollar's plunge continued. By July, the dollar had been pushed down by another 10 percent, a development that French President Georges Pompidou called the "third devaluation of the dollar."

II

The proximate cause of the demise of the Bretton Woods system was massive and unprecedented speculation against the dollar. Currency speculation was hardly a new phenomenon. During the 1920s and 1930s, large amounts of capital and gold crossed national boundaries to escape political and economic disaster. In the early postwar period, however, the dollar was stable, other currencies were weak and exchange controls in Europe were heavy, all of which tended to discourage speculation. This changed after 1958 when most European countries, under U.S. pressure, restored convertibility of their currencies. The U.S. gold pledge weakened under the pressure of the dollar overhang, leading promptly to speculation in the London gold market during the 1960 presidential election. Due to the efforts of Robert Roosa and Charles Coombs, speculation against the dollar was contained, but the volume of hot money circulating in the world's money markets was increasing.

The first currency to succumb to international speculation was not the dollar but the British pound. As Professor Robert Z. Aliber of the University of Chicago points out, it was obvious to all but the British government that the old exchange rate for sterling £1=$2.80 was obsolete by 1964. For three years the British government, with help from the New York Fed, fought the fabled "Gnomes of Zurich" in the currency markets. The epic battle ended in November 1967 when the British threw in the towel and devalued. Less than a year later, when de Gaulle tried to buy labor peace with large wage increases, the speculators jumped on the French franc. This battle lasted only a few rounds. In early 1969, after de Gaulle's departure, the franc was devalued.

Shortly after, the speculators' attention shifted back to the dollar. Uncertainty over the future of the dollar as the dominant world currency and the growing sophistication of international money management increased interest in diversification out of the dollar. Increasingly, international business was being conducted in currencies other than the dollar, particularly in the Euromarket, where Euromarks, Euro-Swiss francs, and Euroyen were readily available. As currencies became increasingly unstable, currency fluctuations loomed larger in determining corporate balance sheet performance. The growth of foreign exchange markets made it possible for corporations and banks to avoid exchange losses and make speculative profits by altering the currency composition of their assets and liabilities. Corporations and banks began to devote more time to currency trading. Moreover, the growing concentration of international trade and investment in the hands of large multinational corporations increased the sensitivity of exchange rates to money flows engineered by the multinationals. In his *Storm Over the Multinationals*, Harvard economist Raymond Vernon puts it this way:

Multinational enterprises in the ordinary course of operations dispose of vast quantities of money across the international exchanges. . . . Most of that flow is concentrated in forty or fifty multinational networks that draw their impressions and their advice regarding the relative stability of different currencies from common sources—half a dozen banks, an even smaller number of financial journals, and an incestuous round of lunches and conferences. Viewed in the abstract, the situation is set up for disaster; a common tilt in the group becomes a source of irresistible pressure on any currency.

The Bretton Woods monetary system collapsed when multinational corporations, banks, and other investors started moving lots of money out of dollars and into other currencies. By the early 1970s, U.S. firms were no more loyal to the dollar than anyone else. As the *Wall Street Journal* put it, they were "betting against" the dollar. Essentially what happened is that the corporations and banks, anticipating a devaluation, sold dollars on Europe's money markets in order to reduce their cash exposure in dollars. Then they snapped up marks, Swiss francs and other currencies that looked stronger than the dollar. This pushed the dollar down and put upward pressure on the others. Foreign central banks fought the inflow of dollars through exchange market intervention. When it got too expensive, they gave up and let their currencies float. This is how floating exchange rates came into the world.

For public relations purposes, most bankers and corporate executives deny that they speculate in currency markets. As the treasurer of one global conglomerate told the *Wall Street Journal* in 1973, "If we took speculative positions . . . , I'd never admit it, because it's the worst kind of public relations imaginable for getting along with various governments, including our own." When they are willing to discuss it at all, bankers prefer more polite and euphemistic terminology to describe how they make money buying and selling currencies: "hedging risks in their managed liabilities" or "serving clients' currency needs." Some admit that they time purchases and sales in currency markets in order to benefit from exchange fluctuations, but insist that this is not speculation. A classic illustration of how bankers dodge the issue of speculation is the following comment that David Rockefeller made to author Martin Mayer:

... What is speculation? A large American company plans to build a plant in Germany, knows they will need a certain amount of marks in six months. I don't consider it speculation for him to move now to get the D-Marks. There is a legitimate reason for doing it.

The "legitimate reason," of course, is to make money on exchange fluctuations. Yet, there are good reasons why the corporations and their bankers like to dodge the issue of their speculative activities. For more than a decade, they have been making tremendous profits speculating against the pound, the dollar and other currencies in international money markets. Professor Aliber estimates that between 1967 and 1978, the net speculative profits of the worldwide network of gnomes totaled $12 billion.

Lesser known wheeler-dealers are not as public relations conscious as the Rockefellers and Wristons. Therefore they tend to be more candid about what is going on. Harry Browne, a parvenu investment adviser and best-selling financial author, defines speculation straightforwardly. ". . . no matter how you try to distinguish 'speculators' from 'investors,' you'll probably return to the basic definition that speculation is the purchase of an investment with the hope of selling it at a higher price."* While Browne's definition may be too inclusive, clearly, during the 1970s, the foreign exchange markets have departed from their stated purpose of financing international trade and become instead preoccupied with speculative activity.

Interestingly enough, the people who actually trade currencies for the major banks talk much more like the Harry Brownes than their bosses. Public relations consciousness is only part of the explanation for this. Another is that bankers like Rockefeller and Wris-

---

* Here is the definition offered by Professor Nicholas Kaldor: "Speculation . . . may be defined as the purchase (or sale) of goods with a view to resale (or repurchase) at a later date where the motive behind such action is the expectation of a change in the relevant price relative to the ruling price. . . . What distinguishes speculative purchases and sales is the expectation of an impending change in the ruling market price as the sole motive of action." As shown in chapter 5, the speculative motive does not always apply to trading that banks undertake for their corporate clients, but it clearly applies to the much larger interbank foreign exchange market.

ton did not rise through the ranks on the basis of their foreign exchange expertise. American banks obtained this expertise by hiring European currency traders. In general, the top managers of American banks are not especially gifted in the foreign exchange area. Lower level managers and trading room bosses are the ones responsible for generating speculative profits. As long as the profits roll in, there is no need for presidents and chairmen to get involved in such arcane areas.

Initially, Americans were novices at currency trading. Except for those who were in Europe with the army or the Marshall Plan, most Americans had little practical experience trading currencies. So as U.S. banks flocked to London during the 1960s and early 1970s, they hired sharp young European traders, often right out of high school. (Europeans, particularly the Swiss and the Germans, have been good at currency trading all along. British traders are considered tops, and many have left conservative British banks to work for more brazen continental or American banks.) Generally, Europeans working for U.S. banks began by dealing in their native currencies, then were promoted to manage currency trading rooms in London, Paris or Frankfurt. The good ones who made money trading graduated to senior management positions in London or New York. As they moved up the ladder, the time and energy devoted to currency dealing increased accordingly.

Opinions differ among bankers and corporate executives on how quickly American banks and corporations became sophisticated speculators. Not all of them do it. Certainly not all are good at it. Even for the good ones, the learning process was not easy. In 1965, Citibank lost $8 million when its Brussels traders misjudged movements in interest rates on a big dollar/sterling deal. After that debacle Citibank went out and found the people it needed to run a foreign exchange business properly. By 1972, the red ink from Citibank's foreign currency trading had been erased and supplanted with a profit. In 1972, Citibank earned over $38 million on its foreign exchange operations. In the turbulent year of 1973, profits increased to $70 million. By the end of the decade, Walter Wriston presided over the premier currency trading operation in the world. In the annual foreign exchange sweepstakes run by *Euromoney* magazine, Citibank has finished number one for the last four years.

In the early 1970s, American banks may not have been quite as adept at currency speculation as their European counterparts but they were learning. A fascinating case study of how sophisticated American banks were in manipulating money markets can be gleaned from a series of internal documents from Chase Manhattan's Frankfurt branch. They show how Chase used its global reach to get around controls imposed by the West German government to limit speculation in its currency markets. When speculation against the dollar (and in favor of the mark) exploded in the early 1970s, the German Bundesbank adopted formal controls to limit the inflow of dollars. To prevent non-German entities from swapping dollars for D-marks in Germany, the Bundesbank placed limits on holdings of D-marks by nonresidents. Secondly, the Bundesbank imposed the so-called "bardepot" rule imposing reserve requirements on loans and credits from foreigners. The bardepot was designed to prevent German corporations from borrowing dollars in the Euromarket and repatriating the funds in order to subvert the Bundesbank's tight money policy. (This was essentially the same problem the Federal Reserve grappled with in 1969 when tight money at home prompted U.S. banks to borrow dollars in Europe to fund domestic loans.) To control short-term speculative inflows, the Bundesbank placed heavy reserve requirements on foreign bank deposits with maturities of less than four years. Banks in Germany that took foreign deposits of less than four years could only use 35 percent for business loans. The balance had to be invested in government bonds or other lower yielding investments. Deposits with maturities of four years or more were exempt from this requirement.

In 1970, Hartwig Bartels, assistant general manager of Chase's German operations, grew concerned about the potential effects of German currency controls on Chase's German business. Bartels warned his superiors in New York that "only the imaginative handling of CMB's German funding base can assure the survival of the bank's operations in this country." Most of the funds for Chase's German loans came from imported Eurodollars. If this source of funds had been cut off, Chase's operations would have been seriously threatened. To avoid German currency controls, Chase created a vehicle called a "Swiss pool," whose purpose was to sustain the flow of Eurodollars into Chase Frankfurt in amounts that exceeded the limits laid down by the German authorities. The Swiss pool routed Eurodollars into Frankfurt by laundering them in Switzerland, thereby concealing the real nature of the transaction from the German authorities.

The Swiss-pool strategy was simple. Chase would buy Eurodollars in Nassau. Without Nassau's hand showing, the funds were forwarded to Chase Switzerland, which invested them in a fiduciary capacity with Frankfurt. Chase led the German authorities to believe that the Swiss deposits were four-year deposits, when in fact they were short-term Eurodollars. The purpose of the Swiss pool was to get short-term Eurodollars into Germany where they could be changed for deutsche marks. This was exactly what the Bundesbank did not want. Once Chase's German branch obtained the funds, they were loaned out to Chase's German customers who used them, among other things, to speculate in the mark. These "four-year deposits" were not subject to the Bundesbank's reserve requirement. As Senior Vice-President Donald Cameron wrote in a February 1972 memorandum:

> These long-term deposits are not subject in Germany to the 65%–35% rule. They may be used in full to fund Germany's loans and investment portfolio. Upon receipt of the dollar deposit from Chase Switzerland, Chase Germany sells the dollars spot to create Deutsche Marks and has always bought the dollars back for forward delivery to coincide with the actual maturity of the underlying dollar deposit.*

The whole transaction was controlled from Frankfurt and Bartels even requested a supply of Nassau's letterheads to expedite the transfers.

* Currencies are traded in both spot and forward markets. Spot transactions are for immediate delivery whereas forward transactions are for some specified date in the future. In the early 1970s, widespread feeling that the dollar would be devalued pushed the value of "forward dollars" below "spot dollars." In essence, Chase converted spot dollars into spot D-marks, profited when the D-mark rose and covered the dollar sale with cheaper forward dollars.

The Swiss pool turned out to be a gold mine, something that Bartels hastened to inform senior management in New York. Since Eurodollars were cheap relative to D-marks this allowed Chase to fund its German loans at a discount, yielding Chase a large 2–3 percent spread on its German loan portfolio, a substantial profit. Chase was not only able to reap large loan spreads, but also to increase its volume of loans.* Bartels bragged about the profitability of the Swiss-pool operation to alert New York "to the contribution made by the money desk people as far as the overall operation of the bank in Germany, with special emphasis on the profit performances. . . ." Bartels resented the notion that loan officers were considered the "kings of the banking business" and wanted New York to know that the contribution of the people who funded Chase's loans was "just as important as the contribution made by the credit officers of the bank. . . ." He also noted with some pride that it took a year for other banks to set up their own Swiss-pool operations modeled on Chase's.

While Bartels crowed to New York about the Swiss pool's profits, one of his charges was troubled by what the Swiss pool-type operations of U.S. banks were doing to German economic policy. Harold Timmeny, who worked for three years in Chase's German branches, conceded that the Swiss pool was "very profitable," but complained to his superiors that it violated the spirit, if not the letter, of German law. Timmeny advised Robert Bloomquist, a senior vice-president in New York, that in his view, "the Swiss Pool functions in a manner contrary to the stated objectives of both the Bundesbank and the German Government as well as to the extraordinary legal measures designed specifically to curtail the growth of the money supply." Timmeny, a classic whistle blower, argued that the Swiss pool could endanger the future of Chase's operations in Germany if the Bundesbank found out about it. Moreover, Timmeny felt that it was wrong for Chase to mislead the Bundesbank. In a letter that must have caused a few chuckles at 1 Chase Manhattan Plaza, Timmeny asserted that the use of the Swiss pool to delude the German government demonstrated a lack of "social re-

---

* One Chase official stressed the importance of disguising short-term Eurodollars as four-year funds. With a normal yield curve, it would have been impossible for Chase to fund short-term lending with four-year funds.

sponsibility" and "moral leadership" on Chase's part. He recommended that it be discontinued.

Chase was not moved. For his concern about social responsibility, Timmeny was transferred to New York, where he would be unable to monitor the Swiss pool. Timmeny got the message and resigned a few months later. Timmeny claims he attempted unsuccessfully to get *Time* magazine and the *International Herald Tribune* to publish his evidence about speculation in the mark.

III

The growing rift among the allies on monetary issues plus the increasing sophistication of private money traders was a sure recipe for a marked increase in speculation against the dollar. During the sterling crisis of 1967, as Professor Jonathan Aronson points out, the banks had learned that "exchange crises could be extremely profitable." The volume of turnover in the world's foreign exchange markets soared. From less than $25 billion per day in 1970, according to calculations of Professor Ian Giddy of Columbia, by early 1973, daily trading had soared to over $50 billion and to $100 billion by year-end. By then, the biggest banks and corporations had become more willing to gamble in the exchange markets and they had the kind of people who could gamble profitably. As instability grew, so did the opportunities to profit from exchange rate changes. Eventually, the speculators took on the most powerful government of all, the United States. After all, they had beaten the British and the French, why not the Americans?

The speculative assault on the old Bretton Woods order came in two stages: in mid-1971 and early 1973. The backdrop to both crises was a massive increase in the dollar overhang that was at the root of the dollar's problems. However, the source of the dollars thrust on the world's money markets was not the familiar problems of a declining trade surplus and Vietnam expenditures; it was large transfers of private capital out of the United States. During 1971, nearly $24 billion in private capital left the United States. By way of contrast, the U.S. trade account was $2 billion in the black in 1970 and the 1971 deficit amounted to less than $3 billion. The capital flight of 1971 flowed through both bank and corporate channels. According to Federal Reserve data, between January 1970 and May 1971 the home offices of U.S. banks loaned about $12 billion to their overseas branches. Mainly, they were repaying funds borrowed from the branches in 1969 to get around the Fed's tight money policies. The $12 billion outflow added substantially to the dollar glut, depressed dollar interest rates and weakened confidence in the ability of the United States to sustain the exchange rate of the dollar. These transfers through the banking system were supplemented in early 1971 by massive speculative flows to the Euromarket. Much of this resulted from an old corporate strategy known as "leads and lags." Corporations utilize leads and lags to profit from exchange fluctuations. For instance, if a U.S. company operating in Germany anticipates the mark will go up against the dollar, it will buy marks and pay its bills before the price of marks goes up. Alternatively, a German company that has payments due in dollars will hold on to marks as long as possible. After the dollar goes down, the firm will receive more dollars per mark. When large numbers of companies engage in leads and lags simultaneously, it leads to what Raymond Vernon called the "common tilt," exerting extreme pressure on a currency. In 1971 this is exactly what happened to the dollar. According to Citibank Vice-President Miroslav A. Kriz:

> Corporate treasurers and others responsible for large amounts of funds . . . sold dollars even when their need for Deutschemarks, Swiss francs or other currencies was well in the future or they postponed sales of such currencies for dollars that they otherwise would have made. By early May these had reached truly colossal proportions.

A technical report of the Committee of 20, established in 1972 by the IMF to study monetary reform issues, concluded that a large part of the billions in unidentified transactions making up the "errors and omissions" segment of the U.S. balance of payments from 1970 to 1972 resulted from corporate leads and lags.

The combination of outflows of dollars through the banking system and corporate leads and lags led to heavy pressure on the dollar in May of 1971, forcing the Germans to close the foreign currency markets and float the mark. The problem was compounded when

Connally and Arthur Burns refused to intervene in the currency markets to help the Europeans support the dollar. The result, as Charles Coombs put it, was that the currency markets "came to resemble a sort of disorderly casino with the odds rigged in favor of the gamblers rather than the house." In retrospect, it had been the May dollar crisis, not the alleged British request for $3 billion in gold, that led to the closing of the gold window and first dollar devaluation.

After the Smithsonian accord, the situation stabilized for a time in 1972. Capital outflows from the United States slowed to a trickle, though a rising trade deficit put the overall U.S. balance of payments deficit at about $10 billion for 1972. Then during the crisis-ridden first quarter of 1973, about $10 billion in private capital flows left the United States. Short-term flows of cash and other liquid assets accounted for a large part of this. (It should be kept in mind that, according to Mendelsohn's estimate, it took only about $10 billion dumped on Europe's money markets during February to force the second dollar devaluation in 14 months.) Most of the funds flowed into the Euromarket where dollars could easily be changed into other currencies. As David Kern, chief economist of London's National Westminster Bank, puts it, "the existence of large and efficient capital markets has undoubtedly provided a sensitive vehicle for the destabilizing flows of short-term capital which have been among the main causes for the breakdown of the Bretton Woods system." International bankers and their clients were shifting out of dollar-denominated financial instruments. This had begun in late 1972, but reached a frenzy in 1973. In her excellent study of multinational banking for the House Banking Committee, economist Jane D'Arista of the Congressional Budget Office calculated that in 1973 foreign currency deposits in foreign branches of U.S. banks grew by $18 billion, a 78 percent increase over 1972. Meanwhile, their foreign currency loans grew by 66 percent. In the critical period between the end of 1972 and March 1973, U.S. banks' foreign branch dollar loans increased by about $4.7 billion while nondollar loans increased by almost $7 billion. Data from Morgan Guaranty confirms that the dollar component of the Euro-currency market fell to a record low of 73 percent in 1973, down from 78 percent in 1972. The banks facilitated speculation against the dollar by changing dollars for foreign currencies and lending them to their customers. In Jane D'Arista's words:

> A large portion of the foreign currency liabilities borrowed by [the overseas branches of U.S. banks] were loaned to non-bank foreign customers. . . . Loans to non-bank foreigners . . . indicate that during the speculative crisis of 1973, *the branches borrowed foreign currency deposits from other banks and loaned a large portion of these funds to non-bank borrowers.*

The banks not only precipitated the currency crisis of 1973, they profited handsomely from it. To quote Jane D'Arista:

> . . . international banks were among the major beneficiaries of currency speculation. They supplied the funds for speculative activity by customers under a system which insured that speculators (and their creditors) were rarely the losers. As had been widely discussed, the overt losers were central banks. . . .

Central banks were "the losers" in two respects. First, as they were mopping up the dollars that were dumped on European currency markets their dollar holdings increased. One indication of the magnitude of speculation that was going on is that official holdings of U.S. government securities (where the proceeds of intervention were invested)* skyrocketed from about $16 billion in 1969 to over $61 billion at the end of 1972. The increase was almost exactly equal to the size of private capital outflows from the United States. Thus, when the devaluations came, central banks' losses were larger because they had been intervening.

Second, the massive inflow of dollars was inflationary. Exchange market intervention fueled inflation because it forced central banks to expand their own money supplies more rapidly than they would have otherwise. At the time, the German Bundesbank was consid-

---

* For a time, some major central banks were reinvesting their dollar reserves in the Euromarket. They stopped when it became clear that the dollars would be reloaned for fresh speculation, starting the whole process over again.

ered the industrialized world's bulwark against inflation. The Germans were certainly running a much tighter monetary policy than was Arthur Burns. The heavy speculation in the currency markets not only exported American inflation to Europe, but also forced Germany out of its anti-inflationary policies. Essentially, Europe lost control over its own monetary policies. The lesson that governments drew from this experience was that they could not control private capital flows, so they might as well stop trying.

IV

It is clear that among the "foreigners" speculating against the U.S. dollar during the currency crises of 1971–73 were the overseas subsidiaries of U.S. corporations and banks. Yet speculation against the dollar by American corporations and banks has been almost totally ignored by economists, policy makers and commentators. Part of this is the result of clever propaganda by the banks. Foreign exchange is an arcane area and when bankers and corporate treasurers deny they speculate, they are seldom challenged. Most conventional economists also deny that large-scale speculation exists. This is not surprising, however, since most economists have probably never been in a bank trading room. Many of the self-proclaimed "authorities" in the area have little practical knowledge of how exchange markets work.

Even sophisticated observers of international economics like C. Fred Bergsten, Thomas Horst and Theodore Moran have written widely respected books on multinationals that are totally off the mark where currency speculation is concerned. In a weighty Brookings Institution tome entitled *American Multinationals and American Interests,* Bergsten, Horst and Moran acknowledge that multinationals play a "powerful role" in international currency markets, but they studiously dilute this fact by echoing the conventional wisdom that global firms "show little interest in reaping profits from successful speculation." They base this conclusion mainly on the findings of a study of the dollar devaluation crises of the early 1970s by the now-defunct Senate Subcommittee on Multinational Corporations headed by former senator Frank Church.

Bergsten, Horst and Moran call the Senate study "the most exhaustive effort to uncover data" on currency speculation by the multinationals. (Bergsten, incidentally, served as a consultant on the study.)

The Church committee mailed a questionnaire to 56 U.S. multinationals and 27 foreign firms requesting information on their currency activities during the 1973 dollar devaluation crisis. Data submitted by the companies demonstrated that, at a minimum, U.S. companies reduced their holdings of dollars during the 1973 crisis and increased their holdings of D-marks, Swiss francs and Dutch guilders. It also showed that they used leads and lags extensively. As Subcommittee Chairman Frank Church put it, "the firms did protect themselves against the anticipated devaluation over a longer term by shifting the currency composition of liquid assets and debts and by prepaying accounts payable in currencies expected to be revalued and by delaying payments in currencies expected to be devalued." The study also confirmed that unusually large outflows of capital from the United States coincided with the crisis period. Yet the subcommittee failed to find evidence "that U.S. multinational corporations . . . [used] the forward market or the banking sector in order to hedge short-term gains against the devaluation of the dollar in the first quarter of 1973. . . ."

In fact, as former staff members of the Senate subcommittee admit, there is reason to believe that the study revealed only the tip of the iceberg. First of all, banks were not included, ironically, in the Senate study. Only Citicorp was asked to respond to the questionnaire, but refused to do so. Since the subcommittee did not force the issue, it stands to reason that Walt Wriston and his colleagues refused to cooperate. Secondly, mailing out a voluntary questionnaire is not a very good way to investigate multibillion-dollar currency speculation. A questionnaire is not a subpoena, and companies were under no obligation to respond fully and candidly.

Bergsten also offers a more sophisticated defense of currency speculation. If the multinationals do engage in currency speculation, he argues, it is a constructive force in the world economy. To the extent that speculation by the multinationals helped bring about a devaluation of the dollar in 1973, it facilitated needed changes in exchange rates. Bergsten credits exchange rate changes with moving the U.S. balance of trade from a $6 billion deficit in 1972 to a small surplus in 1973 and cushioning the effects of the tremendous increase in the cost of petroleum imports in 1974. In other words, if the multinationals helped push the dollar down, they aided U.S. exports and therefore job creation at home.

In part, they are right. The huge devaluations of 1973 made some U.S. products, particularly manufactured goods, more competitive. However, there were also sizable improvements in exports of agricultural products, where price competitiveness is less important than other factors, notably foreign crop failures and the general state of agricultural production abroad.

The devaluation of the dollar was not the only factor behind the improvement in the U.S. trade balance for two reasons. First, the conventional interpretation ignores the effects of world economic growth rates (income effects) on the demand for U.S. products. World economic growth and world trade soared until late 1973, providing a boost to exporters the world over. In 1974, economic growth rates fell off substantially and yet the United States still made impressive gains in manufactured exports. Still, there is more to the story. If it is assumed that countries whose currencies are devalued become more competitive, then countries whose currencies are pushed up should become less competitive. Yet Germany, the main target of the speculative forays of 1971–73, increased its trade surplus from $8 billion in 1972 to nearly $23 billion in 1974, hardly a sign of decreasing competitiveness. Japan, on the contrary, adjusted poorly to the events of 1973–74, and its trade surplus shrank dramatically. The upshot is that the evidence that multinationals performed a public service by pushing the dollar down is not as cut-and-dried as Bergsten, Horst and Moran suggest. They have not proved that exchange rate changes alone did the trick.

While they exaggerate the merits of the dollar devaluations of 1971–73, Bergsten, Horst and Moran soft-pedal the negative effects of massive currency speculation. They acknowledge that devaluation of the dollar worsened inflation in the United States, but they do not mention that the massive stampede of dollars into European currencies between 1971 and 1973 exported U.S. inflation to Europe. In fact, there is good reason to believe that the inflationary effects were greater than they were in the United States. European economies are much smaller than the mammoth U.S. economy and are therefore more vulnerable to destabilization by billions of dollars of capital flows.

More importantly, Bergsten, Horst and Moran fail to appreciate that massive speculation by major financial institutions is dangerous business. The growth of the Eurocurrency interbank market has tied the fortunes of the multinational banks closely together. In such an environment, when banks fail, panic can spread through the Euromarkets like wildfire. Properly managed, bank failures can be contained and their effects limited to the institution involved. But if the banks involved are big or the failures are mismanaged, they can quickly lead to disaster.

In her superb case study of the collapse of the Franklin National Bank, Joan Spero, now an executive at American Express, has demonstrated just how dangerous massive currency speculation can be. Between June and October 1974, two multinational banks, West Germany's Bankhaus I.D. Herstatt and the Franklin National Bank of New York, collapsed from losses suffered in international currency speculation. Herstatt collapsed on June 26 when the bank could no longer cover up huge foreign exchange losses that it had been concealing from the German authorities through phony bookkeeping. At the time of failure, Herstatt had outstanding foreign exchange exposure of $200 million. Four months later, Franklin, the twentieth largest bank in the United States, collapsed. Franklin, which went abroad in the go-go years of the late 1960s and early 1970s, had a poor profit performance, and top management was pressuring its subordinates to increase speculative profits. When it failed, Franklin had exposure of nearly $2 billion.

The failure of two global banks sent shock waves through the Eurocurrency market. By late 1974, foreign exchange trading slowed dramatically and only blue-chip banks were able to obtain funds in the Euromarket. The optimism that accompanied the creation of the elegant international financial mechanism known as the Euromarket gave way to shock and fear. The Euromarket was quickly revealed as a rather shaky arrangement. As Joan Spero writes, "because of the direct linkages of banks through these markets and because of the intangible but very real indirect linkage of bank confidence throughout the system, problems in one bank can spread in a domino fashion throughout the system. . . ."

The international financial system flirted with disaster a number of times during the 1970s, and no one really knows how close to disaster the system has come. Thus far, adept crisis management by governments and good luck have prevented a general financial panic, but no one knows how long this game can go on. People with their fingers on the pulse of financial markets have a much better sense of the seriousness of financial debacles than academic economists. How serious were they? According to Henry Kaufman, chief economist of Wall Street's Salomon Brothers,

> . . . During their most intensive moments, they contained all the ingredients that had fueled the financial debacles of old. How close we came to disaster in 1970, and then again in 1974 and early 1975, no one will ever accurately record. It was a frightening period. . . .

Though the most serious of these crises, the Franklin-Herstatt failures, were successfully contained, who knows what will happen next time? To say that successful management of the Franklin-Herstatt crises proved that today's global financial system is immune from a 1930s-style crash is like saying the Cuban missile crisis proved that a nuclear war is unlikely.

The stakes riding on global currency speculation escalated tremendously in the 1970s. Today, currency speculation is far more than just a game to play against governments to make money. It has transformed the nature of international monetary relations. In the face of the massive flight out of the dollar in 1973, Western governments were pushed into a floating exchange-rate system. Since then, we have been living with the consequences of that fateful decision. Global currency speculation has increased markedly. Moreover, it has been institutionalized through the normal workings of a floating-rate regime.

When floating rates became inevitable because governments were unable to control movements of private capital, economists quickly jumped on the floating-rate bandwagon. Bergsten, Horst and Moran call floating rates the "best international monetary system at the present stage of world economic history." If anything, the experience under floating rates has been the opposite of what the partisans of free floating predicted.* International payments imbalances, which floating rates are supposed to correct, have been larger under floating rates than under fixed rates. Currency fluctuations have been more erratic. Speculative capital flows have distorted economic policy making in industrialized and Third World countries alike.

Still, when the floating rate system survived the bank failures of 1974 and the huge burden of petrodollar recycling, governments were lulled into a false sense of security about its desirability. This was the best of all possible worlds, economists assured them, and hot money flowing in and out of the Euromarket was not a serious problem. The bankers, chastened momentarily by the Herstatt and Franklin failures, cooled their heels for a couple of years. But before long they were back speculating in earnest, and governments would soon find out just how dangerous billions of hot money footloose in the Euromarket could be.

---

* In fairness to the authors of *American Multinationals and American Interests,* they do suggest that some government intervention should help manage the floating rate regime. However, since floating began, intervention has been halfhearted. When Fred Bergsten was a high official in the Treasury Department, Treasury refused to intervene at all until the dollar had nearly collapsed. See chapter 5.

CHAPTER 4

THE ECONOMICS AND POLITICS OF GLOBAL DEBT

The global money market was established to enable Western banks to serve their corporate clients on a global scale. As large numbers of new banks entered the global money game in the early 1970s, however, profit margins on loans to blue-chip corporations, never enormous, fell dramatically. So banks began to look for new customers to lend to. For many, the answer was a return to one of the basics of banking—financing governments. In the nineteenth century, private banks helped countries cope with swings in the trade cycle and made emergency loans to keep governments afloat. During the Franco-Prussian War, the House of Morgan loaned France $50 million. By then, foreign loans by American banks were an important tool of American foreign policy. Even before the United States entered the First World War, Morgan financed Allied purchases of American military supplies. In fact, one of the things bankers disliked about the Bretton Woods Conference was that it created a competing public sector institution, the International Monetary Fund, to provide short-term loans to countries experiencing trade and financial difficulties.

Despite the creation of the IMF, the business of lending to governments was soon taken over by the banks. Even before Oil Shock I in 1973, the Euromarket had grown so rapidly that according to one banker:

The London Market has virtually usurped the role of the IMF and
other international agencies in larger amounts and under less restrictive
terms than usually imposed with regard to rate, maturity and cove-
nants. . . .

The stars of banking were the ones who had gone to Harvard or
Oxford with the world's finance ministers and central bankers.
They had the contacts to bring countries to the money market.
From their perch in the City of London, bankers began to parcel
out enormous quantities of money to a hundred countries around
the world.

By the middle of the decade, the money flowing to Third World
countries from private banks dwarfed that coming from development agencies like the World Bank. The vast industrial combines of
Brazil, the copper, gold and diamond mines of Africa, and the
plantations of Asia were being constructed courtesy of Chase, Citibank, and the Swiss Bank Corporation. Then, as cold war barriers
between East and West fell, the bankers assumed a revolutionary
new function: financing the Soviet Union and its allies. Suddenly,
Moscow began to reap the benefits of inventing the Euromarket.
The square-mile City of London became increasingly cosmopolitan. From the imposing National Westminster Bank Tower on Old
Broad Street, one can see the Moscow Narodny, Poland's Bank
Handlowy, and the Havana International sitting along the Banco
do Brazil, Warburg's, Morgan, and Lloyds.

With a global money market in place, money was available to
any country on earth that was perceived to be creditworthy and
could afford market interest rates. It seldom occurred to bankers or
governments that serious problems could arise. The massive financial failures of the 1920s and 1930s seemed to be ancient history.
For most of the postwar period, such things as defaults and debt
crises were not considered matters of great concern. Bankers, it was
agreed, were among the most conservative of entrepreneurs. Together with central bankers, bankers had the skills and resources to
prevent serious financial problems.

Today, a massive global debt crisis hangs like a great cloud over
the world economic landscape. News of banks' "problem loans" to
Poland and Mexico has moved onto the front pages. What only

Paul Erdman dared say a decade ago has become one of the hottest subjects of financial journalism. Western banks have billions of dollars strung out all over the globe in countries beset by wars, revolutions, and seemingly insurmountable economic problems. The numbers involved are so large they boggle the mind. The Third World owes the Western banking system over half a trillion dollars. Mexico and Brazil are each into the West for around $80 billion. The Soviet Union and its six eastern European allies owe the West over $65 billion, a figure that is projected to reach $100 billion by 1985. The hope that countries will be able to pay back what they borrowed has been given up as a lost cause. The banks are having enough trouble getting them to maintain the interest payments, let alone paying back the principal. The challenge has become one of crisis management. How do you manage half a trillion dollars in global debt, solve problem cases in orderly fashion, and avoid provoking a panic?

I

The global debt crisis had two fundamental causes. The first was the growing importance of Third World countries in the global banking revolution of the 1960s and 1970s. The second was the series of economic shocks that hit the world economy in the 1970s. Together, they led to a marriage of convenience between the global banks and poor Third World countries. Basically, the global banks had money to lend and Third World countries needed it to survive in an increasingly hostile world economic climate.

For big banks, lending money to underdeveloped countries is nothing new. Both commercial and investment banks (in British lexicon, clearing and merchant banks) have long made loans to and floated bonds for foreign companies and governments. Foreign lending was an indispensable part of the expansion of the great European colonial empires in the nineteenth century. After financing much of the development of the European continent early in that century, British merchant banks, such as Baring and Rothschild, later moved heavily into underdeveloped areas. On the eve of the First World War, British banks had loaned substantial amounts to Brazil, Argentina, India and South Africa. By then, British colonial banks had a vast network of international branches around the world. Thirty-two British colonial banks had over 2,000 branches and another 18 British-owned banks possessed another 200 branches.

In the early twentieth century, stimulated by the passage of the Federal Reserve Act in 1913 and the Edge Act in 1919, U.S. banks began to get into the act. Along with the growing importance of U.S. exports and the emergence of the United States as a creditor nation, U.S. banks challenged European financial houses in world financial markets. A handful of U.S. banks had significant operations in Latin America before the Great Depression. National City Bank (Citibank's ancestor), Brown Brothers Harriman, Chase and others were strong in Cuba, Nicaragua, Brazil, Costa Rica and Venezuela. In the 1930s, a picture of the president of Brown Brothers was featured on the currency of Nicaragua.

The overseas expansion of European and U.S. banks was not a gradual uninterrupted process, but instead, ebbed and flowed in response to fluctuations in international trade and financial crises. Generally a period of prosperity led to frantic expansion, speculation and excessive lending, followed by a chain of defaults, panics and liquidations. International bank lending was shattered by the Great Crash of 1929–33. This traumatic experience brought the prolonged expansion of foreign lending to a sudden halt. In his classic *Europe, the World's Banker*, Herbert Feis points out that as a result of the depression:

> ... almost all of the loans that had been made by Americans fell into default. Fortunes were lost. Bankruptcies in Central Europe shook the whole financial and economic structure of the West. Recriminations between lenders and borrowers filled the press and diplomatic dispatches and the board rooms of banks. . . . The American people vowed that never again would they trust their fortunes abroad or respond to the requests of recreant foreign governments.

Those attitudes changed radically after the Second World War. The Bretton Woods institutions provided a more secure climate for private bank lending abroad. Still, its importance to most Third World countries remained marginal. In the 1950s and 1960s, bilateral or multilateral aid programs provided about two-thirds of all foreign loans to Third World countries. The bulk of private money came from investments by the multinational corporations.

In the early 1970s, however, foreign aid failed to keep pace with development financing needs. Countries with ample natural resources and labor supplies turned increasingly to private banks to finance huge mining and manufacturing projects. Concurrently, banks' international activities were growing steadily and so was their appetite for more. Banks had strong incentives to increase their activities in the Third World. Banks went abroad to keep up with their corporate clients. When their clients went to Brazil and Mexico, the banks followed . Beyond that, moving into underdeveloped areas where capital was scarce offered the prospect of much higher returns than capital deployed at home. The multinationals were enjoying greater rates of return in the Third World than at home, and banks anticipated that their Third World loans would be as profitable. As for the security of the loans, banks viewed Third World countries excellent credit risks by virtue of their oil and mineral wealth. In the early 1970s, amid dire predictions of resource shortages and skyrocketing commodity prices, banks rushed to make loans to corporations and government agencies exploiting Third World resources. They viewed large reserves of natural resources as impeccable collateral in the event of default. As bankers are fond of saying, although companies may go out of business, countries never do.

That banks aggressively courted new borrowers and encouraged them to borrow is often ignored in banking literature. Most bankers tend to view themselves as powerless servants of impersonal market forces, supplying credit where demand for it exists. This view was perhaps best expressed by Irving S. Friedman, formerly Citibank's Third World troubleshooter and now a senior adviser at First Boston Corp:

> The process [of debt creation] is demand driven. Borrowing entities, be they private or official, create the demand. The lenders have to determine the magnitude and terms on which they will supply.

Yet this overlooks the role played by international competition among the banks for larger loan portfolios, market shares and profits. As Richard S. Weinert of the New York investment banking firm Leslie, Weinert, & Co. points out:

> Indebtedness is a two-sided relationship. It depends not only on a willing borrower, but equally on a willing lender. . . . LDC indebtedness results as much from the need of lenders to lend as from the need of borrowers to borrow . . . a full analysis of lending to LDCs must take account of both the demand and supply of lending, and see the volume and pattern of loans as a result of their dynamic inter-relationship.

Weinert lists four main factors that he views as responsible for the banks' expansionist thrust into the Third World in the 1970s: servicing client needs, defensive expansion to keep clients, earnings growth, and the opportunities offered by Eurocurrency markets.

The Weinert view, which takes both supply and demand factors into account, is far more convincing. Undoubtedly, Third World countries have an insatiable demand for funds. Yet this would mean little to banks if there was no money in the business and little competition for it. Banks lend to Third World countries, especially the big ones such as Brazil and Mexico, because they have to. Most banks initially became involved as lenders to subsidiaries of their corporate clients. But as economic growth and exports took off, the banks became more deeply involved because there was too much business in those countries to pass up. The growth in the number of banks involved in Eurobanking made competition to manage syndicated loans to prized borrowers intense. Moreover, a country's bargaining power with the banks tends to expand once it becomes a substantial borrower. If a bank shows no interest in managing its syndicated loans, a Brazil or Mexico can always threaten to take billions in trade financing, cash management and other valuable business elsewhere. If Citibank won't do it, Deutschebank will. The result is that banks compete vigorously to win mandates to manage loan syndications. An added incentive to lend is the fact that "front-end" fees awarded to lead banks are collected when the loan is signed. These are treated as current income on banks' balance sheets. Whether or not the loan officer who put together the loan is around when it has to be paid back is of little interest to him. Frequently, having earned a reputation as a gunslinger in the syndicated loan market, he has moved on to a higher paying job elsewhere.

Private bank involvement in Third World countries was already substantial before 1973. In 1972, U.S. banks had over 300 branch offices in Third World countries. That year Third World borrowers accounted for about 38 percent of total publicized international bank credits. In 1973 the total long-term foreign debt of 84 Third World countries was $97 billion, with more than 30 percent held by private banks.

The global banking network was in place before Oil Shock I, but the Third World's addiction to foreign credit began in earnest after 1973. Since then, the Third World has been rocked by a series of economic shocks which have left it substantially in hock to the Western banking system. The banks were looking for borrowers to unload billions of OPEC petrodollars, and oil-importing poor countries needed the money just to stay afloat.

II

The first economic shock of the 1970s was inflation, which hit double digits in 1973, receded slightly and then soared into double digits again late in the decade. World inflationary pressures are generated mainly in the developed countries, though a number of Latin American countries have experienced inflation that rivals history's great hyperinflations. Although Third World exports initially profited from the upsurge in global inflation, the benefits were short-lived. By 1974 the profits of higher raw materials prices were consumed by skyrocketing oil prices and the inflated costs of manufactured products imported from the West. By and large, these countries have lost out to inflation since then.

The most publicized economic shock of the 1970s was the dramatic increase in oil prices from about $3 in early 1973 to over $30 at the end of the decade. That OPEC-inspired oil price increases contributed mightily to the Third World's economic woes is beyond dispute. In fact, the principal victims of both oil shocks were not the industrialized countries, but OPEC's Third World "brothers." Oil is an essential raw material for any country undergoing modernization. Countries that do not have oil have to import it, regardless of the cost. The oil bill of the oil-importing Third World countries rose from about $7 billion in 1973 to $24 billion a year later. By 1981, after the onset of Oil Shock I, their oil import bill reached nearly $100 billion.*

The third major shock was the slowdown in world economic growth, highlighted by the steep recessions of 1974–75, and 1980–82. Third World countries are acutely dependent on exports to the industrialized countries and when economic growth slows down, so does demand for their products. The annual growth rates of the industrialized countries plunged from nearly 5 percent in the decade before Oil Shock I to less than 3 percent between 1973 and 1980. The problem of stagflation in the industrialized world means that in the Third World import prices rise while export markets and export prices suffer. The terms of trade of the oil-importing Third World countries—the relationship between export and import prices—has declined dramatically since 1978.

While OPEC oil shocks get more headlines, the chronic boom and bust cycles of international trade can wreak havoc with Third World countries. In *North-South: Air Program for Survival,* the Brandt Commission, an international commission on development issues chaired by former German Chancellor Willy Brandt, highlighted the case of the African nation of Zambia:

> There was a boom in copper prices from 1972 with the price peaking in April 1974, at $3,034 per ton; then it suddenly fell to $1,290 before the end of that year. But the prices of imports continued to rise so that the volume of imports Zambia could buy fell by 45 percent between 1974 and 1975 and the GDP fell by 15 percent. The gravity of this situation for Zambia is put in perspective when it is contrasted with the "oil shock" of 1974. This resulted in an increased oil bill for the industrialized countries equivalent to about 2.5 percent of their GNP. In numerical terms Zambia's shock was six times greater, in human terms for this poor country, it was severer still.

The fourth economic shock was soaring interest rates. One of the implications of the growing importance of private bank lending to Third World countries is that the cost of borrowing money and ser-

---

* On a net basis, minus oil production in these countries, the oil trade balance went from −$5 billion in 1973 to −$77 billion in 1981.

vicing foreign debts rose substantially. Most private bank loans carry floating interest rates that are adjusted every six months to reflect changes in the cost of money to the banks. Interest rates jumped sharply after the traumatic failures of the Franklin National and Herstatt banks in 1974, but then receded as the global recession spread. In the aftermath of Oil Shock II, however, interest rates rose and remained at levels that are unprecedented in modern economic history. Interest rates on Euromarket bank loans averaged 12 percent in 1979, 14.2 percent in 1980 and 16.6 percent in 1981. For every 1 percent rise in market interest rates, the Third World's debt-servicing costs increase by about $2 billion. In real terms, considering the declines in commodity prices, the pain imposed by higher interest rates is much greater.

The interaction of all these developments has given Third World countries a Hobson's choice of going deeply into debt or facing economic collapse. The gravity of the situation can be illustrated by looking briefly at what economists call the current account balances of the oil-importing Third World for the years since 1973. The current account includes both merchandise trade and services. Even for countries that manage to generate a trade surplus, the costs of servicing the foreign debts and profits repatriated by the multinationals often plunge the current account into the red.

From a fairly modest deficit of $11 billion in 1973, the oil-importing Third World countries plunged to a $37 billion deficit in 1974 and over $46 billion in 1975. After Oil Shock II, the deficit rose from $37 billion to nearly $100 billion by 1981. The deficits, interestingly enough, have remained high despite declining world oil prices, in part because of declining commodity prices and interest costs.

Table 5
NONOIL THIRD WORLD COUNTRIES
CURRENT ACCOUNT BALANCES 1973-1982
(U.S. $ BILLIONS)

1973	1974	1975	1976	1977	1978	1979	1980	1981	1982
−11.6	−37.	−46.5	−32.	−28.3	−39.2	−58.9	−86.2	−99.	−97

SOURCE: IMF, *World Economic Outlook*, 1982, p. 158.

The meaning of these large and growing deficits is that Third World countries have to borrow large amounts of money just to pay their bills. The ones that have consistently lived on borrowed money have become today's biggest global debtors. Most of what they borrow goes to service old debts. The total long-term debt of the nonoil Third World countries exploded from less than $100 billion in 1972 to over $500 billion by 1982. Total Third World debt to the private banks is even larger, really unknown, since published figures do not include billions of short-term debt.* The debt is so massive that it has laid the groundwork for a first-rate debt crisis in the international banking system. As the *Wall Street Journal* observes:

> It doesn't show on any maps, but there's a new mountain on the planet—a towering $500 billion of debt run up by developing countries, nearly all of it within a decade.
> Is the debt mountain also a volcano?

The largest and fastest growing share of the Third World's debt burden is what they owe to private banks. Over the past decade, Third World countries' debts to private banks grew at 25 percent to 30 percent per year. By contrast, their debts to bilateral and multilateral aid agencies grew only about 16 percent per year. In 1973, according to the IMF, private banks accounted for about one-third of the total debt of Third World countries. By 1982, it stood at considerably more than half. What really worries the banks is that their lending is concentrated in a few countries that have pressing debt problems. "If I owe a million dollars," one Brazilian economist told the *Wall Street Journal*, "then I am lost, but if I owe $50 billion, the banks are lost." The ten countries listed in the following table account for the bulk of the Third World's bank debt. Interestingly enough, four of the biggest debtors are major oil-exporting countries. The table also shows that a sizable percentage of the total bank debt is due before the end of 1982.

* In addition, the move away from huge syndicated loans and toward "club" loans involving a few banks means that published data will probably be less comprehensive than in the past.

Table 6
LEADING THIRD WORLD DEBTORS
DEBT OWED TO BANKS
(at end-1981)

| | | Due in one year or less | |
	$ billions	% of total	% of exports
Mexico	$56.9	49	85
Brazil	52.7	35	67
Venezuela	26.2	61	79
Argentina	24.8	47	100
South Korea	19.9	58	37
Chile	10.5	40	77
Philippines	10.2	56	63
Indonesia	7.2	41	14
Taiwan	6.6	62	14
Nigeria	6.0	34	12

SOURCE: Morgan Guaranty, *World Financial Markets*, August 1982, p. 10. Reprinted with permission

The costs of paying the interest and principal on the Third World's foreign debt have grown enormously in recent years. The annual cost of debt service payments rose from $15 billion in 1973 to over $100 billion in 1982. Debt service ratios, the percentage of exports devoted to servicing a nation's foreign debt, rose from less than 14 percent in 1977 to 22 percent in 1982. Interest payments alone rose from under $5 billion in 1974 to $40 billion in 1982. In the late 1970s, Third World countries borrowed heavily from private banks to build up their foreign currency reserves. Now, however, weak export markets, plus higher interest rates, have forced them to dip into these reserves to service their debts. The foreign currency reserves of oil-importing Third World countries fell by 15 percent in 1981. This reduced the safety margin of currency reserve from a high of nearly five months in 1978 to less than 3.5 months.

Just as Third World debt is concentrated in a few countries, most of the lending by American banks is done by a relatively small number of banks. According to Federal Reserve Governor Henry Wallich, who watches over international lending for the U.S. central bank, in 1981, 24 large U.S. banks had over 80 percent of all outstanding U.S. loans to the nonoil Third World countries. For these 24 banks as a group, one dollar in every ten of outstanding loans is to a Third World country. It is sobering to compare U.S. banks' Third World loans to the financial worth of the banks themselves. Theoretically, to diversify risks, a U.S. bank is not supposed to lend more than 10 percent of the value of its capital to any single borrower. The banks have gotten around this limit by convincing bank regulators that different borrowers in the same country are autonomous and thus will be able to service their debts regardless of the fates of other borrowing entities. This allows the banks to loan money to many countries far in excess of the 10 percent rule. Everyone knows, for instance, that Citibank has around $8 billion sunk in Mexico and Brazil, a sum nearly twice as large as the value of Citibank's capital and loan loss reserves. Citibank is not alone. According to Henry Wallich, in June 1979 there were 36 reported instances of a bank having exposure worth more than *30 percent* of its capital to an oil-importing Third World country. Eighteen months later, there were 80 such cases. The loans of the 24 largest U.S. multinational banks to the leading Third World debtors are equal to 180 percent of their capital. For the nine largest banks, loans to nonoil Third World countries stood at 240 percent of their capital in 1980, up from 156 percent three years earlier. They appear to be growing larger all the time.

U.S. banks are more exposed in Third World countries than foreign banks, but the gap is narrowing. One of the reasons Third World debt has grown so rapidly in recent years is the fierce competition between U.S. and foreign banks for beachheads in the Third World. Since the mid-1970s, European and Japanese banks have made serious inroads on the U.S. share of the market. According to the investment banking firm Salomon Brothers, U.S. banks' share of total Third World debt fell from over 54 percent in 1974 to about one-third percent in 1981. From the beginning of 1978 until mid-1979, according to economist Rodney H. Mills of the Federal Reserve System, foreign banks outloaned U.S. banks by an astounding $32 billion to $6 billion, leaving U.S. banks with only about 15 percent of new Third World loans during that period. The European and Japanese onslaught included an erosion of U.S.

banks' traditional monopolies in important Latin American countries, such as Argentina, Brazil and Mexico. In addition, a new generation of Arab banks is increasingly active in international financing. With access to petrodollar billions at favorable interest rates, banks such as Arab Bank Corporation, Gulf International Bank and Union de Banques Arabes et Françaises are involved in a growing number of loan syndications, taking some of the heat off U.S. and European banks.

The Third World is not the only trouble spot in the global debt crisis. One region where the European banks have been more deeply involved than U.S. banks is eastern Europe. Led by German and Austrian banks, Western banks flocked to establish relations with the foreign trade banks of the Soviet bloc.

Loans by private banks to eastern Europe expanded rapidly for a number of reasons. As cold-war tensions ebbed, trade between East and West increased from about $20 billion in 1970 to over $130 billion in 1981. Second, West European governments actively encouraged bank loans to eastern Europe in order to stimulate exports and therefore improve domestic economic performance. East-West economic integration was also perceived as a way to encourage the Soviets to exercise restraint in the world's hot spots and temper their support for Third World revolutions. Thus, government guarantees encouraged the growth of private loans. Third, the Soviet Union possesses larger natural resources, including gold, oil, coal and copper. Like the capitalist-controlled resources of the Third World, bankers viewed vast supplies of Communist resources as sound collateral for loans. On top of this, bankers say the Russians assured them that in a crunch a Soviet "umbrella" would shield COMECON borrowers from default. The Soviets, in other words, would honor East Europe's debts.

As a result, private bank lending to eastern Europe soared. The net debt—gross bank debts minus deposits in Western banks—of the Soviet Union and its satellites (East Germany, Poland, Rumania, Hungary, Bulgaria and Czechoslovakia) grew from a minuscule $7 billion in 1970 to $67 billion by 1981. Poland headed the list with around $25 billion. The USSR and East Germany each had a little over $10 billion, Rumania slightly less than $10 billion, and Hungary about $7 billion. (Bulgaria and Czechoslovakia are relatively minor borrowers.) The costs of servicing the debt also grew enormously. Except for the Soviet Union, which retains a premier credit rating, the debt service ratios of East European borrowers have grown substantially. Poland leads the list of casualties with a debt service ration of more than 100 percent, up from 30 percent in 1975. Hungary's debt service ratio doubled to 45 percent between 1975 and 1981, followed by East Germany with 44 percent and Rumania with 35 percent.

III

For the banks, the meaning of the global debt crisis is simple. Banks earn most of their profits by making loans. If countries cannot repay these huge loans, banks' profits, capital bases and stock prices could suffer grievously. Significant Third World defaults could stretch the financial system to the breaking point, possibly resulting in the collapse of major banks. As Professors Richard Herring and Jack Guttentag of the Wharton School observe:

> . . . a crisis in international banking has become increasingly likely. . . . An insolvency scenario in international banking is likely to begin with a development that substantially raises the expenses, or reduces the revenues of one or more countries with heavy outstanding indebtedness. This could lead to a credit shock to their lending banks, to a loss of confidence in such banks and to a "run" by creditors of such banks including other banks.

Even in the absence of major bank failures, defaults or even the threat of defaults can undermine confidence in the entire financial system and dry up new lending. Since international finance provides the lifeblood for international trade and investment, a crisis in the financial system can quickly disrupt the flow of goods and worsen unemployment and inflation all around.

The growing fear of a global debt crisis led the banks to move more cautiously after Oil Shock II than they did after Oil Shock I. In the aftermath of Oil Shock I, bankers welcomed the opportunity to expand their operations in the Third World via petrodollar recycling. They were not so enthusiastic after Oil Shock II. Oil Shock II, which began with the uprising against the shah of Iran, did not precipitate Paul Erdman's fabled *Crash of '79.* It created almost as many problems, though. Lower Iranian production did not result in a prolonged oil shortage, but fear of one led to frantic buying in the spot market, pushing prices above the official OPEC price and thus encouraging OPEC to raise prices. Prices exploded from about $14 a barrel in 1978, to $30 in early 1980 and reached $40 in early 1981. In the United States, Oil Shock II led to substantial increases in gasoline prices and massive shortages in the summer of 1979. Like Oil Shock I, Oil Shock II was accompanied by other negative economic developments. Before oil prices increased, rampant inflation and a weak U.S. dollar had become hallmarks of the Carter administration. Particularly burdensome were higher interest rates, which rose substantially after Paul Volcker became chairman of the Federal Reserve Board in August 1979.

What was uppermost in the bankers' minds was not gas lines and shortages, but what *Business Week* called the "Petro-Crash of the 1980s." With new shock waves reverberating throughout the world economy, the prospect of recycling billions of new petrodollars from OPEC to the oil-importing Third World looked much less appealing. On top of the existing debt mountain, the Third World faced even larger payment imbalances in the immediate future. The oil import bill of the Third World soared from $26 billion in 1978 to $67 billion in 1980. The current account deficits of the oil-importing Third World soared from $38 billion in 1978 to $82 billion in 1980 and $100 billion in 1981.

With the crushing burden of Oil Shock II, the banks were worried about how much more debt those countries could handle. David Rockefeller was among the first to sound the clarion:

> The seascape facing these same nations in the days ahead, however, is markedly different—and rather more threatening. What we see ahead are treacherous economic seas and gale-force financial winds, strong enough to capsize even large and well-manned ships—unless sails are reefed early, and all hands are ready at their stations when the gale hits.

Fed Chairman Paul Volcker added that if countries were in trouble, so were the banks. "One potential danger in the recycling process is the overloading of the commercial banking system," he declared in early 1980. Volcker said banks can "live with the recycling situation as it is today for a period of time . . . but our capacity to deal with this problem as time passes could increasingly be stretched close to the limit."

The year 1979 had been particularly difficult for the banks. That year the OPEC countries poured nearly $40 billion into the Euromarket. The supply of funds available for Euromarket lending was so vast that the profitability of new bank loans to the Third World fell precipitously. Despite rising indebtedness, the spreads that Third World countries were paying on loans declined throughout the year. Loan maturities lengthened considerably, increasing banks' risks. In short, it was a borrower's market. Third World countries flocked to the Euromarket and absorbed nearly half of all new publicized bank credits in 1979.

For bankers, this raised the specter of Third World debt growing endlessly and embroiling the banks permanently in countries of dubious creditworthiness, leading eventually to massive debt problems and nothing but trouble for the banks. The dangers of heavy private bank lending to the Third World were widely discussed after Oil Shock I, but receded when the OPEC surpluses began to shrink after 1974. Now the fears were back in full force. In the midst of growing pessimism about Third World debt, Citibank's Walter Wriston continued to maintain that things would work out for the best. An ardent free marketeer, Wriston rejects jitters about Third World debt as alarmist. At the 1981 International Monetary Conference, an annual extravaganza sponsored by the American Bankers Association, Wriston laid down the Citibank line:

> It is no secret that over the years a lot of intellectual capital has been invested in the proposition that massive defaults by the Third World will cause a world financial crisis. Those who have taken that view since 1973/74 have been proved wrong, and those of us who believed the market would work proved correct.

To be sure, few bankers shared Wriston's optimism. At the same conference, S.G. Warburg's Eric Roll gave a different view. While acknowledging the past accomplishments of the recycling process,

Roll added that "there is unfortunately reason to believe that recycling and adjustment will be more difficult in the future, particularly for the developing nations." As evidence, Roll cited a catalogue of international economic difficulties, including slower economic growth and balance of payments problems in the industrialized countries, greater competition for funds in the Euromarket and increased risks associated with Third World lending. Another investment banker, Leslie, Weinert, & Co.'s Richard Weinert, pointed in particular to the tremendous burdens imposed on borrowing countries by higher interest rates. "There is a major crisis of LDC debt coming," Weinert said in 1981. "If real interest rates do not come down and export earnings remain depressed, there is no way these debts can be serviced without substantial reschedulings."

If Wriston's position is that the recycling problem need not lead to the collapse of the international financial system, there is undoubtedly some merit to his argument. Much to the embarrassment of its critics, the global financial system has shown a remarkable resilience in the past decade. It has been hit directly by a number of potentially devastating blows—in 1970, during the Penn Central crisis; in 1974, when the Herstatt and Franklin failures dried up the foreign exchange markets; the silver market collapse and economic warfare between the United States and Iran. Each time, the system has bent, but never broken.

Still, the recycling problem has clearly become more difficult in the aftermath of Oil Shock II. A glance at the figures shows that the banks, including Citibank, radically changed their lending behavior in 1980. The banks knew they were headed for trouble if they continued to lend at 1979 levels. So in 1980, when Third World countries brought their annual borrowing plans to market, they asked for as much money as they obtained in 1979 on virtually the same terms. The banks refused. Fortunately for the banks, the countries needed the money more than the banks needed more Third World paper. The countries backed down.

In 1980, according to Morgan Guaranty, new bank lending to the Third World fell by 18 percent. The oil-importing Third World countries fared even worse. Publicized new loans fell to $23 billion in 1980, down from $35 billion in 1979, a staggering 35 percent decline. Countries affected by the cutback included the biggest Third

World debtors. Brazil's new borrowing fell from $6.7 to $4.3 billion. South Korea's fell to $1.3 billion from $3.2 billion. Though the data is less precise, COMECON borrowers also got considerably less in 1980.

After an early year standoff, the banks did open the money bags again, though the terms of lending changed dramatically. On top of higher interest rates, loan spreads increased substantially. Brazil, for instance, which used to pay spreads of less than 1 percent began to pay over 2 percent. Spreads for all Third World borrowers increased in 1980, increasing the profitability of the loans, though not as much as the banks would have liked.* Loan maturities shortened and the banks became more demanding about receiving accurate economic and financial data from borrowing countries.

Despite the banks' cautious attitudes toward some countries, the debt crisis came anyway. It just took a little longer than some people expected. While bankers' eyes were riveted on the Third World, a major debt crisis broke out in Poland. Bankers had rushed into eastern Europe on a wave of optimism, but the great eastern European illusion was bared for all to see when Poland finally defaulted in 1981. Poland's difficulties were symptomatic of the debt problems encountered by eastern Europe; but it was by far the most extreme example of excessive borrowing and lending. In 1972, according to the U.S. Treasury Department, Poland had a gross debt to the West of about $1.6 billion. Eight years later, the debt stood at $25 billion, a staggering 15-fold increase. Of Poland's total debt, some $16 billion was owed to private banks. In 1972, the combined payments of interest and principal due on Poland's foreign debt stood at a scant $300 million. By 1980, that had soared to $8 billion. The ratio of Poland's annual debt-servicing costs to its export revenues in 1972 was 15 percent, a manageable burden. In 1980, Poland's external debt payments *exceeded* its hard-currency exports by 8 percent.

---

* Focusing on spreads alone can be misleading because the banks can inflate their profits, increasing front-end fees and other charges attached to syndicated loans. Borrowers also have an incentive to go along, since published spreads are an important indicator of a country's standing in the financial community. They would rather pay large (and largely unpublicized) fees and low margins. So not all of the bankers' chronic complaints about low margins are justified.

Throughout the 1970s, the Polish authorities played the classic game of borrowing heavily abroad in order to avoid difficult economic and political choices at home. When the government of former party chief Edward Gierek launched a massive industrialization drive, it was financed largely by foreign borrowing. For political reasons, Gierek tried to avoid raising food prices and slowing down the growth of consumption to support the industrialization drive. Food riots had toppled his predecessor, Wladyslaw Gomulka, and Gierek wanted to avoid a similar fate. Yet Poland was trying to increase simultaneously both investment and consumption with limited resources. Production and exports were not growing sufficiently to service Poland's foreign debt, which was growing by leaps and bounds. The crunch finally came in 1980, when the Polish authorities moved to squeeze more hard currency out of the economy by diverting products to shops that accepted only foreign currencies. The purpose was to reduce domestic consumption in order to improve Poland's external financial viability. Before long, however, this policy produced an unprecedented explosion of strikes and confrontations between the government and workers and consumers. Unable to quell the disturbances peacefully, the government began to make concessions. The confrontations culminated in August 1980 with official recognition of Solidarity, the independent labor confederation. Although the political settlement raised hopes about Poland's future, in the short run the strikes and wage increases damaged copper, coal and other exports. The debt burden was becoming increasingly unmanageable.

Still, the banks kept lending. In the midst of the August political crisis, a $325 million loan by U.S., European and Japanese banks, plus the Moscow Narodny Bank, was signed in London. The bankers, apparently determined to hang with Poland, if only to salvage their existing loans, were not dismayed by the raging internal struggle. As one London-based banker told the *Wall Street Journal* in August, "the big banks are confident that the situation isn't out of control and that it will be resolved within two weeks. That seems to be the general feeling of the Polish government as well." In October, a 25-member consortium of German banks completed a $666-million-dollar Eurocredit to Poland, one-third of which was guaranteed by the West German government. No doubt the bankers consoled themselves that the stiff margins Poland was paying in 1980 made loans to that country more profitable. But this is small consolation when a debtor is unable to pay back what it has already borrowed. At the signing ceremony, Polish officials predicted that Poland would run a trade surplus with the West in 1981 and encounter no problems meeting 1981 borrowing targets. Asked if Poland was borrowing new funds in order to keep up its debt payments to the banks, Bank Handlowy President Marian Minkiewicz replied that "with funds from all sources in an account it [was] difficult to establish any specific payment's origin." "Money is money," he chirped.

Whether or not it could have been foreseen, the political settlement reached at Gdansk did not resolve the economic crisis but made things worse. Once Polish workers had political power, they used it to demand shorter hours and higher pay. Consumers wanted more goods on the shelves. Yet the government and the banks wanted exactly the opposite: higher labor productivity and resources diverted from domestic consumption to servicing the foreign debt. Objectively speaking, Solidarity's demands were probably unrealistic given the state of the economy, but after the hard-fought gains of August 1981, they were in no mood to start making concessions to party bureaucrats. The political impasse hastened the economy's deterioration.

In April 1981, Western governments moved to ease the position of both Poland and the banks by rescheduling Poland's government to government debt on lenient terms. Then Poland approached the banks to talk about rescheduling. European banks, particularly the Germans, had a lot riding on Poland, an estimated $6 billion in outstanding loans; Austrian banks were in for another $2 billion. U.S. banks had only about $2 billion in outstanding loans to Poland, much of it guaranteed by the U.S. government. Only First Chicago and Bank of America stood to lose substantial amounts. This is undoubtedly why U.S. banks refused to participate in the initial rescheduling talks.

The U.S. coordinating committee of leaders to Poland rejected a settlement, which the steering committee of Poland's lenders had hammered out with the Polish authorities, and sacked the Bank of America officer who had represented them at the meeting. Frederick Schwartz of Bankers Trust took his place at the next negotiating session. He maintained a hard line at the June negotiations, rattling off a series of conditions U.S. banks demanded the Poles meet. This included better numbers on Polish economic trends and sensitive information on Soviet loans to Poland. This annoyed the European bankers—and no doubt the Poles as well—who felt the U.S. bankers were backing the Polish authorities into a corner. The U.S. bankers were not moved.

In the meantime, political unrest continued to take a toll on production and exports. According to Daniel Singer, a leading authority on Soviet bloc economies, Poland's national income declined by about 16 percent in 1981, after a 7 percent fall in 1980. During the first ten months of 1981, while money incomes rose by more than 25 percent, the supply of goods and services the country was actually producing fell 11 percent. Coal exports, Poland's principal hard-currency earner, fell dramatically.

Sooner or later, something had to give. Eventually, it was Solidarity. For obvious reasons, no Western banker will go on the record in support of the government's December 1981 crackdown on Solidarity. But during the interim between the Gdansk agreement and the imposition of martial law on December 13, 1981, bankers openly sympathized with the government's desires to get the workers back to work and out of politics. On September 11, 1981, Paul McCarthy of New York's Chemical Bank said on "The MacNeil-Lehrer Report" that "Solidarity has to become understanding of how serious the financial problems are. . . . It has to be willing to work with the government to retain centralized control over the economy until such time as a stabilization program begins to take effect." A European banker, speaking to *Institutional Investor*, but not for attribution, was even blunter: "It's nice to take a year off," he said, "but now they have to go back to work." With its arrears to the banks piling up, Poland tried to buy time by applying for membership in the International Monetary Fund and World Bank in November 1981. Membership would not only increase the flow of hard currencies into Poland, but it would also place the Polish economy under the watchful eyes of the IMF's technocrats, something bankers find tremendously reassuring.

In the midst of a deepening economic crisis, the Polish generals moved to crush Solidarity. On the morning of December 13, perhaps in a last-ditch attempt to prevent Soviet intervention, martial law was imposed on Poland. The government now had a free hand to squeeze more out of the domestic economy to pay Poland's external debts. Yet despite the "benefits" of martial law, when 1981 came to an end, Poland still had not paid more than $500 million in interest and $2.5 billion in principal on its 1981 debt. Poland had defaulted.

Poland's 1981 debt repayments remained in limbo for several months. At times, it seemed that no one was quite sure if Poland had paid or not, but finally, on March 27, 1982, the remaining interest of $500 million left over from 1981 was paid. Once this was done, Poland's 460 bank creditors agreed to reschedule $2.5 billion in principal payments that Poland could not meet in 1981. The military government agreed to pay about 5 percent of this, or $120 million, in 1982, with the balance due in installments beginning in 1985. Yet no sooner were the 1981 rescheduling negotiations complete than Poland began talking with its bankers about rescheduling the payments that would fall due in 1982. Virtually no one believes Poland will have the hard currency needed to meet even a small portion of those payments. In a brash move, Poland has attempted to exploit its inability to pay its debts as a bargaining chip in its dealings with the banks. As Bank Handlowy's Jan Woloszyn told the *Wall Street Journal*, "If the banks want their money back, they will have to help us."

Initially, the Poles proposed borrowing a fresh $3 billion. The banks would have no part of this, and a compromise solution was agreed upon wherein the Poles will receive back half of the $1 billion in 1982 interest payments in the form of new credits. This gives the Poles an incentive to maintain interest payments while the billions in principal payments it owes will be rescheduled into the future. Although this may solve the banks' immediate problems, there should be no mistake about what it involves. Poland is broke and the banks are lending it new money to pay off its old debts. Still, the banks have not formally declared Poland in default and have no intention of doing so. Default is a bad word in today's global money market, something that bankers seek to avoid at almost any cost. The banks have too many billions strung out all over the globe to go around declaring countries that can't pay their debts in default. Instead, the watchword is "rescheduling." It has better connotations than default and preserves the illusion that the banks' Polish loans are good loans. As one French banker told the *New York Times,* "You've got to be cynical. Everyone knows Poland is in default. But if we say so, we admit we're bad bankers who made loans we never should have made."

While the bankers were crossing the t's and dotting the i's on the 1982 Polish rescheduling, a much bigger debt crisis exploded virtually overnight in Mexico.* This time American banks were not so smug. They were far more deeply involved in Mexico than the Europeans were in Poland. Mexico's total foreign bank debt is over $60 billion, with U.S. banks in for well over $20 billion. At the top of the list stand Walter Wriston's Citibank and Bank of America.

Mexico has traditionally been a large Euromarket borrower, but it became the leading Third World debtor, ironically, when oil exports soared in the late 1970s. Oil has lured the banks into scores of Third World countries and Mexico was no exception. With oil prices expected to rise indefinitely, Mexico embarked on an aggressive industrialization drive fueled by oil revenues, which also served as collateral for billions more in bank credits. Headed by the state oil company Pemex (Petroleos Mexicanos), Mexico became the most active borrower in the international money markets. Mexico's total foreign debt increased an astounding $60 billion in six years, from $20 billion in 1976 to over $80 billion by 1982. Mexico suffered briefly during the general reduction in Third World lending in 1980, but in 1981 Mexico was back in the credit markets with full force. The world recession, high interest rates and a global oil glut cut deeply into Mexico's exports and government revenues. None of this apparently fazed the banks. Faced with a deteriorating economic outlook, the banks hung with Mexico. Competition to lend to Mexico was intense. Bank of America boasted about a

---

* Some sources have suggested that Poland had an easier time in 1982 because of the banks' mounting problems in Latin America. This apparently had two effects. First, the U.S. banks needed the Europeans and Japanese to weather the Latin crisis. Second, while the Latin crisis was developing, a major upset over Poland could have sapped confidence in the whole international financial system.

mammoth $4 billion trade credit it had arranged for Mexico, the largest of its kind in Euromarket history. Unlike most Third World countries, Mexico's loan spreads fell in 1981. Estimates prepared by *The Banker*'s Basil Caplan show that Mexico's foreign debt increased by $18 billion in 1981 with Pemex alone borrowing $10 billion. On top of bank credits, Mexico tapped the bond markets for billions more. As the oil glut worsened Mexico's outlook in 1982, loan spreads rose and maturities fell but the lending binge continued. According to Morgan, Mexico borrowed $7.5 billion in the first six months of 1982, much of it to defend the peso. Mexico also raised another $1.8 billion in the bond markets.

In the middle of 1982, however, the Mexican economy fell apart, forcing Mexico to suspend its foreign debt payments and delivering a rude shock to the international banking community. The glamour stock of the Euromarket was suddenly a basket case. Initially the problem surfaced in Mexico's largest private enterprise, Grupo Industrial Alfa. Beset by inflation, mismanagement and high interest rates, in April the steel-based conglomerate suspended payments on its $2 billion foreign debt. While Alfa discussed a debt renegotiation with its bankers, rot spread throughout Mexico's entire economic and financial systems. Capital fled the country, and in a desperate attempt to restore confidence the government borrowed more to support the peso. Like Alfa and Pemex, Mexico had been living on borrowed money. Billions in debt payments, which the government could not honor, were falling due. A massive black market sprang up in Mexican pesos, which pushed the currency down from about 25 to the dollar early in the year to over 100 in a few months. By summer, Alfa's troubles, recurrent speculation against the peso and the crippling world recession ignited a general financial panic in Mexico. In August, the central bank ran out of dollars. Rumors swept a stunned Wall Street that Citibank and Bank of America were in trouble.

After closing the currency markets, Mexico's finance minister Jesús Silva Herzog jumped on a plane to seek emergency financial assistance in Washington, which was quickly promised by Treasury and the Federal Reserve. Then came the inevitable proposal from the Mexicans to restructure Mexico's foreign debt. In a meeting with more than 100 bankers at the New York Federal Reserve Bank on August 20, Silva Herzog proposed a 90-day suspension on Mexico's repayments of the principal on its foreign debt. He also asked the banks for another $1 billion in loans to ease the country's financial stress. In contrast to their stance in the 1981 Polish talks, U.S. bankers were receptive to the proposal, which had the backing of the U.S. Treasury and Federal Reserve. While the Fed, Treasury and IMF assembled a multibillion-dollar bail-out package, the situation continued to deteriorate. Renewed speculation against the peso forced the government to nationalize private banks and toughen its exchange control measures, resulting in huge losses to foreign investors. Two weeks after the banks had agreed to the 90-day moratorium, Silva Herzog announced that new projections of Mexico's foreign currency shortfall showed that Mexico would be unable to resume amortization payments on its foreign debt before the end of 1983. Like Poland, the Third World's biggest debtor was broke.

IV

The Mexican and Polish cases exploded two stubborn myths about global banking. The first is that the banking system is essentially sound and that the banks are not carrying large amounts of questionable loans on their books. The second is that when problems arise, "the market" solves them handily.

That the banks' aggressive lending has led to problems in major countries like Poland and Mexico, not to mention lesser cases like Costa Rica, Zaire and Sudan, is clear. What is not generally appreciated is that the situation is probably worse than it seems. When Walter Wriston claims that the loss record on international loans is much better than losses on domestic loans, what he doesn't mention is that what the banks classify as "loan losses" is only the tip of the iceberg. For each international loan that the banks have written off as a loser, there are many more that are highly questionable. When countries default, the banks theoretically have to set aside reserves to cover their exposure. As long as countries like Mexico keep up their interest payments, however, the banks are not required to classify the loans as "nonperforming," even though the principal will never be repaid. As Henry Wallich observes, "It is harder to recognize a loss on a sovereign loan than on a commercial loan. On a loan to business, the loss is final when the borrower goes out of business. That kind of tap on the head with a two-by-four usually does not happen in the international field." This is purely an accounting fiction that allows management to avoid the embarrassment of admitting it made bad loans and dipping into profits to compensate for them. To avoid declaring countries in default, the banks are increasingly relying on debt reschedulings. When countries can't pay, the banks restructure the terms to allow countries to maintain interest payments. That way, the loans remain on the banks' books as good loans.*

The banks are perfectly happy with this arrangement, but the Fed's Wallich is not. In a speech to bank supervisors in September 1981, Wallich put it bluntly:

> We, as supervisors, should begin looking seriously at the treatment of rescheduled loans. In particular, the question arises at what point the banks should begin to set up reserves against such loans. A recent multi-country review of banking practices by the Bank for International Settlements found that in no major country are delays in payment of interest on sovereign loans automatically classified as doubtful assets. In most countries the banks themselves have considerable leeway with regard to the accounting treatment of loans to sovereign borrowers that are in arrears. In the United States, only loans that are explicitly delinquent must be placed in a non-accrual status by the banks. Rescheduled loans seldom reach this state: as an illustration, loans to Poland and Turkey are not now considered in a non-accrual status by U.S. banks.

While rescheduling solves the immediate problems of both the banks and their troubled customers, papering over bad loans is tantamount to debasing credit standards. No doubt Wriston and his colleagues understand what a dangerous game this is, but they are gambling that so long as the problem loans come in dribs and drabs

---

* On October 26, 1982, the Securities and Exchange Commission took a small step in the direction of greater disclosure of potential sovereign loan losses. The SEC Staff Accounting Bulletin 49 requires banks to disclose the amount of their loans to countries with liquidity problems that may have a material impact on public and private sector borrowers' ability to repay U.S. banks, when such loans exceed 1 percent of the bank's outstanding collectibles. Still, the banks determine which countries go into that category.

rather than all at once, confidence in the integrity of the financial system will be maintained. In any event they have no other options.*

Although the merits of the banks' approach to reschedulings can be debated, it is patently clear that they get a good deal of help from governments in averting some potentially serious financial disasters. Global banks operate on the premise that governments will always bail out a bank of any significance that is in difficulty. Indeed, one of the reasons why international bank lending has become so reckless is that it is assumed no major financial institution will be allowed to go under. The global bankers are the strongest believers in laissez-faire, yet they look to the government, and ultimately the taxpayers, in times of trouble.

In the case of Poland, the U.S. government has so far picked up the tab for delinquent Polish loans. For six weeks after the imposition of martial law in Poland, the Reagan administration inveighed against Poland's military junta and their Russian sponsors. When the Poles failed to come up with the money to pay interest to Western banks, hard-line anti-Communists beseeched Reagan to formally declare Poland in default. Had the administration done so, in all likelihood, U.S. banks, European governments and European banks would have followed suit. Poland would have been closed out of world credit markets. Much of the rest of eastern Europe, particularly Rumania, would have experienced severe difficulties in obtaining new financing. The Soviets, in turn, would have had to assume the burden of paying eastern Europe's bills.

Instead of declaring Poland in default, Reagan chose to preserve the fiction that Poland is creditworthy in order to protect the banks. On February 1, 1982, the Reagan administration ordered the Agriculture Department to reimburse American banks, including Citi-

---

* Debt reschedulings have become so common that advising countries on how to negotiate with commercial banks has become big business for a number of investment banks. Probably the most famous advisory service is the troika formed in 1977 by Warburg, Lehman Brothers Kuhn Loeb, and Lazard Frères. Representatives of the three banks met in Indonesia when each was trying to solicit a contract to advise the government on its debt rescheduling. The group was formed shortly thereafter and has handled about a dozen reschedulings, including Turkey, Zaire and Gabon.

bank, Chase Manhattan, Morgan, Bank of America, First Chicago and others $71 million in interest that Poland had failed to pay on U.S. government-guaranteed loans. Yet the administration did not force the banks to declare Poland in default. For all of 1982, the U.S. government reimbursed U.S. banks $344 million for delinquent Polish loan payments. Over the next two years, the banks stand to collect another $495 million from the government.

A more blatant example of the government bail-out operation to protect U.S. banks was the U.S. government's handling of the Mexican crisis. The banks were scared stiff over the Mexican crisis, and the government moved swiftly to avoid serious damage to the financial system. First, the U.S. Treasury gave Mexico an immediate $1 billion dollar currency swap line to support the government's financial position. (Later the swap line, in effect, was used to pay Mexico for $1 billion worth of oil exported to the United States for stockpiling in the strategic petroleum reserve.) Second, the Federal Reserve contributed $925 million to a "bridge loan" of nearly $2 billion, organized through the Bank for International Settlements in Switzerland. (The BIS, formed in 1930 to handle problems of German repatriations payments, is the only effective international "lender of last resort" for the international banking system. It is sometimes called the "central bank of central bankers.") Third, the U.S. government's Commodity Credit Corporation agreed to guarantee $1 billion in credits allowing Mexico to purchase food. Finally, the U.S. government backed a huge package assembled by the International Monetary Fund for Mexico. Combined with some new money from the banks, the infusion of money into Mexico totaled about $5 billion. The package amounted to a bail-out for Mexico, but it was also designed to ease the situation of the banks and prevent a Mexican default from provoking an even larger crisis. Six months later, President Reagan handed Brazilian President Figueralo a check for $1 billion to prevent a default by the Third World's next largest debtor. Through the BIS the Fed kicked in another $500 million.

The supreme irony of the global debt crisis is that the banks are in so deep that they can't get out without bringing down the whole house of cards. They have loaned so much money to the Brazils, Mexicos and Polands that they can't cut them off without triggering the crisis they are hoping to avoid. In the aftermath of the Mexican crisis, a number of smaller banks started demanding their money back and refused to participate in new syndications. The big banks, already shell-shocked from developments in Mexico, were panic-stricken that without new money Brazil and Argentina would quickly go the way of Mexico. Chase Manhattan convened a major conference of leading banks, known as the Ditchley group, in October to drum up support for continued lending. The Ditchley group, chaired by Chase Vice-Chairman William Ogden, formally agreed to establish a new banking institute to exchange information on borrowing countries, but the real reason for the gathering was to convince the world that the big banks would not abandon the biggest debtors. Almost half of the money they owe the banks falls due in 1983 and without new money they will be unable to pay. The only place they can get enough money is from the banks. Shortly after the October conference, the big six U.S. banks quickly assembled an emergency $600 million package for Brazil.

This situation probably gives the bankers more sleepless nights than any other dilemma they face. When a country gets into trouble, the banks are under tremendous pressure to cover their existing exposure by throwing good money after bad. One investment banker with experience in tangled Third World debt messes explains why: "Look, you've got people out there who don't want to show a lot of red ink to the stockholders. They've got families and homes and they don't want to wind up out there on the street. The banks don't want to lend Poland or Turkey any more, but they lend to them because they have to."

V

In more than four decades in the international financial business, Irving S. Friedman has seen it all. A soft-spoken, likable 68-year-old with snow-white hair, Friedman started out working as one of the bright young economists in Harry Dexter White's Treasury Department. Later, Friedman moved to the World Bank and the International Monetary Fund, where he pioneered the development of the fund's system of annual policy consultations with member countries. Friedman, who considers himself the high priest of IMF "conditionality" for the use of IMF credit, spent 25 years in the IMF-World Bank complex before moving to Citibank in 1974. Citibank's most important Third World troubleshooter continued to live in Bethesda, Maryland, shuttling to New York every week, and almost as often to some remote country to salvage bad Citibank loans. When he retired from Citibank in 1980, he joined Wall Street's First Boston as a senior adviser and statesman.

Irving Friedman believes that the global debt crisis is a permanent part of the world economic landscape. Debtor countries, he says, can't do without the money. When bankers express anxieties about their "exposure" in the Third World, he tells them, "If you're scared, you don't belong. That's when you could have real problems." He refuses to talk apocalyptically about the global debt problem, but he gives the impression that he keeps his fingers crossed. Unlike dogmatic free marketeers, he openly admits that the private banks need help, mainly from the International Monetary Fund. Today Irving Friedman believes that the IMF should become a genuine global "lender of last resort" for the private banking system. He believes the IMF's resources should be increased from the present level of about $60 billion to as much as $300 billion. He dwells on the importance of the perception that a powerful IMF is there to help countries and their banks in times of trouble. "In order to have a truly central role, I think the Fund has to be perceived as having the capability of defending the system," Friedman says.

The global debt crisis gave the International Monetary Fund a new lease on life. Throughout the postwar period, the Fund was gradually edged out of the center of the action in global finance by the private banks. Today, the IMF has fewer resources as 'a percentage of world trade than at any time in its history. As the Fund's influence waned, senior people such as Friedman left for more power and money in the private sector. What changed the Fund's fate was the debt crisis. Today the IMF's main area of responsibility is mopping up messy global debt problems, mainly in the Third World. As COMECON's debt troubles have grown, so has their interest in joining the IMF. What Moscow used to condemn as an agent of Western imperialism has become another source of hard currency for the financially strapped members of COMECON.

The IMF provides a kind of intensive care unit for countries in trouble. The IMF's role is straightforward. When countries can't pay their debts, the IMF steps in with a series of recommendations on how it thinks the country can get back on its feet and regain creditworthiness. Increasingly, private banks look to the IMF to discipline debtor countries so that they can get their money back. Banks normally do not agree to lend to countries in difficulty unless the government has agreed to do what the Fund says it must to set its financial affairs in order.

As the global debt crisis mounted, the number of bankers shuttling to Washington to visit the IMF increased dramatically. Having lunch with a banker in Washington generally means eating at the Hay-Adams, up the street from the Treasury Department, or at Dominique's, around the corner from the Fund. Increasingly, the banks rely on the Fund's advice and expertise. "Commercial banks," Gabriel Hauge, the late chairman of the board of Manufacturers Hanover Trust, once put it, "tend to feel more at ease with their country's credits after the IMF has stepped in and . . . established a viable adjustment program." Private banks, says Irving Friedman, view the IMF as a kind of "fire department," to cope with potential defaults. As more and more countries have become overextended, private banks have looked increasingly to the IMF to certify their creditworthiness before agreeing to reschedule loan payments or extend new credits. With the exceptions of Poland and Nicaragua, banks have seldom rescheduled the loans of debtor countries that refuse to submit to the dictums of IMF economic "stabilization programs."*

The IMF's role in resolving the global debt crisis is not primarily its financial contribution. In the years after 1973, the Fund loaned its members only a small fraction of what they needed to buy oil and other necessities. From 1974 to 1979 the IMF loaned all of its members approximately $12 billion, or about $2 billion per year. During this period industrialized countries took a large part of the

---

* At the time of its reschedulings, Poland was not a member of the Fund. Nicaragua refused to accept an IMF stabilization program. The Sandinista government, with financial advice provided by New York's Leslie, Weinert, & Co., and the strong support of then-creditworthy Mexico, received a full rescheduling on highly favorable terms.

IMF's credit, so that left the Third World with about $7 billion. With the Third World facing hundreds of billions of dollars of deficits, $7 billion doesn't go very far. What the Fund has to offer is experience in dealing with the economic difficulties of individual countries. Only a few big banks, such as Citibank or Morgan, have an adequate number of in-house economists who pore over the economic indicators of countries on a daily basis. Citibank's Jack Guenther, who also took his training at the IMF, argues that the IMF's experts are actually in a better position to evaluate country trends than are bankers. Bankers, he says, are frequently "under pressure to lend" to countries the bank deals with and that the normal tendency "is always to lend more," which means their reports must be optimistic. He cites as evidence the rosy reports about the future of Somoza's Nicaragua written in the mid-1970s by Citibank's Central American "experts." Not long after, Somoza suspended payments on Nicaragua's foreign debt, and in 1979 a civil war toppled Somoza. It may be difficult to be objective, muses Friedman, "when you're playing golf with Somoza."

The IMF also has something else individual banks often don't, political clout with poor countries, particularly those with severe financial problems. As a makeshift "lender of last resort," when countries in trouble can't borrow money from anybody else they go to the IMF. The IMF doesn't dish out money to good customers as commercial banks do. Unlike the World Bank, it does not finance specific projects such as steel mills or oil exploration. The IMF lends general purpose funds but with strings attached. Interest rates are concessional; the real price is what the country must do to qualify.

The love affair between the banks and the IMF was a product of growing Third World debt delinquency. At first, the big banks thought they could go it alone. What changed their minds was Peru's brush with default in 1976. Following the military coup of 1968, which brought a reform-minded regime to power, commercial banks poured money into Peru. Peru's external debt quadrupled from roughly $1 billion in 1968 to $4.4 billion by 1975. The banks seemed convinced that high copper prices would provide Peru with stable export income, while new oil discoveries were expected to produce a future bonanza. By early 1976, these hopes were dashed and Peru was nearly bankrupt.

Peru needed help, but the government wanted to avoid the conditions attached to IMF borrowing. So President Francisco Morales Bermudez, who succeeded General Juan Velasco Alvarez, asked the banks to reschedule Peru's debt payments. With Irving Friedman at the helm, a steering committee of six U.S. banks agreed to refinance $400 million in payments without demanding that Peru seek IMF help. In addition, the U.S. banks promised Peru $250 million of new financing, if the government could raise another $100 million from European and Japanese banks and curb the spending habits of the military.

For a variety of reasons, the banks found it difficult to turn the country's economy around. The government did not make good on its promises to the banks. As Peru's economic crisis worsened, the prospect of default again loomed on the horizon. This time the banks would not play ball. Instead, they demanded that Peru reach an agreement with the IMF, which, they decided, was better equipped to enforce an economic stabilization program. E. Walter Robichek, head of the IMF's powerful Western Hemisphere Department, called this sequence of events a "watershed" in the history of the IMF's relations with the banks. As for Friedman, he likes to downplay the significance of the incident.

After a couple of false starts, the IMF and Peru finally reached an agreement in August 1978 which gave Peru access to about $200 million in IMF credits over a two-year period. With Peru back in the Fund's good graces, the banks were ready to talk about refinancing. With access to the Fund's credit, Peru would now have the cash to pay off some of their pressing private bank debts. More importantly, the government's economic policies would be under strict scrutiny by the Fund. The debt refinancing agreement was tied directly to the government's compliance with the specific performance targets of the IMF agreement.

Since the Peruvian fiasco, the banks have never strayed very far from the skirts of the IMF. The close working relationship that has evolved between the banks and the IMF helps the banks considerably. First, by injecting fresh funds into debtor countries, the IMF makes it easier for them to maintain payments to the banks. Second, if the Fund can remedy countries' economic problems it may help salvage potentially sour bank loans. Finally, the IMF has legitimacy as an official multilateral institution which allows it to impose "adjustment policies" on member countries more effectively than the banks. The IMF, points out Willard Butcher, David Rockefeller's successor as chairman of Chase Manhattan, "can exert the political muscle that banks cannot, in ensuring that an adjustment process is inaugurated and maintained." When the IMF gives a country its "seal of good housekeeping," as Arthur Burns used to call it, the banks feel confident.

In the aftermath of Oil Shock II, the Fund's role in the global debt crisis expanded considerably. For the banks, the IMF has become indispensable in coping with the global debt crisis, casting a long shadow of doubt over Walter Wriston's assertion that "the market" can solve the recycling problem. In 1979, a heavy borrowing year, the banks felt countries were exploiting their willingness to lend to avoid going to the IMF. The banks were right. As their worries about their exposure in overburdened Third World countries escalated, a massive campaign to upgrade the Fund began. On the eve of the 1980 IMF annual meeting, *The Banker* editorialized that the Fund should "take the lead" in resolving the global debt mess by

> either loosening its own purse strings or by acting as a catalyst in attracting funds from the markets or by a combination of the two approaches. In granting member countries access to its resources, however, it has to be prepared to take risks that market institutions could not assume.

To enhance its role in the recycling process, the Fund arranged to borrow about $10 billion from the Saudi Arabian Monetary Authority (SAMA). When private bank lending to Third World countries declined in 1980, the Fund moved in to take up the slack. During 1980 and 1981, the Fund made loan commitments of more than $22 billion to its member countries to support stabilization programs, more than it had spent in the previous seven years. An unprecedented number of countries have undertaken stabilization programs under the auspices of the IMF. By early 1982, 39 countries had agreed to take the IMF medicine. By the end of the year, so did Mexico, Brazil and Argentina.

IMF stabilization programs have thus become the logical and necessary complement to private bank reschedulings. In the absence of a genuine solution to the global debt crisis, the banks have been content to salvage their loans on a case-by-case basis. What happens essentially is that an IMF technical mission jets into a troubled country with the magic computer printouts that tell a country how to cough up enough hard currency to maintain debt payments to the banks. For poor countries, this involves more than reshuffling interest payments. Generally, it means making politically explosive changes in economic policy. Often, under pressure from foreign banks and the IMF, poor countries must use their scarce foreign currency reserves to pay off foreign banks while ignoring the pressing needs of impoverished populations. As Jamaica's former Prime Minister Michael Manley put it at the nadir of his country's debt crisis in 1980, the choice often comes down to "using your last foreign exchange to pay off Citibank and Chase Manhattan or buying food and medicine for your people."

VI

One of the things John Maynard Keynes and Harry White used to argue about was how much authority the Bretton Woods institutions, particularly the IMF, would have to intervene in domestic economic policy decisions. White, liberal though he was, represented a creditor country, and understandably he favored using financial leverage as a way to force countries to shape up. Keynes, representing a debtor country, categorically rejected the notion of a supranational agency intervening in domestic policy decisions. One of the reasons Keynes despised the gold standard was that, in effect, it forced countries to submit to foreign financial pressures. In the postwar world, the IMF took the place of the gold standard.

In theory, IMF officials sit down with government ministers to work out solutions to a country's economic problems. In reality the relationship is inevitably adversarial, and the country's bargaining power is limited by the knowledge that if it does not accept the IMF's conditions, it will be closed out of world credit markets. Basically, the Fund lays down a series of conditions, spelled out in what is known as a standby arrangement, which the country agrees to meet before it gets IMF money.* The amount of money a country can borrow from the Fund depends on how much it pays in, its "quota" in IMF jargon. Countries with minor problems may borrow 25 percent to 50 percent of the quota. Basket cases can get as much as 450 percent. The IMF lends hard currencies—dollars, German marks, or Japanese yen†—in "tranches," or slices of credit, in the literal French meaning. Each successive tranche is governed by progressively harder conditions. If a country fails to meet them, the disbursements stop. In the words of former IMF staff economist John Williamson:

A standby is an agreement that a country has the right to draw up to a specified sum during a determined period subject to the observances of certain conditions. It is also now standard policy for the total drawing to be made available in a series of installments rather than all released immediately, and for these installments to be subject to the country satisfying a series of performance criteria agreed before the standby is granted.

When a country violates the performance criteria, the IMF tears up the agreement. Generally the finance minister is sacked and frequently the government falls.

IMF economic "stabilization" programs have traditionally been austere. Like the old gold standard, they emphasize cutting government spending, devaluing the currency, increasing unemployment

* The core of most IMF programs consists of four, specific, monetary targets. They are net domestic assets, net foreign assets, bank credit to the public sector and total bank credit.

† For accounting purposes, IMF credits are denominated in Special Drawing Rights, or SDRs, the IMF's official unit of account. In IMF terminology, countries do not receive "loans," instead they "purchase" hard currencies from the Fund with their own currencies. Paying the IMF back is known as "repurchasing."

and raising interest rates in order to restore financial integrity. Essentially what the Fund does to a country in trouble is administer a tough, quick-fix solution to its balance of payments problems. The IMF, which does not consider itself a development institution, is less concerned with solving the structural dilemmas of development than with generating a quick improvement in a country's balance of payments. In the aftermath of Oil Shock II, and particularly following the election of Ronald Reagan, IMF programs became especially rigid. The Treasury Department's monetarists, led by Beryl Sprinkel, argued that after Oil Shock I countries received too much financing instead of making the cuts necessary to adjust to balance of payments difficulties. At the Fund, the watchword quickly became "adjustment" rather than financing.

What the Fund strategy boils down to is making radical cuts in domestic consumption in order to free up resources to service the foreign debt. Wages must fall dramatically in real terms in hopes that exports will become more competitive. Simultaneously, currency devaluation and lifting price controls pushes up prices beyond the reach of many consumers. Imports will decline and new production will be diverted to the export market. The hope of the IMF technocrats is that rising exports and falling imports will lead to "equilibrium" in the balance of payments, thereby restoring creditworthiness. If it does, the IMF then leans on the banks to contribute more money as a reward for being successful. Occasionally, for important Western allies, such as Turkey, Pakistan or Seaga's Jamaica, the United States and western Europe assemble massive supplementary financing that makes the IMF medicine easier to swallow.

In poor countries IMF programs typically bring economic and social disaster. When a country reduces domestic consumption to free up resources to pay off its creditors, somebody else must get less. When the IMF and the banks get together to "solve" a Third World country's foreign debt problems, the usual losers are the urban workers and the rural poor. Devaluing the currency and abolishing price controls on food and other necessities sends the cost of living skyward, so the majority of the population is forced to spend most of its income just to survive. Cuts in government spending inevitably lead to recession, increasing unemployment and lowering wages.* Meanwhile, the incomes of the rich go up—by design. The rich, according to conventional economic theory, are society's principal savers. Since it is out of savings that the funds for investment come, particularly if foreign borrowing is curtailed, the rich must be encouraged to save more so they can invest more. The IMF has never come up with a satisfactory solution of what to do if the rich put their additional income in Swiss banks or use it to buy real estate in Paris or Manhattan.

The injustices of IMF programs have led to food riots in Lima, Cairo, Kinshasa and Rabat. The political fallout from IMF programs has toppled governments in Turkey and Jamaica. In 1977, the rigors of the IMF's approach nearly brought down the government of Anwar Sadat. The governments that have survived a dose of IMF economics frequently are military governments. In Turkey the overthrow of democracy by the military in 1980 was a direct result of an IMF stabilization program. The IMF, one observer told the *New York Times*, "has overthrown more governments than Marx and Lenin combined."

Despite the costs of the IMF's policies, countries might not be so reluctant to submit to the Fund's shock treatment if the programs had a reasonably successful track record. That they do not is confirmed by the Fund's own staff. According to an analysis performed by T. R. Reichmann, an economist in the Fund's powerful Trade and Exchange Relations Department, 21 stabilization programs initiated after Oil Shock I had only about a 33 percent success rate. The mixed results of more recent Fund programs were described candidly in a speech by IMF Managing Director Jacques de Larosière. In a survey of 23 programs implemented in 1978 and 1979, according to Larosière, only half of them could be considered successes. Moreover, the success stories tended to be concentrated in lesser developed European economies such as Turkey and Portugal, not in the poor countries of Asia, Africa, Latin America and the Caribbean. In only half the cases did the programs reduce external

---

* The IMF often reasons that when food prices go up, poor farmers will be among the main beneficiaries. Yet, even if food prices rise, the increasing costs of fuels, fertilizers and credit are often sufficient to render the impact of higher food prices negligible.

deficits and inflation in line with the targets established by the Fund. While the 50 percent success rate is an improvement over the results of the early 1970s, the dilemma facing a government with massive debt problems is whether the costs of the Fund's approach can be justified by the benefits.

In fairness to the Fund, not all of this is due to its own shortcomings. One of the reasons why the Fund is forced to rely on quick-fix programs is its lack of resources, which are minuscule compared to the balance of payments problems with which it is supposed to cope. Only the massive debt crises in Mexico and Brazil prompted the Reagan administration to drop its outspoken opposition to a major increase in the IMF's resources. The major industrialized countries are now preparing to approximately double the Fund's $60 billion in resources to shore up a badly strained banking system.

Yet no amount of money can compensate for the basic flaw of the IMF's approach to the economic problems of Third World countries. No three-year economic program can remedy problems that have been decades or even centuries in the making. IMF stabilization programs assume that the problems that led to instability result from bad domestic policies. To be sure, inefficiencies, corruption and rotten governments abound. But these are not the main causes of the massive balance of payments problems of the 1970s and early 1980s. The principal causes remain the structural dilemmas of development and global economic fluctuations over which Third World countries have little influence. The most immediate example of this is the dramatic increase in world oil prices in the 1970s. Oil is an essential raw material in the industrialization process. For countries that do not have oil, no amount of tinkering with domestic monetary policy can make OPEC price increases easier to swallow.

The IMF bases its faith in monetary manipulation largely on the experience of the industrial economies. In these countries, technological prowess plus tremendous financial resources make it possible to design macroeconomic policies that allow them to cope with severe dislocations such as oil price increases. In the Third World, short-run macroeconomic policies are often secondary to the real economic problems characteristic of underdevelopment. In a speech to the 1980 IMF annual meeting, Amir Jamal, the finance minister of Tanzania, put it this way:

> If in an industrial economy a boiler explodes, the results are of a purely micro nature, and anyhow, it can probably be replaced in 48 hours. With us, it can be very different. If the boiler of a large, remote coffee curing works explodes, it may take 48 weeks to obtain a replacement. And in the meantime, the effects on overall exports, government revenue and bank borrowing, as well as storage capacity, are significant at a macro as well as a micro level. I very much doubt that indicators and targets related to cyclical demand management within industrial economies are the best yardsticks for measuring these realities. . . . Added to this is a wholly unrealistic time-frame quite unrelated to time for recovery from external bettering of achievement of real adjustments in production. These factors, plus the imponderables which make any single figure projection arbitrary, make of "conditionality" either a procrustean bed or a carte blanche for further Fund policy prescriptions.

In short, grinding down an economy to restore temporary equilibrium in the balance of payments not only imposes undue hardship on the population, it may be irrelevant to the real problems at hand.

The banks' increasing reliance on the International Monetary Fund may make their global exposure more manageable in the short run, but relying on the Fund is no solution to the fundamental economic problems that led to the debt crisis in the first place. Yet the bankers are preoccupied with getting their money back. It is not surprising that they are pushing eastern Europe's debtors, who dropped out of the Fund years ago, to rejoin and accept a strong dose of IMF austerity. Rumania and Hungary are members already. Poland has applied for membership. Like the Polish generals, the strategies of the IMF's technocrats involved squeezing domestic consumption and lowering wages to pay off the banks. The strategy is perfectly compatible with martial law, even a full-scale Soviet invasion. From the banks' point of view, as the *Village Voice*'s Alexander Cockburn observes, the optimal solution to the Polish debt crisis would be "Russian tanks pouring in from the East and IMF panzer divisions from the West."

CHAPTER 5

THE DECLINE OF THE DOLLAR

Shortly before noon on Friday, June 24, 1977, Treasury Secretary W. Michael Blumenthal arrived at the headquarters of the Organization for Economic Cooperation and Development (OECD) in Paris. The OECD was holding its annual gathering of the Western world's twenty-four leading industrial powers. The main agenda item in Paris was how the Western powers would manage the sluggish recovery from the deep 1974–75 recession.

Though no one knew it at the time, the Paris meeting would ignite one of the greatest currency speculations in history. The target of the speculation was the U.S. dollar. The dollar had been strong in the money markets since 1974, but by the end of the decade, it was being kicked around like the British pound or the Italian lira.

I

W. Michael Blumenthal seemed to be an ideal choice for secretary of the treasury. A highly successful businessman, Blumenthal had a Ph.D. in economics and broad experience in international trade. Formerly chairman of Bendix, he represented the United States at the highly acclaimed "Kennedy Round" on international trade negotiations in the 1960s. To the Europeans, who had spent most of the 1970s grappling with abrasive Treasury men like John Connally and William Simon, the amiable Blumenthal seemed a welcome change.

President Jimmy Carter sent Blumenthal to Paris to inform the Europeans and Japanese that the United States would no longer shoulder the whole burden of leading the world out of the steep 1974–75 recession. In Paris, the discussions centered on the so-called "locomotive theory" cooked up by the OECD's economists. According to the locomotive theory, the United States, Germany and Japan had to stimulate their economies through government spending in order to drag the rest of the world out of recession. When Germany and Japan refused to cooperate, the whole burden fell on the United States. The Germans, who in 1923 suffered the century's worst inflation, argued that the German economy could not grow any faster without risking additional inflation. To avoid this, they seemed willing to accept a lower rate of economic growth. The Japanese, for their part, seemed content to fuel recovery by exporting Toyotas and Sonys to the rest of the world. The high rate of economic growth in the United States meant that we were importing heavily from the rest of the world. One result was a huge U.S. trade deficit, projected to reach $30 billion by the end of 1977.

When President Carter assumed office, the United States had privately urged Bonn and Toyko to reflate their economies and buy more U.S. products. In January, Vice-President Walter Mondale headed a mission to Japan, where the United States complained about large Japanese trade surpluses with the United States. Mondale accused the Japanese of manipulating currency markets to hold down the value of the yen and therefore make Japanese products cheaper in world markets. Since the adoption of floating exchange rates in 1973, exchange rates were supposed to fluctuate freely in response to supply and demand. The U.S. accused the Japanese of engineering a "dirty float" to keep the yen down and help exports. "We knew what the Japanese were doing," says Fred Bergsten, who accompanied Mondale, "and we told them to knock it off."

Throughout the spring Japanese and German exports to the United States continued to increase. In May, at the annual economic summit of the seven major industrial powers, Carter pressed U.S. grievances with Chancellor Helmut Schmidt and Prime Minister Takeo Fukuda. A month later, with no discernible change in German and Japanese policy, the U.S. trade deficit was piling up.

Carter sent Blumenthal to Paris to force the issue. The United States was willing to help the world out of recession, Blumenthal acknowledged in his keynote speech, but only if Germany and Japan were willing to do the same. The United States was not about to let basic industries like autos and steel drown in a flood of imports. No nation, he said, in an unmistakable slap at Japan, "could expect to be an island of prosperity in a sea of economic troubles." If Germany and Japan did not act to increase their imports of U.S. products, Blumenthal suggested the United States would act unilaterally. "Exchange rate adjustments," he said, should "play their appropriate role" in remedying the U.S. trade deficit and equalizing trade relations between the United States and its trading partners. This could only mean that the Treasury secretary thought that a declining U.S. dollar would restore the competitiveness of U.S. products in world markets. If need be, Blumenthal was saying, the U.S. would push down the value of the dollar. By making U.S. products cheaper, a lower dollar would restore the U.S. competitive edge over Japanese autos, German steel and French tires. Conversely, a rising mark and yen would diminish German and Japanese competitiveness.

Bankers in New York were still having breakfast when news of Blumenthal's remarks flashed across the green Reuters screens that lined the walls of offices of U.S. and foreign banks in Paris, London and Zurich. At first the bankers were puzzled by the spectacle of a U.S. Treasury secretary "talking down" the U.S. dollar. The dollar was, after all, the chief vehicle of international trade and commerce. If the bankers harbored any doubts about Blumenthal's intentions, a spate of news leaks from the Treasury Department over the next few weeks would confirm that the U.S. government was "talking down" the dollar.

II

The big multinational banks that dominate the world's money markets are in business to move money from people who have it to those who want it. To them, money is a commodity like pork bellies or soybeans. In recent years, currency trading has also become an indispensable part of the banks' operations. In the United States, most currency trading is done by a few big banks in New York, Chicago and San Francisco. These banks trade currencies for themselves, their corporate clients, and individual customers. On any given day, a bank will provide foreign currencies for American tourists to spend in Europe, for General Motors to build automobile plants in Latin America, or for Exxon to construct oil refineries in the Middle East.

The foreign exchange "market," unlike the stock market, is not located in a single building. The "market" consists of an intricate web of telephones, telexes and computerized information systems which flash currency quotations to banks' trading rooms around the world. The world's foreign exchange trading rooms operate 24 hours a day. On Monday morning, when the New York market opens, London has already been trading for five hours, and by the time San Francisco closes, Singapore and Tokyo will still have a full day of trading left. By the time London opens the next day, some banks will already be trading dollars, pounds and Swiss francs "backward" out of Bahrain.

Currency trading has become big business for large U.S. and foreign banks. Trading volumes are enormous. On an average business day, the 200 or so banks that comprise the New York foreign exchange market will turn over $40 billion worth of dollars, marks, yen and other currencies. London's average daily turnover is $50 billion. In 1977, according to an estimate by Shearman and Sterling, the main law firm for Citibank, $50 trillion in foreign exchange changed hands in the world's currency markets. That year, by way of contrast, the total volume of world trade was slightly more than $2 trillion. The total volume of trading in the world's currency markets dwarfs the amount of trading in gold, silver and even oil.

Before the 1970s, notwithstanding a few assaults on the British pound, currency trading was relatively insignificant. In the early 1970s, however, the growing weakness of the dollar, the emergence of strong currencies like the mark and yen and the increasing sophistication of the major banks led to a meteoric rise in trading volumes. The biggest stimulant to increased trading was the move to floating exchange rates in 1973. Henceforth, currency values would fluctuate according to supply and demand in the marketplace. With the values of more than 100 currencies moving around in response to economic forces, speculation, news events and plain gossip, the potential gains and losses to global companies and banks increased dramatically. The banks that wanted to be global banks became foreign exchange traders.

At first glance, the business of foreign exchange trading is one of the most mystifying aspects of the world of international finance. "Foreign exchange and the markets in which national currencies are traded," Federal Reserve Board Chairman Paul Volcker has written, "have always had an aura of mystery, seemingly involving an arcane art not quite comprehensible to anyone but a professional trader." Yet every tourist who has traveled abroad has probably been an amateur foreign exchange trader. In hotels and airports around the world, an American can usually swap dollars for more units of the local currency than are offered at local banks. The decisions to buy or sell currencies, which all traders, large and small, make in a single day, constitute the global foreign exchange market. Currency trading provides a classic example of the law of supply and demand. Those currencies people want to acquire but which are scarce tend to go up or appreciate in value. Those in which the supply exceeds demand tend to depreciate in value. The foreign exchange trading business carried on by the world's major banks and corporations has become highly sophisticated. But its governing principles are the same as those that impel the amateur to swap U.S. dollars for a Caribbean or African currency: to buy a currency as cheaply as possible and sell it for a profit.

In a world of floating exchange rates, currency consciousness became crucial to the balance sheet performance of companies that operate globally. It introduces an element of uncertainty that must be dealt with. To safeguard the company's funds against the effects of foreign exchange fluctuations, the firm hedges its cash in the foreign exchange market. How this can be done is explained by Roger Kubarych, a foreign exchange expert at the Federal Reserve Bank of New York:

A U.S. importer of cheese from Great Britain may arrange in July for a special holiday shipment to arrive in December. The contract with the British cheese wholesaler may call for payment in sterling on December

10. Between July and December, however, the pound might rise against the dollar. So if the importer waits until December to buy the sterling needed to cover the payment for the cheese, it might cost more dollars. To avoid that risk, one alternative for the importer is to buy pounds for spot value in July, invest them in Britain for four months or so, and use the proceeds of the maturing investment to pay the cheese wholesaler.

In the epoch of global production, finance and marketing, multinational corporations have become increasingly dependent on their bankers to manage their "exposure" in foreign currencies. Banks compete actively for corporate foreign exchange business, especially the big multinational firms to whom the banks provide a wide variety of other services. As in any other line of banking, a bank that falls behind in the foreign exchange business risks losing other corporate business. European bankers initiated their American counterparts into the mystical art of currency trading, but the rampant growth of world trade and investment in recent decades forced U.S. banks to become the leading practitioners in order to remain competitive. Though London remains the largest foreign exchange market, most major New York banks have established foreign exchange departments situated alongside their domestic money market operations on Wall Street.

Many U.S. banks, needing quick expertise in the practices of foreign exchange trading, hired top-notch European dealers to run their trading operations. Today, of the 200 or so banks that constitute the New York foreign exchange market, many are run by Europeans, especially experienced British dealers. However, there are also some home-grown experts. First Chicago, once a laggard in the foreign exchange business, hired Charles Coombs, who supervised foreign exchange operations at the New York Federal Reserve Board for over a decade, to beef up its New York trading operation. First Chicago now trades for over 100 blue-chip New York-based corporations and turns a handsome profit.

The revolution in communications technology has transformed foreign exchange trading. Twenty years ago, according to Stuart Bass, an Englishman who heads the New York trading operations of Manufacturers Hanover Trust Company, completing a single foreign exchange transaction took as long as one hour. A typical transaction involved several long-distance telephone calls plus an exchange of cables between a U.S. firm in New York and a U.S. or British bank in London. As the markets grew in volume and volatility, a demand for sophisticated communications technology, which could flash currency quotations and news that could affect currency prices around the world instantaneously, was created. Today, traders move millions of dollars, marks and yen in a few seconds. Many deals involve customers whose business the banks value, so foreign currency traders must give instant quotes that are competitive with those a corporation can obtain from other banks.

Most corporations rely on the banks to manage their foreign exchange business. But they do try to avoid becoming overly dependent on one bank for all their foreign exchange needs. When fewer banks were in the foreign exchange business, a firm like GM or IBM did virtually all its business with a Morgan Guaranty. Today, it is rare to find a corporation that gives one bank most of its foreign exchange business. "They don't trust the banks," says one foreign exchange veteran, "and they shouldn't." So corporate treasurers at blue-chip companies, such as Exxon or Texaco, may get as many as three banks on the phone simultaneously and ask for the quotations of each on the same deal. The bank that delivers the best quote gets the business. The one that offers the worst price will probably wait a long time before it receives another call from the firm.

Surprisingly few American corporations have developed their own foreign exchange expertise, though it is common in Europe. Few admit publicly that they actively speculate in the foreign exchange markets for profit, but more are moving in this direction. One of the famous corporate speculators is the Dow Chemical Company. Dow divides up its global money management among six area treasurers. Any resulting gains and losses arising from foreign exchange trading are credited to the area treasurers, so there are strong incentives for them to wring profits from the currency markets. Wilson Gay, Dow's corporate treasurer, points out that "our principal business is to finance the business of Dow Chemical Co. . . . and while we're doing that, if we see some opportunities to make money for the company, we're going to try to do it." Dow Chemical, he says, uses money "like any other raw material: we try to make some money on it."

As in any other kind of business transaction, a good deal of posturing and maneuvering goes on between participants in a foreign exchange deal. How the market actually works can be illustrated as follows. When a foreign exchange trader receives a call from a corporate customer, the caller may ask, "Where's sterling?" without indicating whether he is interested in buying or selling. Thus the trader is frequently required to give two-way quotes, e.g., the dollar price at which his bank will buy or sell sterling. Traders frame quotations in terms of "basis points"; i.e., a change of 100 basis points equals a change of one full percentage point. If, for example, the British pound is hovering around 2.40 ($2.40 = £1) the trader may offer to buy sterling at 2.4010 and sell it at 2.4016; or simply 10/16. This difference of 2 basis points is known as a spread, which compensates the bank for making the transaction. If the caller likes the price quotation, he may offer to buy £2 million at 2.4016. Once the trader gives his word, the transaction is history. If the transaction is a spot transaction, the sterling must be delivered within two business days, so the trader must have the £2 million on hand or go into the market immediately and obtain it. If it is a forward transaction, the bank trader may purchase it immediately or wait until rates are more favorable for the bank.

Occasionally, when a close relationship has developed between a corporation and a bank, the bank trader may offer to go into the market with the understanding that he will try to obtain the currency at the best possible price. Naturally, the big multinational firms are in the best position to get top foreign exchange service. As one corporate executive told *Institutional Investor,* "I'd hate to be a $250 million company looking for first-rate service."

On a normal trading day, the difference between the traders' purchases and sales may make the bank a net buyer of some currencies and a net seller of others. In the jargon of the trading rooms, a bank that is holding more or less of a currency than it needs to cover current transactions has take a "position" in a currency. (A net buyer of dollars has a "long" position in dollars, a net seller is holding a "short" position.) Banks obviously prefer to be "long" in currencies that are expected to appreciate in value and "short" in those expected to decline.

Banks enter the risky foreign exchange business for the same reason they enter other financial markets: to make money. In the heated atmosphere of the trading room, large profits—and losses—come from taking positions in currencies and guessing correctly where they are going. Traders are frequently supervised by a senior economist or vice-president, but the bank's performance in the market ultimately depends on the competitive skills of its traders. Good foreign exchange traders make profits for the bank, bad ones cost the bank money. How much money a trader can make determines how long he or she will last in the dizzying foreign exchange business. Traders who consistently present large losses to the trading room boss at the end of the day get fired or transferred to another department of the bank where the pace is slower. A good foreign exchange trader makes money by guessing which way the market is going and, as one New York trader puts it, "getting there about ten minutes before everybody else." Mavericks do not necessarily make good foreign exchange traders. "You can't make money by trying to take the sheep where they don't want to go," he says, "you have to decide where the sheep are going and get there a little bit sooner."

III

The men and women who trade currencies for the world's largest banks are a breed apart from other bankers. Whereas corporations and banks pay high-priced economists to study foreign exchange market trends, the people who are on the frenetic firing lines in the trading rooms of the world's biggest banks have more modest credentials. "Foreign exchange traders," notes Charles C. Coombs, the former chief foreign exchange expert at the New York Federal Reserve Bank,

> for better or worse, are not a bunch of scholarly Ph.D.'s, searching through reams of statistical evidence for proof that a certain currency rate is becoming over or under valued and thereby triggering their decision to buy or sell. Anyone who has ever spent any time in a foreign exchange trading room knows only too well that traders focus primarily on short run developments. Foreign exchange traders have been taught by harsh experience that betting on the longer term fundamentals is an

excellent way of losing your shirt. The name of the game is to anticipate market reaction to each new report coming over the ticker. . . .

A trader who must give instantaneous two-way quotes on multi-million dollar transactions to the bank's prized customers relies only on the pale green screen in front of him which gives him the latest price quotations of the major currencies. If he is lucky, a trader may have time to catch the latest Reuters wire service news on the computerized wall in the trading room.

Today's typical currency trader is a 28-year-old, riveted to his Reuters screen at least eight hours a day. During hectic trading, New York traders report to work at 3 A.M. to be ready for the start of the London trading day. The trader may have never touched a deutsche mark or a Swiss franc. To him, they are only numbers on a screen that links him with his counterparts across town and around the world. His is a cold and impersonal world. The way some traders talk, it is hard to tell if they view the machine as an extension of their persona or view themselves as an extension of the machine. After his morning briefing from the trading room boss, the trader is virtually on his own. His telephones have dozens of lines connecting him to corporate clients, money brokers and other banks. Frequently, half a dozen of them light up at the same time.

Normally, a new trader in a major New York bank begins his career by trading marginal currencies like Swedish kroner or Belgian francs. He will trade these primarily against dollars. This keeps his workload manageable and prevents a novice from losing too much money. A promotion frequently means a year's appointment in one of the bank's European branches. There he will learn to trade Swedish kroner or Belgian francs against a dozen other currencies.

Unless the bank spots a young Paul Volcker or Walter Wriston in its trading room, the chances for fame or fortune in the foreign exchange business are limited. Today's typical money dealer generally has little more than a high school education—a B.A. at most. Starting salaries are under $20,000. For those who survive in the foreign exchange pressure cooker, a step up in the world is to become the trading room boss or the trader of the aristocratic currencies: marks, yen, Swiss francs. In these, the potential for profit and loss is much greater and so are the salaries, at present running as high as $100,000 a year. Perhaps the greatest honor in the business is to be named "the world's greatest foreign exchange dealer" in the annual sweepstakes sponsored by the prestigious financial magazine *Euromoney.*

One young trader recalls the week of June 24, 1977. When he arrived at work, the Wall Street trading room was already abuzz with activity. New York trading rooms are usually active when European markets are still open, but it hadn't been this busy for a while—especially on a Friday. The trading room boss was storming around complaining that Blumenthal was "shooting off his mouth." The trader was puzzled by all the commotion. "Those Treasury guys were always giving speeches," he recalls, "so I couldn't figure out what the big deal was." The trader didn't know it at the time, but he was about to join one of the biggest currency speculations in history. Before it ended, he and the other traders in the world's biggest banks almost killed off the once mighty U.S. dollar.

IV

"The best way to destroy the capitalist system," Lenin is quoted by Keynes as having said, "is to debauch the currency." By the late 1970s, however, it was not Lenin's disciples who were debauching the dollar, but the capitalists themselves. Among the biggest speculators against the dollar were the bastions of American capitalism, the largest U.S. banks.

In 1977, conditions were ripe for a new run on the dollar. The dollar had been relatively strong since 1974 but only because of extraordinary circumstances. The deep slump of 1974–75 slashed imports and yielded an unusual $9 billion trade surplus in 1975. High interest rates in the United States helped the dollar, as did the overly cautious currency trading which was an outgrowth of the traumatic bank failures of 1974. Trading volumes fell dramatically in late 1974 and recovered only slowly. But when Carter's Keynesians came into office, they wanted the economy to grow. Unemployment still hovered at 7 percent and Carter had pledged to do something about it. But the world's money men knew something it would take the Carterites years to learn: a strong and growing U.S. economy meant a weak U.S. dollar. When the economy started to grow, imports and inflation would soar. As night follows day, so did the dollar overhang. None of the so-called monetary "reforms" of the early 1970s had touched the problem of the dollar overhang, but merely tried to sweep it under the rug. Yet as long as the global supply of dollars exceeded demand, the dollar would be a chronically weak currency.

The effect of Blumenthal's speech was to pour gasoline on smoldering embers. "Blumenthal," one trader remarked, "gave everybody the excuse to kick the hell out of the dollar." Naturally, the banks took advantage of this. The initial impact of Blumenthal's June 24 speech on the exchange markets was to depress the value of the dollar mildly. But there was still a residue of disbelief among bankers about Treasury's tactics. Then Treasury Department officials began to leak stories to the *Washington Post* that a declining dollar was desirable because it would reverse America's trade and balance of payments problems. The pressure on the dollar mounted. "We knocked it down 50–100 [basis] points," one trader recalled, and "it didn't come back."

In the 16 months following June 24, 1977, U.S. and foreign banks were decidedly bearish on the U.S. dollar. They dumped dollars in favor of marks, yen and Swiss francs and advised their corporate and individual clients to do the same. The turnover in foreign exchange markets soared as firms scrambled to get out of dollar-denominated assets. Eventually this process became self-propelling and created a full-blown speculative raid. "Such speculation," according to Charles Coombs, "naturally takes on a sort of self-fulfilling quality. As an exchange rate depreciates, therefore, it takes a pretty brave if not foolhardy trader to buck the tide. The astute trader will instead be content to play along with the crowd. . . ."

By the end of 1977, the dollar had lost a fifth of its value against the yen, 10 percent against the Swiss franc and 7 percent against the mark. The dollar was sinking fast and the U.S. government did nothing about it. As one trading room boss remarked: "The feeling was very definite that the situation was way out of control. . . . Sure Blumenthal was talking the dollar down. But the question was how far he would let it go."

"Every few days," Charles Coombs recalled, "some dumb bastard from Treasury would get up and say that the U.S. would not intervene to fix the value of the dollar, only to counter disorderly markets. When people heard that, the cry went up: 'sell the bucks.' " At year-end 1977, the U.S. reported a whopping $31 billion trade deficit and an overall $35 billion balance of payments gap. This added billions more to the huge oversupply of dollars sloshing around in the international money markets and added fuel to the speculative fires.

Soon bankers and European statesmen gave the administration's dollar policy a name: "malign neglect." As the situation went from bad to worse, bankers and foreign governments watched in amazement as the U.S. government did nothing to arrest the seemingly endless downward drift of the dollar. Like John Connally before him, Blumenthal forbade the Fed to intervene on the scale required and would not even discuss new bond sales. Arthur Burns, who was trying to earn Carter's favor in order to win another term as Fed chairman, apparently accepted Treasury's dictates. In the absence of Fed intervention, the dollar resumed its "natural" downward course. By 1978, the sprawling foreign exchange markets had become so sensitive and so volatile that the banks took Treasury's statements and ran wild with them, turning Blumenthal's "exchange rate adjustment" into a veritable rout of the dollar.

In the foreign exchange business, bluffs don't work very well. Amid harsh European criticism of malign neglect and threats that OPEC would raise oil prices to recoup losses they suffered from a declining dollar, Treasury finally exhibited some concern. In a sudden change of heart, the administration announced in early 1978 that the Treasury would allow the Fed to activate its foreign currency swap lines and intervene in the market to shore up the dollar. Treasury would also mop up some dollars with increased gold sales. Temporarily the announcement buoyed the dollar. Some bankers thought that this signaled a fundamental change in U.S. policy and quickly began buying back some of the dollars they had sold in previous months, but the smart money viewed the announcement with suspicion. The dollar's strength turned out to be short-lived. One New York trader, who mistakenly anticipated that the dollar would continue to improve, lost $700,000 one January day when the market beat back the Fed's halfhearted efforts at intervention. "There is nothing worse than crossed signals," he later mourned over his beer.

"If a foreign exchange trader gets patriotic, he's an idiot." Other bankers were less troubled by the dollar's problems. "I don't know if it's un-American or not," says a smiling Jeffrey Kiel of Republic National Bank, a big gold and foreign exchange dealer, "but that's life."

As the run on the dollar resumed in early 1978, Blumenthal's house economists urged him to fight the speculative assault on the dollar with good news about the "fundamentals" of the U.S. economy—economic growth, reducing government deficits, and falling oil imports—by asserting that these factors would ultimately strengthen the dollar. Blumenthal quickly absorbed the new dogma. The speculators just laughed. Blumenthal jokes became increasingly popular among European traders, but the governments of western Europe were not amused by what was going on. They were the real losers in the global game of chicken between the U.S. government and the banks. Since Lyndon Johnson's time, the United States had deliberately forced them to hold more dollars than they wanted—to finance America's overseas expenditures. Now, the United States was not only adding to their accumulation of dollars by running a two-year balance of payments deficit of nearly $70 billion, but took no responsibility at all for guaranteeing the value of the dollar. So these governments were the real losers. To cut their losses, they had to do what the United States refused to do: intervene in the money markets to shore up the value of the dollar. When the banks dumped dollars in the market, the governments of western Europe and Japan moved to mop them up. In effect, this became a massive support operation on behalf of the dollar. Without one, there is no telling how far the dollar would have dropped.

Western Europe and Japan had powerful incentives to do so. First, since most countries' currency reserves consist mainly of dollars, a falling dollar actually diminishes the value of these reserves, effectively depleting their national treasuries. Second, a steep decline in the dollar's value makes U.S. products more competitive and hurts European and Japanese exports.

The overriding considerations, however, are the political and economic implications of the world's dependence on the dollar. A collapse of the dollar could well bring down the whole elaborate system of international trade and payments, in which Europe and Japan have an enormous stake. As Jelle Zijilstra, head of the Bank for International Settlements once put it, "When the pound went, we could go to the dollar. If the dollar went, where could we go? To the moon?"

Yet as Europe and Japan learned in the early 1970s, "intervention" is not a painless procedure. In 1977 the central banks of Western Europe and Japan spent approximately $35 billion to support the dollar in the exchange markets. The irony is that supporting the dollar actually increased their dollar holdings. Thus the international role of the dollar gave the United States virtually unlimited access to a bottomless pool of free credit, and Europe and Japan were picking up the tab.

Intervention also fuels inflation. In order to purchase dollars, other central banks had to sell their own currencies: marks, yen and Swiss francs. This, of course, meant expanding their domestic money supplies by giving banks more money to lend.* Moreover, because the value of the dollar is, in Paul Volcker's words, "the world's most important price since so many other prices here and abroad depend on it," when the dollar declines, it encourages everyone from the OPEC countries to Toyota to raise prices to maintain the real value of their prices in dollars.

While the Carter policy of malign neglect was universally criticized as disastrous for the world economy, the banks were having a field day speculating against the dollar. (Banks do not conspire to speculate against currencies. The markets are too competitive. No trader in his right mind would tip his hand before he was properly positioned. When the big banks all jump on the same bandwagon, however, they can just about kill any currency.) The banks advised their customers to get out of dollars and were taking big positions with their own money and making hefty profits in the process. Since the adoption of floating exchange rates in 1973, increased speculative activities have boosted bank profits in general, but in 1978, for-

* Some sources have suggested that this is what the Carterites had in mind all along, forcing Europe and Japan to expand money supplies through exchange market intervention in order to speed up economic growth and imports of U.S. products. This is an intriguing hypothesis, but in retrospect it is hard to imagine Jimmy Carter's Treasury Department being that sophisticated.

eign exchange trading was exceedingly profitable. Citibank, New York's leading bank, recorded a 700 percent increase in profits from foreign exchange trading, from $13 million in 1977 to $105 million in 1978. In 1978 Chase Manhattan recorded a 54 percent gain in foreign exchange profits; Morgan Guaranty's jumped from $40 to $56 million. Republic National Bank, a big gold and currency dealer, reported profit increases of 350 percent between 1976 and 1978.

Citibank's stellar performance in speculating against the dollar in 1978 earned it the reputation of being the "world's best foreign exchange dealer" by *Euromoney*. The bank has held that distinction for four consecutive years. By 1978, Citibank had become the Exxon of the foreign trading business. "The supermen of Citibank," as *Euromoney* calls them, control more of the world's foreign exchange trading than Exxon does of the international oil market. Citibank's share of the mammoth global foreign exchange market is about 10 percent, nearly three times as much as its nearest rival, Chase Manhattan.

V

Probably the most detailed information regarding currency speculation by a major bank became public through the so-called Edwards case, a major international banking scandal involving Citibank. David Edwards was a trader for Citibank who was fired in February 1978 after bringing management's attention to irregularities in Citibank's foreign exchange trading practices.

Edwards, a sandy-haired young Texan, broke into international banking in London, working at the old merchant bank Samuel Montagu & Co. In 1972, he joined Citibank's international staff and helped set up Citi's "Nassau" operation, in reality, a desk in the bank's Eurocurrency Department in Manhattan. Later, he was assigned to Citibank's Paris branch. In 1975, Edwards became aware of what seemed to be irregularities in Paris' trading operations, including the possibility that officers were receiving kickbacks on foreign exchange deals. Apparently intrigued by what he had discovered, Edwards probed further. He eventually discovered evidence that Citibank's European branches were violating tax and foreign exchange control laws on a massive scale. The violations were of two varieties. First, Citibank was using phony international currency transactions to shift profits out of high-tax European countries to tax havens like Nassau. Secondly, Citibank was hiding speculative positions in nondollar currencies from local bank inspectors by "parking" them in Nassau.

For more than a year after Edwards' initial charges, he pestered his superiors in Europe and New York to look seriously into his allegations. Apparently in good faith, Edwards told senior New York officers that if Citibank got caught in unsavory dealing practices, it could endanger the future of the bank's operations abroad. Despite reprimands from his superiors, Edwards refused to be quiet. By late 1977, it was clear that Citibank was fed up with David Edwards. In December, he received a letter from Citibank Executive Vice-President Thomas Theobald requesting his resignation, asserting that "your continued allegations were detrimental to the best interests of Citibank." Failing to move top management, Edwards approached the Audit Committee of Citibank's Board of Directors, a star-studded collection of business luminaries chaired by Lawrence Fouraker, dean of the Harvard Business School. When Edwards delivered his famous "blue book" of allegations to the board, he was fired by Theobald, who is one of the top runners to succeed Chairman Walter Wriston. Edwards responded by retaining New York attorney Jonathan Lubell to sue Citibank for $14 million on grounds of wrongful dismissal.

Evidence unearthed in connection with the case provides a rare glimpse of the internal workings of banks' global foreign exchange activities. His charges caused a major uproar at Citibank because of the importance of currency trading to the global banks in general and Citibank in particular.

The tax avoidance issue is fairly straightforward. Essentially, Citibank rigged transactions among different branches to move currency trading profits out of high-tax areas into lower tax areas. On June 11, 1976, for instance, Citibank's Paris branch instructed Citibank Nassau via telex to buy $6 million at the rate of 4.7275 French francs to the dollar. Later the same day, Paris instructed Nassau to sell $4 million to New York and $2 million to Brussels at the rate of 4.7374 francs per dollar, which yielded Nassau a profit of 60,000

French francs. Paris then repurchased the $6 million from New York and Brussels at the higher rate; in effect, creating a loss on the whole transaction in Paris. Then, through an internal accounting mechanism called a Management Profit Report, Paris had the 60,000 French francs profit credited to its own account for generating the profit "parked" in Nassau. For tax purposes, Paris lost money and Nassau made money, but the entire transaction was controlled by Paris, which received the kudos for generating the profit.

Edwards provided government investigators with the telexes and other documents that revealed that numerous transactions of this kind were undertaken to shift foreign exchange profits out of Europe. The transactions were wholly artificial and controlled by the "parking" branch, such as Paris. The artificial nature of the transactions was revealed in a comical incident wherein a Milan trader was forced to change the delivery date of a transaction involving $5 million worth of Italian lire he channeled to Nassau. His telex read:

HI THERE FRIENDS
GOOD DAY
ON SEPT 27 I SENT YOU A SPECIAL TRANSACTION, BY
WHICH YOU BOUGHT 5 MIOS DOLLIES AGST LIT FROM
LONDON AT 850 00
THE POINT IS THAT I THINK I WAS DRUNK AT THAT
TIME, BECAUSE I SET THE VALUE DATE OCT 10 WHICH
IS SUNDAY. . . .
WUD YOU MIND CHANGING IT IN OCT 12 PLS
(I HAVE ALREADY ADVISED LONDON FOR THE AMENDING)
TKS ALOT AND SORRY FOR THE TROUBLE

The practice of parking exchange positions to avoid taxes and, as we will show below, to hide speculative positions was not limited to a few random transactions. According to a memorandum by the enforcement staff of the Securities and Exchange Commission, which investigated Edwards' charges, the practice was widespread. Of these instances that were uncovered, between 1973 and 1977 about 10 percent of the dollar volume of foreign exchange business done in Citibank Frankfurt consisted of parking transactions. In Milan, parking accounted for anywhere from 13 percent to 30 percent of transactions. In Paris, the estimate was 3 percent. In London, the world's biggest foreign exchange trading center, the SEC staff found it was done on a "daily" basis.

The documents Edwards passed to government officials showed how Citibank used artificial transactions to avoid European taxes, but focusing on the tax issue obscures the more fundamental problem of currency speculation by large multinational banks. Speculation by Citibank and other banks had contributed mightily to global exchange rate instability. In economic terms, this has had far greater consequences than tax avoidance. As far as Citibank was concerned, what the bank was saving in taxes was negligible compared to what it was making by speculating against the dollar and other currencies.

As shown in chapter 3, since the early 1970s, European countries had been plagued by speculation in their currency markets. After the Herstatt and Franklin failures, speculation subsided for a time. But as a result of Blumenthal's "malign neglect," European central banks were again taking a beating in absorbing huge amounts of dollars. This was the same thing that had happened earlier in the decade, but now it was happening on a much larger scale, provoking even greater disturbances in the currency markets.

Citibank provides a case study of how global banks speculate against currencies. Although it can be argued that in the early 1970s multinational banks simply traded currencies to protect their customers against exchange fluctuations, as the decade wore on the banks were clearly speculating with their own money and for their customers' accounts. At Citibank, this change in emphasis is reflected in the bank's own internal documents. On January 16, 1970, for instance, Citibank's comptroller adviced Executive Vice-President (later vice-chairman) G.A. Costanzo that "We want to confine exchange trading essentially to transactions facilitating commercial business; i.e., no speculation, although in practice it's recognized we have to do some pure trading as long as the limits are observed." "The limits" referred to are the bank's internal controls on traders and the limits on currency positions imposed by foreign governments. With the move to the floating exchange rates in 1973, however, Citibank unleashed its traders and encouraged them to ignore

European government trading limits. Thus, on May 26, 1974, Arthur Natvig, a vice-president in the comptroller's division, wrote that "New senior management has loosened our former internal constraints on FX trading and widened our traders' horizons"; i.e., gave them greater leeway to speculate.

Parking currency positions was as important for speculative purposes as it was for tax avoidance. Parking became crucial in the aftermath of the Franklin-Herstatt failures, when European governments tightened regulations on currency trading to prevent excessive speculation. But governments had no sooner imposed new controls on currency speculation than Citibank employed new tactics to get around them. Essentially, Citibank's European branches took larger positions in deutsche marks, Swiss francs and other currencies than were allowed by local authorities. They would then park the excess positions in Nassau or New York, effectively removing them from local books and thereby concealing them from local authorities. To facilitate speculation, Citibank's senior management allowed European branch managers to take positions *four times larger* than local governments allowed. In Switzerland, for instance, Swiss authorities allowed Citibank an overnight position in Swiss francs of between $16 and $20 million. Citibank's internal limit for its Swiss branch was $75 million. As SEC attorneys Thomson von Stein, David Doherty and Robert Ryan pointed out, Citibank "considered its overnight position limits from a business risk standpoint regardless of governmental limits." In a January 1974 memo to Costanzo, Senior Vice-President Freeman H. Huntington summed up the rationale for parking:

> ... it was common practice in most European countries for trading branches to park their positions overnight or otherwise ... when in the interest of the institution. We continue to feel that this is of vital necessity to give us the worldwide flexibility which we require to capitalize on the existing volatile exchange markets. ...

During this period, Citibank's internal overnight currency position limits were about $200 million, enabling the bank to profit substantially from exchange rate movements.

Still, banking mythology has it that after the 1974 Herstatt and Franklin failures, speculation declined because banks imposed greater internal controls on traders. At Citibank, in January 1975, Wriston did order a comprehensive review of worldwide trading practices, but the only result was to make it more difficult for foreign governments to detect parking and other illicit practices, not to reduce speculation. This was amply illustrated by attitudes Citibank officials displayed at a May 1975 conference in London, which was convened to discuss trading practices as part of the review. In a memo written for the London meeting, Natvig made it clear that despite Herstatt and Franklin, for Citibank's European branches it was still business as usual. He wrote: "to continue previous trading volume (and profits), and to keep large overnight positions, the Europeans have been 'parking' positions." In fact, the aim of the whole 1975 exercise was to improve Citibank's methods of concealing parking and other illicit techniques from government authorities. One of Natvig's suggestions was to switch the parking place from Nassau to New York because "just the name Nassau raises suspicions." But Natvig and other Citibank officials were emphatic that the bank wanted to maintain its capacity to engage in heavy exchange market speculation. Referring to the bank's Milan branch, for instance, Natvig put it bluntly: "Why do we want to take positions larger than allowed? . . . usual reason is that we want to trade and take an overnight position on which we think we will make a profit." At the London conference similar presentations were made regarding other trading centers, including Frankfurt and Paris.

No substantive changes were made in Citibank's dealing practices as a result of the 1975 review. The final report, which was read by Wriston and other senior officers, spelled out the methods Citibank traders were using to hoodwink European governments. Despite clear evidence that some of these practices were illegal, Citibank's top officers, including Wriston, apparently did nothing to encourage foreign branches to start obeying the law. As SEC attorney Thomson von Stein observed, ". . . although the survey pointed out clearly to the top management how Citibank parking practices violated the law, its only suggestions for change were cosmetic," mainly eliminating written references to parking and placing positions with New York rather than Nassau.

Despite the cosmetic changes prompted by the 1975 review, European government regulations against speculation continued to concern Citibank. In June 1976, Francesco Redi, a vice-president in London, notified Freeman Huntington about

> growing intervention on the part of Central Banks to prevent locally domiciled banks taking FX positions in their domestic currency. To avoid these growing restrictions, a number of CMDS have developed "parking of positions," that is they have been selling these positions to other CMDS located in countries not subject to the same type of restrictions.

Redi also warned Huntington about the "potential risk of correspondence which would make obvious the nature of the transaction" leading to, among other things, "severely upsetting the local Central Bank. . . ."

A few months later, Redi's fears were confirmed when David Edwards discovered that Citibank's European branches were violating tax and exchange control laws. In March 1977, Edwards approached Edwin Pomeroy of the comptroller's division to voice his concerns about parking. Pomeroy knew plenty about the parking since he had participated in the 1975 foreign exchange review. Edwards pressed his charges but was repeatedly told that they could not be substantiated. In May, Pomeroy suggested that Citibank find a way of "unloading" David Edwards. As an interim step, Edwards was transferred to a different area of the bank. Unfortunately for Citibank, when Edwards was transferred he was assigned to an office formerly occupied by Paolo Cugnasca, a trader from Milan who in 1975 had been asked to set up a new unit to monitor position taking. When Cugnasca moved to Freeman Huntington's staff in New York, he inadvertently left a number of documents in a desk which Edwards discovered. After Theobald asked Edwards to resign in December, Edwards copied the documents and sent them to the audit committee of the Board of Directors. When Theobald fired him in February, Edwards flew to Washington and handed the documents to Stanley Sporkin, director of enforcement at the Securities and Exchange Commission.

VI

From Citibank's perspective, the Edwards revelations were a potential disaster that threatened to blow the lid off the global currency trading business like no other event since the 1974 Franklin and Herstatt failures. Coming in the midst of the heavy run on the dollar in 1978, the Edwards revelations could have been catastrophic for the world's biggest foreign exchange dealer. What David Edwards was doing must have given Walter Wriston nightmares. On top of his $14 million lawsuit, Edwards was passing out confidential Citibank documents, including telexes and other records of rigged currency transactions, to hordes of government investigators and journalists. His allegations eventually prompted at least five federal agencies—the departments of Justice and Treasury, Comptroller of the Currency, the Internal Revenue Service and the SEC—to undertake investigations of banks' foreign exchange trading. Edwards was meeting with congressmen who were planning hearings on foreign currency manipulation by American banks. He was telling friends that he was planning to write a book-length exposé on his experiences.

Faced with a potentially disastrous public examination of its foreign currency trading practices at a time when the dollar was dropping like a stone in the money markets, Citibank dug in its heels. With top people assigned to containing the crisis, Citibank took the offensive. The crucial element in Citibank's cover-up was initiating its own self-serving investigation of Edwards' allegations. Soon after Edwards was fired, the Audit Committee of Citibank's Board of Directors asked the Wall Street law firm Shearman and Sterling, Citibank's main outside counsel, to investigate the bank's currency trading practices in a number of European countries. The audit committee of Citibank asked Shearman and Sterling to "determine whether the bank was engaged in any pattern of violations of foreign exchange and tax laws in the countries under review." With the assistance of the big accounting firm Peat Marwick Mitchell, Shearman Sterling presented local counsel in a number of European countries with various "scenarios" of Citibank trading procedures and asked them to pass judgment on possible legal challenges.

When the report was released in November 1978, Citibank heralded it as ringing confirmation that Edwards' charges were groundless. In a press release announcing the results of the investigation, Citibank proclaimed that "eight months of intensive investigation revealed no pattern of violation and foreign exchange regulations in any country reviewed...." and "... no institutional pattern of transferring tax liabilities from one country to another in violation of local tax laws." Despite its apologetic tone, the Shearman and Sterling report acknowledged that in a number of countries legal challenges to Citibank's dealing practices had a "high probability of success." Nevertheless, Citibank made extensive use of the Shearman and Sterling report for public relations purposes. Audit Committee Chairman Fouraker told the *Wall Street Journal* that the Shearman and Sterling report made it "clear" that Citibank had a "general policy" of complying with relevant laws and regulations. Elaborating on Shearman and Sterling's findings, Citicorp Vice-Chairman G.A. Costanzo took the art of justifying corporate crime to a new low. Costanzo said that "there exist hundreds of pages of foreign exchange regulations in the countries involved. These regulations are constantly being changed and interpreted and none have the precision of a fifty-five mile speed limit which one either exceeds or does not."

The Shearman and Sterling report was, SEC attorney Thomson von Stein concluded, a "whitewash" from beginning to end. Citibank's Audit Committee asked Shearman and Sterling to investigate whether or not the bank had a "pattern" of violations of tax and exchange control laws. This phraseology made any discovery of violations of European laws look coincidental, not like deliberate corporate policy. Moreover, as the SEC staff noted, when Shearman and Sterling asked local European counsel to pass judgment on certain "scenarios," they neglected to inform them that management had explicitly authorized such transactions to get around European laws. As the SEC enforcement staff put it, the Shearman and Sterling report was "written as if hundreds of Citibank documents in their possession did not exist, documents which show how senior management directed its [trading] procedures, including false documents to hide it from the authorities ... which show ... management knew it was done to circumvent local laws."

Shearman and Sterling's rosy conclusions also rested on a straw man buried deep in the report. After reviewing the periodic changes in Citibank's trading practices in 1973, undertaken in order to conceal parking from the authorities, Shearman and Sterling concluded that "In short, the story of foreign exchange position parking at Citibank is not a history of uniform practices or widely agreed upon procedures." This hardly vitiates the fact that Citibank specifically engineered phony transactions to get around local tax and exchange control laws. All it says is that these practices did not remain constant over time. Naturally, Citibank's trading practices changed as laws and market conditions changed. Moreover, the answer to Costanzo's apologia is, of course, that governments typically adopt new foreign exchange regulations to keep up with the banks, not vice versa. Even before the new laws are in place the banks and their lawyers are looking for new ways around them.

European governments did not accept Shearman and Sterling's whitewash. When the Shearman and Sterling report reached banking authorities in Europe, it prompted new investigations that found Citibank liable for millions of dollars in back taxes and other administrative fees. Citibank was even caught violating banking laws in Switzerland. In September of 1969, the Geneva office of Citibank made a formal declaration to Swiss authorities that it would "not undertake anything controversing the monetary and credit policy of the Swiss National Bank." Yet the bank's practice of parking currency transactions was, in the words of the Swiss Federal Banking Commission, "incompatible with this assurance and the formal declaration of September 15, 1969." At the conclusion of the Swiss investigation, Fritz Leutweiler, former head of the Swiss National Bank and now president of the Bank for International Settlements, told the Swiss weekly *Die Weltwoche:*

We can assume that there was not an absence of guilt in all cases. . . . There were several operations however which are difficult to square with our laws. The bank maintained foreign exchange positions abroad in conflict with our laws on an overnight basis or for several days and then transferred the foreign exchange back to Switzerland when the air was clear.

For its transgressions in Switzerland, Citibank was hit with a bill for over $5 million in back taxes, along with another $4.5 million in Germany and $700,000 in France.

At home, however, the Shearman and Sterling report, combined with the dismissal of Edwards' suit,* solved Citibank's immediate crisis by undermining Edwards' credibility. As Citibank quietly settled its tax violations in Europe, media and congressional interest in the Edwards revelations waned. Edwards' exposé about Citibank never materialized. Increasingly isolated and disillusioned, Edwards dropped his crusade and spent his time scouring the New York financial district looking for a job. Not surprisingly, he received few offers. Eventually, he returned to Wichita Falls, Texas. "They destroyed him," volunteered one former associate.

In retrospect, probably Edwards' biggest mistake was to believe he could change Citibank policies by appealing to Walter Wriston's sense of corporate responsibility. Had Edwards ageed to shut up when he was told, he might have gotten somewhere in the vast Citibank hierarchy, with all of the trimmings of fancy lunches, subsidized luxury apartments and ski weekends in Gstaad. Instead, his career disappeared into paper shredders atop the Citibank skyscraper at 399 Park Avenue. At various times, Citibank officials gave at least three reasons why Edwards was fired. Wriston said he was incompetent, whereas Theobald said he refused to accept a transfer and was acting against the best interests of Citibank. The real reason, of course, was that he blew the whistle. The SEC's von Stein concluded that Edwards was the only Citibank employee who "acted with honor" in the whole affair. The clever Sporkin eventually pried this out of Citibank's chief lawyer, Hans Angermuller, who admitted that firing Edwards was "not fair."

VII

With David Edwards out of the way, Citibank still faced a federal investigation of its currency trading practices at a particularly sensitive time. Citibank was making record foreign exchange gains in

---

* The dismissal of Edwards' civil suit implied nothing about the content of his charges. The judge rejected Edwards' contention that he had been illegally fired, because he had no outstanding employment contract with Citibank.

the turbulent markets of 1978. For the global banking community as a whole, the stakes were also high. In response to recurrent instability in the Euromarket, the Bank for International Settlements was sponsoring discussions aimed at imposing greater regulations on Eurobanking. One concrete proposal was to roll back the Euromarket's chief competitive advantage by imposing reserve requirements on international lending and deposit taking. The U.S. delegate to the BIS, Henry Wallich, had openly voiced support for the measure, which would have had the effect of slowing down the growth of the Euromarket. (Separately, Representative Jim Leach, a moderate Republican from Iowa, was launching a congressional investigation of the Euromarket with an eye toward greater regulation.) Regulation is the bane of Eurobanking. As the Euromarket's chief laissez-faire ideologue, Wriston would have been humiliated if his bank's misconduct had been used as an excuse to impose greater regulations.

For a time, things continued to go Wriston's way. Most of the federal investigations were half-hearted and eventually petered out. Ironically, one of Citibank's biggest defenders was the Treasury Department. Treasury took the lead in trying to convince Congress that banks do not speculate against currencies. The standard reasoning behind this conclusion is that published government reports on banks' foreign currency positions show no correlation between large position taking and weakness of the dollar. If one examines the regularly published accounts of bank positions in foreign currencies during this period, they do show fluctuations, but they are small by foreign exchange market standards. (It is noteworthy, however, that U.S. banks did dump at least $1 billion between October 18 and October 25, the week preceding the climax of the 1978 dollar crisis.) The SEC staff concluded in its investigation of Citibank that the bank's management regularly misled European governments about the dimensions of their positions in local currencies. As the SEC enforcement staff put it, European "books and records were false as they did not reflect the true nature of the [foreign exchange] transactions." In addition, the staff found that in 1977, in both Switzerland and Italy, internal documents were changed "to make it appear to local authorities" that Citibank's internal foreign exchange position limits were the same as those permitted by local authorities. The U.S. Treasury was even less adept than its European counterparts at spotting Euromarket loopholes. Convinced that banks do not speculate, Treasury took no action.

However, the Office of the Comptroller of the Currency, under the knowledgeable John Heimann, now a top official of Warburg's in New York, conducted a more thorough investigation. The comptroller's office is part of Treasury, but maintains considerable independence. Like the SEC, Heimann concluded that many of the foreign exchange transactions reviewed accomplished "essentially what David Edwards alleged," adding that the violations were "more serious than portrayed in the Shearman and Sterling report." Heimann took no action against Citibank, but in December 1980 sent a stern letter to Citibank's Board of Directors asserting that "a number of foreign exchange transactions reviewed were inconsistent with sound banking principles." The letter was accompanied by a report from his staff on Citibank's currency dealings, which said that "the question of why the practices were not eliminated when initially disclosed to bank management in 1975 is not clear." The letter was sent at the time news surfaced that Wriston was being considered for the post of Treasury secretary in the Reagan administration. Individuals familiar with the Citibank investigation say that it was timed to prevent Wriston from getting the job, which went to Merrill Lynch's Donald Regan.

The one government body that investigated the Citibank matter vigorously was the enforcement staff of the Securities and Exchange Commission. After convincing reluctant commissioners of the importance of the case, former SEC enforcement chief Stanley Sporkin launched a probe of Citibank in May 1978. By then, Sporkin had become the scourge of Wall Street for his vigorous enforcement of the nation's securities laws. To head the investigation, Sporkin recruited the sharp investigative attorney Thomson von Stein, a Sporkin protégé who had moved on to the Federal Energy Regulatory Commission. Von Stein conducted an exhaustive investigation of Citibank's foreign exchange dealing, including scores of interviews with leading Citibank officials. The investigation resulted in a strong 32-page memo from the enforcement staff to the Commission recommending an administrative proceeding to determine Citibank's culpability.

By the time von Stein, David Doherty and Robert Ryan took their case to the commission in December 1981, however, the SEC had changed radically. Their chief ally, Sporkin, had departed to become general counsel of the CIA. He had been replaced as enforcement chief by corporate lawyer John Fedders. The new chairman was John Shad, formerly of E.F. Hutton, who replaced Harold Williams. Both Shad and Fedders shared Ronald Reagan's desire to limit government regulation of business and pare back the activist role the SEC had assumed under Sporkin.

For von Stein and company the issue was not bank speculation against the dollar as such, but whether Citibank's illicit trading practices violated federal securities laws. Buttressed by the comptroller's assertion that Citibank had engaged in "unsound" banking practices, the SEC staff made three specific charges. First, Citibank's management had approved measures designed to cover up questionable trading procedures, including cooking the books to make phony transactions appear legitimate. Second, in its regular reports to the federal government, Citibank routinely presented the phony transactions outlined above as "arm's length." In reality, these were intracorporate transfers designed to delude tax and banking inspectors around the world.* Normally, the IRS requires that such transactions be flagged so that any income from them can be properly allocated to different branches and subsidiaries. Finally, Citibank had misled its shareholders on the extent of risks involved in foreign exchange trading. Citicorp's 1977 second quarter report to shareholders included a speech by Freeman Huntington stating, falsely, that Citibank's traders acted independently and assuring stockholders that foreign exchange trading was subject to tight internal controls. Yet Citibank was breaking laws in Europe, incurring risks the shareholders were not informed of. In the staff's view, Citibank's predeliction for breaking foreign laws and covering them up through bogus accounting went "to the heart of the securities laws." They recommended that an administrative proceeding be brought against Citibank to force Citibank to correct its prior disclosure regarding its foreign exchange dealing.

The changes that had taken place at the SEC made the staff's po-

---

* This is the equivalent of "transfer pricing" by multinational corporations.

sition much weaker without Sporkin's formidable presence. His replacement, John Fedders, vigorously opposed bringing about action. He argued that the staff had not proved that Citibank had violated the securities laws and that senior management did not understand that the conduct in question was illegal. Besides, he added, the case was old. At bottom, however, Fedders' position was that Citibank's European transgressions were no business of the SEC:

> I do not subscribe to the theory that a company that violates tax and exchange control laws is a bad corporation and that disclosure of illegal conduct should be forced as a prophylactic measure.

Fedders prevailed. The Reagan SEC voted three to one with one abstention against bringing an action. The Citibank case was dead.

The case remained sealed from public view until February 1982 when someone leaked the proceedings of the December meeting, along with the staff memo, to Jeff Gerth of the *New York Times.* When the award-winning reporter plastered long quotations from the staff memo over the business section of the *Times,* complete with an imposing photo of the 6'4" chairman, Wriston exploded. He fired off a letter to the editor accusing the *Times* of employing McCarthyite tactics. An SEC attempt to find and fire Gerth's source proved futile.

VIII

When banks and other speculators make money, somebody has to lose. Part of the profits banks make by trading foreign exchange come at the expense of other private speculators. But a more predictable source of profits is trading against central banks. The resources the big private banks have to trade in foreign exchange markets not only dwarf those of the central banks, but central banks frequently absorb losses in the foreign exchange markets in attempting to stabilize their currencies. They buy, in other words, when others are selling and vice-versa.

The Federal Reserve's position is particularly ludicrous because the Fed enters the foreign exchange market through the private banks. When a trader gets a call from the Fed to buy or sell currencies for the Fed's account, the cry goes up around the trading room: "Fed's in." More importantly, it is usually not hard to guess which way the Fed is going. Thus the Fed, unlike any good poker player, telegraphs its hand to the other players.

That is why, on a profit and loss basis, the Fed and other central banks are frequently losers in the foreign exchange markets. As Professor Dean Taylor points out, "the actions of central banks have become an important tool for private speculators.... Central bank losses become . . . a subsidy to private speculators and traders who gamble against the government." In a recent survey published by the Group of 30, a blue-chip financial affairs committee, many banks openly admitted that their foreign exchange trading profits come disproportionately at the expense of central banks. The irony is that central bank intervention is frequently the only alternative to full-scale chaos in the exchange markets.

Throughout 1978, the banks milked the dollar's slide for all it was worth, but by the fall, even they felt things had gotten out of hand. By October 1978, a sickening feeling of panic had gripped the foreign exchange markets. In 13 months the dollar had lost 67 percent of its value against the Swiss franc, 55 percent against the yen and nearly 35 percent against the deutsche mark. The dollar even fell against the British pound. Yet, as late as mid-October, important U.S. officials still denied that there was a problem with the dollar. In October, as the banks watched in disbelief, the United States allowed the dollar to fall 6 percent against the Swiss franc, 7 percent against the yen and a whopping 12 percent against the mark.

Profitable or not, even the banks finally decided that the run on the dollar had gone far enough. "The fun and games are over," said Willard Butcher, David Rockefeller's successor as chairman of Chase Manhattan. Wall Street was deeply concerned about the potential ripple effects of a genuine collapse of the dollar. As the *Wall Street Journal* pointed out:

Pessimism about the dollar and the administration's economic management had become so rampant that the nation was on the brink of, in the words of one New York banker, "a nineteenth century kind of financial panic from which a genuine depression could have developed."

On Wednesday, November 1, Carter gave up. He complained that the dollar's decline was "clearly not warranted" by the underlying "fundamentals" of the U.S. economy. Speculation, in other words, played a major role in the dollar's decline. After beating the Germans and Japanese over the head for two years to try to get them to reflate their economies, Carter suddenly decided that inflation was the nation's number one economic problem. That is what the bankers and their ideological acolytes had been pushing for years. Carter's conversion to their viewpoint was based on one simple fact: if he had any hope of rescuing the dollar, Carter had to get the banks to play ball. The president still lauded the U.S. economic "fundamentals," but in case the speculators weren't impressed by the fundamentals, he announced the most massive currency support operation in history.

The November 1 dollar defense package, which Blumenthal, Treasury Under Secretary Anthony Solomon, Federal Reserve Chairman G. William Miller and Carter had drafted in a secret meeting the previous Saturday evening, had two component parts. The centerpiece was a $30 billion war chest of foreign currencies which the Fed would use to buy dollars and beat back speculation in the currency markets. Second, the Federal Reserve raised interest by a full percentage point. The November 1 policy package signified that for the first time since the United States set up the old Bretton Woods system in 1944, U.S. domestic economic policy was subject to ratification—and veto—by the international money men. A first-rate crisis in the international monetary system forced Carter to embrace a program of economic austerity—higher interest rates, slower economic growth and probably a recession—bad politics for someone with a traditional Democratic party base.

CHAPTER 6

THE GREATEST HIGH

The greatest high is making money for my clients and myself.

JAMES SINCLAIR
noted gold trader

Just about anything you buy, rather than paper, is better. You're bound to come out ahead, in the long pull. If you don't like gold, use silver. Or diamonds, or copper, but something. Any damn fool can run a printing press.

NELSON BUNKER HUNT

The success of Jimmy Carter's November 1 dollar-defense program was short-lived. Sophisticated money men knew the November 1 package could only be a temporary palliative because it did not go to the heart of the problem: the vast oversupply—or overhang—of dollars in the world's money markets. This was the legacy of the United States' exploitation of the world's dependence on the dollar to maintain politically acceptable rates of economic growth and employment at home. Carter had aggravated the problem considerably. For the two years 1977–78, more than $70 billion flowed out of

165

the United States, flooding the money markets with dollars.* An editorial in the *Times* of London put the point succinctly:

> Intervention in the markets by central banks, no matter how massive the scale, can, however, do nothing but buy time. . . . It is simply the case that the number of dollars around the world is out of proportion to the size of the American economy. There are more dollars around than people want. This, far more than the American trade deficit, has been the cause of the recent flight from the dollar. . . . We have to move to a situation where the relative amount of dollars in circulation is reduced. It remains to be seen how far and how fast the United States itself is prepared to go in this process. If it is only interested in token gestures, it is certain that once the psychological impact of the [November 1] package has worn off, the dollar will once more come under pressure.

The November 1 program was not a complete failure. The dollar did strengthen temporarily, but only because the Federal Reserve spent record amounts of money to defend it. On November 1, the Fed spent as much as $300 million an hour in the currency markets and the dollar rose 4 percent. In November and December, the New York Fed spent nearly $7 billion worth of foreign currencies to buy dollars and even this did not prevent the currency from falling substantially throughout December.

Two other developments helped strengthen the dollar through mid-1979. First, the dollar received a boost when higher oil prices occasioned by Oil Shock II filtered throughout the world economy. Oil price increases initially strengthen the dollar. Though they add to U.S. trade deficits, they also underscore the dollar's indispensability in world commerce. As long as Saudi Arabia accepts payment for oil in dollars, other countries must first buy dollars before they buy oil. Then in July, as the dollar showed new signs of weakness, Carter responded by axing Blumenthal, shifting William Miller to Treasury and appointing Paul Volcker chairman of the Federal Reserve System. Bankers and foreign officials applauded

---

* According to the *Federal Reserve Bulletin* (April 1979) this consisted of a current account deficit of $31 billion for 1977–78 and private capital outflows of more than $42 billion. This was accompanied by a $71 billion increase in official foreign assets in the United States, reflecting heavy exchange-market intervention to support the dollar.

the appointment of Volcker. A conservative Democrat and dyed-in-the-wool inflation fighter, Volcker was a known quantity in European and Japanese financial circles. He alone had tried to smooth some of the rough edges of the Nixon-Connally nationalism of the early 1970s. French President Valéry Giscard d'Estaing and German Chancellor Helmut Schmidt, both former finance ministers, had personally dealt with Volcker in those days and apparently thought highly of him. Volcker was perceived as one person in the Carter camp who knew what he was doing.

After the short-lived "Volcker rally," the dollar's slide resumed. By the fall, the dollar was as low against the deutsche mark as it had been in the depths of October 1978. The fundamental weakness of the dollar was reinforced in early 1979 by the divergence between the inflation rate and interest rates in the United States. Even before the onset of Oil Shock II, inflation was reeling out of control. Despite the modest rise in interest rates associated with the November 1 dollar-defense program, the Carter administration resisted dramatically higher interest rates in order to avoid a recession. As a result, the "real" returns on dollar-denominated assets were negligible compared to what was available in other currencies, particularly deutsche marks. As the following tables demonstrate, real U.S. interest rates were flat from mid-1978 to mid-1979 while German rates were rising rapidly.

The emergence of the Eurocurrency market means that corporations, banks and investors can shift in and out of different currencies with relative ease. Banks and corporations view currency operations as profit centers. Thus they increase their holdings of currencies that offer high real interest rates and prospects for exchange rate gains while reducing their holdings of those that do not. Consequently, short-term capital flowed out of the United States to the Euromarket where dollars were exchanged for deutsche marks and other hard currencies. Leading economic consultant Alan Greenspan worked out the arithmetic in hearings before the Joint Economic Committee:

Earlier this year, 3 month CDs, offered both in the United States and in the Eurodollar market, were holding relatively steady in the area of 10 to 10½ percent. However, with inflation in the United States running

Table 7

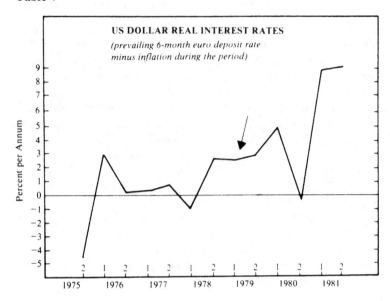

Table 8

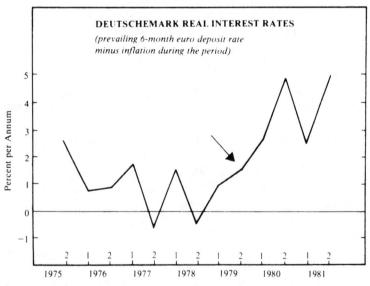

SOURCE: *AMEX Bank Review*, November 30, 1981
Reprinted with permission

persistently in the double digits and expected to continue far above that of Germany the dollar was being heavily discounted in the forward exchange markets.

At the same time, according to Greenspan,

... 3-month forward deliveries of the mark were being quoted at approximately a 6 percent premium—at an annual rate—above the spot position. Not surprisingly, therefore, the 10 percent dollar interest rates arbitraged into a 4 percent 3 month inter-bank deposit rate for DMs in Germany.

Essentially what happened is that speculators, including the largest U.S.-based multinational corporations and banks, dumped dollars in the spot market and acquired deutsche marks, which they placed in short-term bank deposits. Because of the dollar's weakness, they covered their short dollar positions in the forward market at hefty discounts. As a result, the dollar plunged.

This run on the dollar was not just a replay of 1978. It had a new wrinkle. When investors dumped dollars in 1979 they were not only snapping up marks and yen as they had a year earlier. They were also heading into the last refuge of scared investors: gold and silver. Gold began 1979 at a little over $200, passed $300 at midyear and headed toward $400 in the fall. During the last week of September, the price of gold jumped $27 one day and $16 a couple of days later. Silver jumped from $6 an ounce in early 1979 to $12 by the fall.

Volcker would have an opportunity to discuss the latest turmoil in the currency markets with the Europeans, Japanese and Arabs at the annual meeting of the World Bank and IMF at Belgrade, Yugoslavia, in early October. But by the time the IMF-World Bank representatives had assembled in Belgrade, mere turmoil in the money and gold markets had degenerated into pure panic. During the first week of October, everybody who mattered in the financial world— banks, industrialists, the oil sheiks, and central banks—were bearish on the dollar and bullish on gold. There were only net buyers of gold, virtually no sellers. That week prices hit $450. "The gold market," one trader told *Newsweek*, "has gone absolutely mad."

Among the biggest goldbugs were big Middle Eastern investors. The air of Belgrade was vividly captured in one account:

Each day, sometimes twice or three times a day, small groups of Arabs, wearing gold Rolex watches, whose value in the past six months has nearly doubled, slip into a second floor suite of the Intercontinental Hotel here.

They listen quietly for a half-hour, sometimes an hour, while G. William Miller, Secretary of the Treasury, and Anthony Solomon, Under Secretary for Monetary Affairs, explain why they should help support it and why they should trust the dollar over gold, which many have come to favor.

Then they leave, mostly unconvinced.

The Arabs were not only down on the dollar, but the petrodollar recycling process was breaking down. Although the banks had always performed the bulk of recycling, a special effort had been made to lure OPEC money into Treasury securities. In this way, the OPEC countries would be financing U.S. government budget deficits and it would also take some pressure off the banks. In late 1974, Treasury Secretary William Simon and his deputy, Jack Bennett, after extensive consultations with the Saudi Arabian Monetary Agency (SAMA), established a special facility in the Federal Reserve Bank of New York to administer Saudi purchases of Treasury securities. A similar arrangement was later concluded with Kuwait. The quid pro quo was a Treasury guarantee that the extent of the investments would never be divulged to Congress or the public. Simon's success in this area was an important factor in turning U.S. policy toward OPEC from confrontation to cooperation. The money that was going out to pay for oil was flowing right back into the United States.

After Oil Shock II, this neat arrangement began to unravel. Because the Carter administration was trying to keep interest rates down, the OPEC countries were not buying U.S. Treasury securities. Interest rates on Euromarket deposits soared above T-bill rates and the OPEC countries dumped virtually all of the investable surplus they had accumulated in the first three quarters of 1979 into the Eurobanks. One banker who was at Belgrade explains why: "At the time, you would have had to be pretty stupid to be buying treasuries, when you could put your money into marks or Swiss francs. And remember there was a lot of gold and silver buying." Regardless of the currency composition of the deposits, the OPEC money flowing into the Euromarket complicated life for Paul Volcker. The banks were using the OPEC money to finance an orgy of credit expansion in the United States. There was also a torrent of lending to Third World countries at low margin spreads which, to Volcker, began to look increasingly imprudent. In addition, the OPEC surplus was no longer financing the government's budget deficit, which meant that the Fed would have to do so through monetary expansion. This was directly at odds with Volcker's anti-inflationary policies. There was no way out save a dramatic increase in U.S. interest rates.

II

Man's attraction to gold has perplexed such great thinkers as Freud, Shakespeare and Keynes. Keynes ridiculed the sentimental, subconscious attachment to the yellow metal. In 1930, he called the use of gold in monetary matters a "barbarous relic." Some years earlier, Lenin predicted that under socialism gold would be used to decorate the walls and floors of latrines.

Most goldbugs could not care less about the deeper psychological or philosophical meaning of man's attraction to gold. They recite a catalogue of economic facts to show why gold should be a treasured commodity. Gold is relatively scarce, which ensures its value. Gold production has grown only erratically, and new discoveries have been few and far between. The supply is what economists call price unelastic. Even when prices rose dramatically, production did not increase. In *Essays in Persuasion,* Keynes quipped that "A modern liner could convey across the Atlantic in a single voyage all the gold which has been dredged or mined in seven thousand years." Gold's use in monetary affairs has been enhanced by its physical qualities. Gold is so hard, it is virtually indestructible, yet it can be divided into infinitely small quantities.

What matters to goldbugs is gold's usefulness as a store of value. Gold has survived countless international catastrophes and maintained, or even increased its value. Gold is panic money. When currencies collapse, depressions set in and nations go to war, individuals and governments want gold because they know that for much of modern history, gold has been the common denominator of monetary relations.

Gold prices were essentially fixed by governments at $35 an ounce for 25 years. Gold began a comeback in the late 1950s as the dollar-based monetary system came under pressure, but a series of patchwork arrangements managed to keep the benchmark gold price under $40 until 1971. After 1971, the United States intensified its efforts to downgrade the role of gold in international commerce. The IMF ratified the 1971 decision to demonetize gold four and a half years later. Henceforth, governments were supposed to be only sellers of gold, not buyers. The effect was to leave the Western world totally dependent on the U.S. dollar.

The unsettled state of international monetary relations also makes gold attractive. Officially speaking, gold may be "demonetized," but it still functions as panic money. Throughout the 1970s, as international economic disorder spread, private interest in gold accelerated. Gold prices in the major trading centers—London, Zurich, New York and Chicago—became a veritable barometer of confidence in the future of the Western economic system.

Similarly, the ebb and flow of international tensions usually affects gold prices. When nations go to war, governments rely on inflation to finance war expenditures. One obvious result is that the value of the currency goes down. Governments also typically hoard their gold in wartime. Since the accumulation of fabulous oil wealth in the Persian Gulf, hot Arab money rushes into gold whenever the masses get restless or East-West tensions heat up.

The "Gold Rush of 79," as *Newsweek* called it, was essentially caused by the same kind of developments that have caused gold panics throughout history. A principal factor behind the gold price was the growing U.S. inflation rate. In 1979, inflation exceeded 13 percent, the highest annual increase since wartime controls were lifted in 1946. Oil prices had skyrocketed and more increases were on the way. At the end of 1978, world oil prices averaged $13 per barrel. By June of 1979, prices reached $17 and soared to $22 in October. Moreover, the United States was heading into an election year in 1980. U.S. presidents since Johnson have generally preferred more inflation to deep recessions, and there was no reason to believe Jimmy Carter would behave any differently. With Carter trailing Senator Edward Kennedy in the polls, no one really believed that he would slow down the economy enough to reduce inflation. If he did, it would bring on a recession that would push unemployment to intolerably high levels. Paul Volcker had said all the right things about controlling inflation, and in fact raised interest rates to slow the economy. But in the past, when push came to shove, politics usually had won out over "sound monetary management." If Volcker pushed interest rates too high, Carter's "Georgia Mafia" might try to force him out of the Fed and appoint a Bert Lance to the post.

On top of a deteriorating economic climate, there was a complete lack of confidence in the Carter administration. The banks and other speculators had already made the administration look foolish in 1978. Why couldn't they do it again? Even with the addition of Volcker, the Carter team was perceived as incompetent and simply unable to assert influence over critical world events. "The Europeans were looking for leadership," Robert Roosa recalls, "and we were not providing it." For 25 years, the Western world had grown accustomed to powerful American leadership. The Carter administration proved impotent during the revolution that toppled the shah of Iran. These fears would be unmistakably confirmed in the second week of November when Islamic militants stormed the American embassy in Tehran and took its employees hostage, and again, shortly after Christmas, when Soviet troops marched unimpeded into Afghanistan.

The very existence of the gold panic demonstrated that the United States, despite the pretensions of its policymakers, was unable to purge gold from the monetary system. "The U.S. has failed in its efforts to demonetize gold," one European banker told *Business Week*, "and what is important is that previously the United States had always succeeded in imposing its view on this sort of question. Now it can no longer do so."

When the world's financiers gathered in Belgrade, the consensus was that the world economic system was floundering around like a rudderless ship. There was panic in the gold and silver markets, high oil prices, new OPEC ultimatums, a weak U.S. dollar, mounting Third World debt, a rumored Chrysler bankruptcy, and threats of recession.

The flight into gold combined with the continuing weakness of the dollar meant that once again the role of the dollar as the world's key currency was being seriously questioned. When the Europeans threatened to suspend support for the dollar in the currency markets, Volcker must have shivered. As Nancy Teeters, a liberal member of the Federal Reserve Board, put it, the October gold speculation was "wild and scary." Another Fed member, J. Charles Partee, worried that the United States was facing "a real speculative blow-off—a run from currency that is extremely rare in economic history."

In an article entitled "Manic Gold Trading Poses a Global Threat," *Business Week* summed up everybody's feelings:

> The panic in gold is beginning to spill over into the foreign exchange markets and central bankers are starting to worry that, unless the pell-mell speculation is curbed soon, a major international financial crisis may be brewing. In just one day recently, the British pound fell by 2% as hot money from the Mideast rushed out of sterling—into gold. . . . For the global financial system as a whole the gambling now going on in the gold market is for high stakes.

On October 2, Paul Volcker suddenly dropped out of sight. By then, the financial markets were so touchy that his disappearance set off a minor panic when rumors circulated suggesting that Volcker had either resigned or died. (Volcker later denied that he had considered either.) But Volcker apparently had heard enough in Europe to convince him of the gravity of the situation. So he left the IMF meetings to return to Washington to draft the second major dollar rescue program in less than a year.

III

After returning to New York on October 2, Volcker spent the night with his family and shuttled to Washington early the next morning. On Saturday evening, October 6, after an emergency meeting at the

Federal Reserve, Volcker announced a dramatic series of measures. The centerpiece was higher interest rates. First, the Fed increased its "discount rate" from 11 percent to 12 percent. The discount rate is what banks pay when they borrow money from the Federal Reserve. When the Fed raises the discount rate, banks raise their rates and this usually means that tight money is on the way. Second, the Fed drastically altered the way it makes monetary policy. In a major concession to Milton Friedman and the monetarists, the Fed announced that henceforth it would focus on controlling the growth of the money supply, rather than trying to peg interest rates at any specific level. In practice, the Fed's new operating procedure meant that the Fed would squeeze the nation's bank reserves as much as possible to reduce lending. Dollars had been cheap and consequently bank lending soared. Commercial bank loans in the United States had increased by over $200 billion since the end of 1977. Less bank lending, the Fed reasoned, should slow economic activity and help ease inflation, though interest rates might skyrocket. Third, the Fed imposed new "reserve requirements" on banks' Eurodollar borrowings. Reserve requirements are funds banks must set aside in interest-free accounts with the Fed. In the fall of 1979, about half of the increase in domestic credit originated with funds borrowed from OPEC via banks' overseas branches. The banks were using their access to OPEC money to finance credit expansion at home. Until October 6, the reserve requirement on these funds was zero. The new regulations meant that if the banks loaned these funds to corporations in the United States, they would have to keep a certain percentage—8 percent for starters—on deposit with the Fed, thus limiting the scope for credit expansion.

Another measure, where compliance was not mandatory, addressed the issue of speculation. Concerned about developments in the gold market, Volcker requested that banks restrict lending for purely speculative purposes; i.e., commodity speculation and financing of unproductive corporate mergers. The request expressed in the October 6 announcement was underscored in letters sent to all U.S. banks, branches and agencies of foreign banks operating in the United States, and foreign central banks.

The reaction of bankers and the business community in general to the October 6 package was universally positive. Adjectives like "forceful," "decisive," and "radical" were used to describe Volcker's actions. David Jones, chief economist of the Wall Street firm Aubrey G. Lanston, called the October 6 package the Fed's "knockout punch" against inflation. In its Monday edition, the *Wall Street Journal's* lead editorial, entitled "Support Mr. Volcker," typified bankers' reactions:

> The new Federal Reserve anti-inflation package is the most hopeful economic policy development in over a decade, clearly signalling a determination to break the back of inflation that has wracked the economy. It is not as sharp a break with preceding policy as the dollar support package of a year ago, but it is a change of a far more sweeping and fundamental character.

It was openly conceded that higher interest rates, which depress vital industries such as housing and automobiles, increased the risks of recession. But as the Fed's Charles Partee put it, given the chaos that had preceded it, the October 6 package "started to look like the lower risk course." And in any case, Paul Volcker didn't have to run for reelection, Jimmy Carter did.

IV

After the chaotic events of early October, it is hard to imagine how things could have gotten much worse for Paul Volcker and the American economy, but they did, as the Fed's October 6 package quickly came unraveled. Inflation increased. During the first two months of 1980, propelled by gold, silver and oil prices, wholesale prices rose at an annual rate of nearly 20 percent. Consumer prices were advancing at a 17 percent clip. Despite a tighter monetary policy, credit expansion did not slow down. Despite higher interest rates, corporations continued to borrow and the banks continued to lend. The Fed's new reserve requirements on the banks' Eurodollar borrowings were totally ineffective. Instead of borrowing in New York, U.S. companies shifted their borrowing to London and other overseas branches, where the new rules did not apply. In fact, corporate borrowing speeded up for fear that the Fed might impose credit controls. Undaunted, the banks continued to lend money to speculators to support speculation in the gold and silver markets. When it became clear that the Fed's new policies were not working, speculation in gold took off again. Gold prices, which had fallen back to $370 from $450 after the October 6 announcement, resumed their upward course. Though the Federal Reserve's October 6 package failed to stem the growth of credit that was feeding speculation, the Fed hardly deserved all of the blame. International political events beyond the Fed's or anyone else's control traumatized the financial markets and contributed substantially to speculation in gold and silver.

The first shock came in the aftermath of the kidnapping of the U.S. hostages in Iran. On November 4, after President Carter admitted the deposed shah into the United States, the Iranians seized the American embassy and its employees. When the Iranian government refused to do anything about it, a virulent war of words broke out between Washington and Tehran. Ten days later, Foreign Minister Abolhassan Bani-Sadr was quoted as saying that the Iranians would withdraw their money from American banks. Unbeknownst to the Iranians, contingency plans had been in place since February of 1979, long before the taking of the hostages, to seize Iran's foreign assets. If the new regime attempted to disrupt the financial markets, the United States was prepared to seize Iran's money before it left the banks.

The day after Bani-Sadr's remark, President Carter did exactly that and shocked the international financial markets in the process. He froze the deposits of Iran in domestic and foreign branches of U.S. banks, plus gold and other Iranian assets on deposit with the Federal Reserve Bank of New York. Shortly after the initial announcement, the U.S government amended the freeze order to allow U.S. banks to "offset" outstanding loans to the government of Iran with Iran's frozen deposits. Led by Chase Manhattan and Citicorp, the banks declared all loans to the government of Iran in default and seized over $5 billion of Iranian money. Since Iran had more billions on deposit with the big banks than it owed them, the big banks benefited handsomely from the Carter freeze. Smaller U.S. banks, which had no OPEC deposits, were not so lucky. Under the Carter freeze order, the Iranians couldn't pay what they owed and they had no deposits to offset the debts.

This kind of asset seizure was unprecedented in the history of the Euromarket. It quickly revealed the so-called "apolitical" nature of the Euromarket as a grand illusion and sent a message to the OPEC money men that if the United States so decreed, their mountains of petrodollars were not worth the paper they were printed on. On November 14, you might say, the Euromarket lost its virginity. That accelerated the flight of hot Arab money into gold.

Then, in late December, Soviet troops poured into Afghanistan to put down a guerrilla rebellion and install a loyal pro-Moscow regime. President Carter called the Soviet action the "gravest threat to peace" since World War II and threatened the Soviets with World War III if they moved toward the vital oil lifelines of the Persian Gulf. This not only drove the last nail in the coffin of détente, escalating East-West tensions, but it frightened the daylights out of the oil sheiks of the Persian Gulf. For it is probably a safe assumption that either superpower would level the oil rigs of the Gulf rather than allow them to be seized by the other. The Saudi royal family was already reeling from an attack on the Grand Mosque in Mecca. A superpower war over the oil fields was an even more frightening thought.

The upshot was new panic in the gold market. Henry Wallich of the Federal Reserve called events in the gold market a "sideshow." But there is no doubt that, as far as investors were concerned, gold was the main attraction in late 1979 and early 1980. After Iran and Afghanistan, gold prices took off again: $500, $600, $700 an ounce. On January 21, gold reached an all-time high of $875, closing at $825. Operating through Swiss and German banks, Arab interests were buying heavily into gold and so were a lot of other people. *Business Week* stated flatly that Arab fears over Afghanistan and Iran were behind the surge in prices:*

* In the Arab world, financial matters are shrouded in secrecy so it is virtually impossible to know how extensively Arab governments were involved in gold speculation. Arab financial expert John Law, the author of a major Chase Manhattan study on Arab investments, believes the gold buying was confined to private investors. In *Beyond Greed*, a book about the Hunt brothers, Stephen Fay of the London *Times* has traced Saudi activity in the silver market as high

In New York and London gold markets, there is universal agreement that Washington's freezing of Iranian assets triggered the flight out of paper currency into gold. The move has been reinforced by the buying of gold by thousands of rich Arab merchants afraid for their lives in the wake of the Russian invasion of Afghanistan and the recent uprising in Saudi Arabia. Arab purchases have continued unabated through gold's sharp rise to $875 per ounce, its low of $585 and its climb back to more than $700 because the metal is being bought out of fear—as a mechanism of escape.

For the third time in six months, genuine panic had gripped the financial markets. All the familiar symptoms were there: double digit inflation, a flight from the currency, and $700 gold prices. Rising U.S. interest rates had strengthened the dollar, but the price was a destructive international interest rate war between the Fed and other major central banks. This was plunging everybody into recession, while speculation in precious metals markets were contributing to still more inflation. No one disagreed that there was panic, only about its causes. Congressman Reuss, angered at the way U.S. banks flaunted the Fed's request to restrain lending for speculative purposes, condemned the speculative "joy ride" in gold and silver. The next day in its lead editorial, the *Wall Street Journal* excoriated Reuss' glib remark and mourned that the gold panic signaled the end of "American economic and political hegemony."

Paul Volcker had no time for polemics. His job was to stop the panic. By early March the Fed chairman had concluded that the October 6 package was inadequate. Credit expansion had not slowed down, except for auto and housing installment loans. Even as the prime rate shot over 20 percent, the banks kept lending. The economy stubbornly resisted falling into a recession deep enough to bring down inflation. (The only other possible remedy was wage and price controls; but Senator Edward Kennedy had upstaged Carter in calling for controls.) This time Volcker would attack the problem at its roots. Nothing else had worked. If the growth in credit that was fueling inflation would not slow down by itself,

---

as Crown Prince (now King) Fahd. In any event, as Fay observes, the Saudi royal family *is* Saudi Arabia and so the question of government versus private speculation in gold may well be irrelevant.

Volcker had no choice but to bring about a "credit crunch," i.e., force the banks to stop lending. On March 14, the Fed imposed mandatory credit controls on the economy.

Unlike the October 6 package, controls did the trick. Credit expansion stopped. The U.S. economy sank like a stone. In the second quarter of 1980, the U.S. economy declined at an annual rate of nearly 10 percent, the worst quarterly drop in memory. With the economy sinking rapidly, inflationary pressures eased somewhat. After another brief increase, interest rates did start to come down. Gold prices fell quickly as speculators, now convinced that Volcker was serious, dumped gold and rushed to lock in the high interest rates available on dollar assets. The dollar surged above other currencies.

Yet on Wednesday, March 26, twelve days after the announcement of the credit controls, Volcker received a call from the brokerage firm Bache Halsey Stuart Shields that one of America's wealthiest families, the Hunts of Texas, was in financial trouble. The Hunts' troubles were rumored to be so big that they threatened to take some big institutions down with them.

The next day, March 27, the silver market crashed.

The crisis wasn't over yet.

V

In an interview with *Barron's* in 1974, Nelson Bunker Hunt, scion of the late oil magnate H. L. Hunt, and H.L.'s successor as head of one of America's wealthiest families, was clearly bearish on the future of the U.S. dollar as a store of wealth:

> Just about anything you buy, rather than paper, is better. You're bound to come out ahead, in the long pull. If you don't like gold, use silver. Or diamonds, or copper, but something. Any damn fool can run a printing press.

Even before H.L. died, Bunker spearheaded family speculative ventures in various commodities including sugar, soybeans and silver. In 1977, Bunker and his brother acquired nearly 24 billion bushels of soybeans, an essential crop for oils and animal feed. The Commodity Futures Trading Commission (CFTC), the federal agency that regulates the nation's commodity markets, took the Hunts to court on the grounds that they had violated CFTC regulations prohibiting any individual firm from acquiring more than 3 million bushels. Bunker and Herbert countered that the family's holdings were within the CFTC's limits because their children and other Hunt family enterprises and trusts traded soybeans individually, not in concert with the two brothers. After making millions, the Hunts were fined $500,000 by the CFTC.

Silver was destined to be the biggest Hunt scheme of all. After the nationalization of the Hunt oil interests in Libya by Colonel Qaddafi in 1973, Bunker used his Libyan compensation to acquire about $200 million worth of silver bullion. Herbert also got into the silver market in 1973, when prices averaged less than $3 per ounce. They also purchased a sizable interest in the Sunshine Mining Co., one of the largest producers of silver in the United States, but lost control of the firm in a proxy fight.

As the 1970s wore on, silver loomed larger in Hunt portfolios. Silver was not just another investment. It was more like a religion. In the tradition of H.L., the Hunt boys viewed Washington as a hotbed of big-spending socialists who used inflation to finance extravagant welfare programs. An inevitable by-product of these policies, they believed, was debasement of the dollar and with it the fortunes of the rich. For the Hunts, the answer was to accumulate wealth in a commodity other than paper dollars. When Herbert and Bunker Hunt added up the numbers, they concluded that the price of silver was headed up. Annual world consumption outruns annual production by at least 100 million ounces a year. The deficit is made up by U.S. government stockpile sales, meltdowns and dislodging of the ancient silver hoards of India. Higher prices seem to do little to encourage more production. In testimony before a congressional committee, Herbert spelled out the reasons why he felt silver was bound to be a winner.

A study of the facts and figures led me to believe that silver was a wise, good and conservative investment. My research revealed that the price of silver had been kept artificially low by various government actions. Furthermore, in 1972 free world silver consumption was approximately 426.7 million ounces while production was barely in excess of 294.2 million ounces. U.S. demand in 1972 was five times domestic production.

Demand was greater than supply and therefore prices were bound to go up.

The Hunts became involved increasingly in silver market speculation in both the "spot" and "futures" market. In the spot markets of London, New York and Chicago, investors take deliveries of physical silver. The spot market is used by businesses that consume silver, as well as by the hoarders and speculators. Silver has a wide variety of industrial uses, including photographic film, electrical machinery, sterling flatware and jewelry. Like dozens of other commodities, silver is also traded in futures markets in the United States and Europe. The main difference between spot and futures markets is that only a small percentage of silver bought in futures markets is ever delivered to the buyer. Most futures contracts, which in silver means 5,000 ounces per contract, are liquidated before they mature.

Futures markets have evolved into largely speculative devices. In futures markets, speculators try to anticipate price movements in various commodities in order to buy contracts cheap and sell them dear. A speculator in silver, for instance, might believe that the prevailing price—say $6 an ounce—is unrealistically low. Banking on a price rise, the speculator will go "long" in silver; i.e., he will buy a contract enabling him to receive 5,000 ounces of silver at $6 per ounce at some specified date in the future. If silver prices rise to $9, for example, the speculator can sell his contract at a higher price just before it matures. To sell a commodity in futures markets, you need not own it. Thus, another speculator, who anticipates a price drop, may enter into a contract to "short" or sell silver in three months at $6 an ounce. He or she is hoping the price will drop below $6, at which point the speculator can buy the silver he had already "sold" at a cheaper price, cover the contract and pocket the difference.

In futures markets, investors or speculators do not purchase futures contracts at face value. Typically, all that is required is a small fraction of the value of the contract, or "margin," which is usually about 5 percent of the face value. A margin is a kind of down pay-ment that allows speculators to buy a 5,000-ounce silver futures contract priced at $10 an ounce for about $1,000. And sometimes a billionaire speculator, such as Bunker or Herbert Hunt, doesn't even have to put up a cash margin. Instead, he can present a letter of credit from a bank indicating that credit is available if needed.

Operating through the spot and futures markets in Zurich, Lon-don, New York and Chicago, the Hunts amassed huge quantities of silver and pushed the price steadily higher. From $6 per ounce in early 1979, silver rose to $10 in August and closed out in November at over $18, a 300 percent rise in less than a year. But there was more to come. Silver soared over $20 in December and topped out at more than $50 in mid-January.

Some of the increase in silver prices, no doubt, was propelled by the same forces that moved the gold market: inflation, Iran and Afghanistan. But it was clear by the summer of 1979 that unlike the gold market, silver was dominated by a few buyers. On July 27, the staff of the Commodity Futures Trading Corporation (CFTC) esti-mated that the Hunts held 10,000 contracts representing 50 million ounces of silver in U.S. futures markets alone. In October, Bunker told the CFTC that he had a "substantial quantity" of silver stored in banks in Chicago and New York as well as London and Zurich. He informed the CFTC that he and Herbert were also buying silver through a corporation called IMIC, an offshore venture incor-porated in Bermuda, owned by the Hunts and two Saudi Arabian businessmen. Since the mid-1970s, the Hunts had been trying to woo big OPEC money, including the shah of Iran and King Faisal of Saudi Arabia, to invest in silver, presumably to boost the value of their own holdings. But they were unsuccessful until early 1978, when former Treasury Secretary John Connally provided the Hunts with the right Saudi contacts. Arab money began to flow into silver through IMIC, as well as Conti-Commodities, the commodities trading arm of the Continental Grain Corporation.

The Hunts' holdings had grown so large that they became the dominant force in the market. Yet the CFTC, which is supposed to prevent such situations from arising, did nothing about it until very late in the game. The CFTC is fundamentally a weak agency com-pared to older regulatory bodies like the Securities and Exchange

Commission. Consequently, it is in a poor position to police the markets. On top of this, Jimmy Carter had appointed as chairman a young consumer advocate named James Stone, who had no prior experience in commodity trading. The appointment was resented by the industry as well as by the other commissioners, who took a much more laissez-faire attitude toward the commodities markets than did Stone. The upshot was that the CFTC stood on the sidelines while the Hunts and their cohorts bought up about two-thirds of the silver in the United States.

The first visible expression of concern about developments in the silver market came from Treasury Under Secretary Anthony Solomon, just after the Belgrade meetings. CFTC officials were summoned to Treasury where Solomon relayed his concerns about the effects of gold and silver speculation on the dollar. He wanted to know what the CFTC could do to curtail speculation. As the dominant market position of the Hunts became clearer, the CFTC moved to make speculation in the market more expensive. Under prodding from the CFTC, the Commodity Exchange in New York and the Chicago Board of Trade, which establish trading rules in their respective markets, substantially raised the margins required to purchase silver futures contracts. Then they placed limits on the number of outstanding futures contracts individual market participants could hold. Finally, in January 1980, they all but forced the big players to stop buying silver in U.S. markets.

The Hunts complained vigorously to the CFTC that the new rules imposed by the exchange were unfair. They argued that the exchanges were dominated by individuals representing silver users (for example, the photo industry) and who therefore had an interest in seeing prices fall. Whatever complaints they had, the new rules did not make a bit of difference as far as Herbert and Bunker were concerned. They were still buying silver. As the *Washington Post* put it:

> The talks between the Hunts and federal regulators showed that restrictions imposed on the silver futures market at the urging of the CFTC did nothing to stop the Hunts' silver buying spree. When limits were imposed on the number of silver futures contracts any single investor could own, the Hunts stopped buying their silver in the futures market

and got it from U.S. metal dealers in London. When the down payment on silver futures contracts were raised to 40%, the Hunts found they could finance cash purchases with only 20% down.

By early 1980, there was no doubt that the Hunts had a huge hoard of silver. How much probably no one knows. Bunker later told Congressman Benjamin Rosenthal that he had no idea how much silver he owned. The CFTC estimated that the Hunts and related interests owned more than 150 million ounces. Fed Chairman Paul Volcker said the Hunts probably owned about two-thirds of the silver in the United States. Alan Trustman, a lawyer and commodities speculator not unsympathetic to the Hunts, estimated that they owned somewhere between 50 and 500 million ounces.

The Hunts and their Arab cohorts were not alone in the silver game. Even the billionaire Hunts do not have the kind of ready cash to finance such huge silver purchases. To do what they were doing, they needed credit, lots of it. They borrowed money on the upside of the market to finance ever larger purchases of the metal. When the commodity exchanges began to raise the stakes in order to discourage speculation, they borrowed more in order to stay in the market. Finally, when prices headed down, they borrowed still more to cover their paper losses so they could avoid massive liquidation of their position, destroying prices.

A glance at the list of the Hunts' creditors listed in Table 9, shows that the biggest banks and brokerage houses in the world were up to their ears in the silver game. Among the Hunts' creditors were Morgan Guaranty, First Chicago, Merrill Lynch, Citibank, Bache Halsey Stuart Shields, and Swiss Bank Corporation, not to speak of respectable country banks like the First National Bank of Dallas. Not all were direct lenders to the Hunts; many were lenders to the Hunts' brokers, like Bache, which borrowed money from the banks and loaned it to the Hunts. (This was not surprising, since the Hunts held 6 percent of Bache's stock.) Other banks loaned to the strongest Hunt family enterprise, Placid Oil, to finance silver purchases. When the Federal Reserve added up all of the money the Hunts and their associates had borrowed to finance silver speculation, the total came to a stunning $1.7 billion. As expected, collateral for the loans was mainly silver. In February and March of 1980, according to former Representative Henry Reuss, the Hunts consumed about 9 percent of all new bank credit in the United States. They consumed nearly 13 percent of new business loans. Remember that Paul Volcker had asked the banks in October 1979 not to make loans for speculative purposes, but compliance was voluntary and Volcker claimed that he had no legal authority to force the banks not to loan to support speculation. Given the secrecy that surrounds banking activities, it is reasonable to assume that Volcker was not aware of the silver loans. What Volcker didn't know couldn't hurt the banks or the Hunts. Under these circumstances, what loan officer could turn down the wealthiest family in America? Who was more creditworthy than Bunker Hunt, especially since he was offering huge supplies of silver bullion as collat-

Table 9
HUNT SILVER-RELATED BORROWINGS
(August 1979–March 1980)
($ Millions)

Principal Lenders	Loan balance (8/1/79)	Loan balance (1/17/80)	Loan balance (3/27/80)
ACLI International	$29.8	$80.5	$134.2
Bache	$38.	$43.7	$235.5
Swiss Bank Corp.	$70.	$150.	$200.
First Chicago	$30.	$10.	$100.*
E.F. Hutton	---	$100.5	$100.
Citibank	---	$25.	$90.
First National Bank of Dallas	---	---	$79.2
Merrill Lynch	---	$54.	$169.
Placid Oil	---	---	$110.

SOURCE: Securities and Exchange Commission, *The Silver Crisis of 1980*, October 1982.
* This actually understates the extent of First Chicago's involvement with the Hunts. The bank had a total of $223 million in loans to Hunt interests, plus another $75 million loan to Bache which lent the money to the Hunts.

eral? As soon as Bunker threatened to take the Hunt family business up the street, bank loan officers came up with the money fast.

One bank which became heavily involved with the Hunts was the First Chicago Bank, the ninth largest U.S. commercial bank. In 1979, First Chicago had loaned $75 million to the brokerage firm, Bache Halsey Stuart Shields, which in turn loaned the money to the Hunts to finance silver speculation. Then in 1980, as the silver market was collapsing, First Chicago loaned the three Hunt brothers another $100 million, so that the Hunts "could avoid precipitous liquidation of the [silver] position." In testimony before a congressional committee, Richard Thomas tried to justify the loans by pointing out that Chicago "had a relationship with the parent for 35 years" and with Bache's metals subsidiary for 5 years. As for the Hunts, Thomas explained, they had been "very productive customers for us over the years," implying that First Chicago could hardly turn them down.

The biggest banks in the United States loaned the Hunts hundreds of millions of dollars to finance silver speculation at a time when consumers were having a difficult time securing credit to buy autos and houses. The huge loans to the Hunts, as Representative Reuss pointed out, accelerated the expansion of bank credit in early 1980 that led directly to the imposition of harsh credit controls in March. The March 14 package not only squeezed consumers, it drove the U.S. economy into the deepest quarterly economic decline in memory, putting millions of Americans out of work. From the banks' point of view, these were still "good" loans. Even after prices dropped from their January peak, prices were still high by historical standards. The banks were not in any trouble as long as silver prices stayed around $30. Prices stabilized at $35 until early March.

Then the roof fell in on the Hunts and their bankers. A combination of events—the new regulations imposed on the silver market by the exchanges, the Fed's credit controls and a growing recognition that Volcker was serious about inflation—pulled the legs out from under the Hunts' plan to dominate world silver markets. Silver prices dropped precipitously during the second and third weeks of March. On March 26, prices plunged to $16 and below $11 on

"Black Thursday," as the silver brokers call it. As the Hunts' losses multiplied, their brokers demanded that they put up more cash to cover their paper losses, margin calls as they are known in the trade. The Hunts didn't have the money.

Paul Volcker became directly involved in the silver gambit at midday on Wednesday, March 26, when he learned that falling silver prices had created serious financial problems for a major New York brokerage house. The firm, Bache Halsey Stuart Shields, was threatened with huge losses, a run on its stock and possible bankruptcy when the Hunts failed to meet margin calls of more than $100 million. With prices tumbling and the news circulating that the Hunts were unable to come up with the cash to meet their margin calls, Bache panicked and sold sizable quantities of the Hunts' silver, which further depressed the market. It soon became clear that no matter how much of the Hunts' silver Bache dumped, the firm was facing big losses.

Volcker convened an emergency meeting of key officials for 2 P.M. in his office. The meeting lasted four hours. Because the Hunts owned so much silver through a myriad of fronts, Volcker's first job was to decipher what was going on. By the end of the afternoon, at least two things were clear. First, if the silver plunge continued on Thursday, the Hunts, Bache and other brokers, including Conti-Commodities and Merrill Lynch, could be in serious financial difficulty. Second, the Hunts' huge bank loans were backed with high-priced silver as collateral. As silver prices dropped toward $10, the loans were seriously under-collateralized. If Bache and the Hunts went belly-up, what would this do to the banks? James Stone, the 32-year-old chairman of the CFTC, came away from the March 26 meeting with the distinct impression that Paul Volcker was worried about the possibility of a financial crash. Under questioning by Representative Benjamin Rosenthal, Stone admitted that those present at the meeting were concerned "that there could be a situation of financial panic which could affect not only the commodities markets, but the stock market and possibly financial institutions as well."

The silver market plunge continued on Thursday. Silver fell more than $5 an ounce and closed out the day at $10.85. The chaos immediately spilled over into the stock market. "A classic panic" is how brokers described the market. At one point, the stock market had fallen more than 25 points. With rumors flying everywhere, officials of the Securities and Exchange Commission suspended trading in Bache's shares to forestall a complete collapse of the stock. (SEC officials also suspended trading in Shearson Loeb Rhodes, Wall Street's second-largest brokerage concern, because of rumors that Shearson was big in silver. Some months earlier, Shearson had wisely passed up the silver gambit and told the Hunts to take a walk.)

Miraculously for Bache, the Hunts and Volcker, the slide of the silver market did not resume on Friday. Still, there was no rest for the weary. During the last week of March 1980, the silver market crashed, the prime rate hit 20 percent, First Pennsylvania Bank was on the ropes and Chrysler was in the intensive care unit. While he was juggling the fate of First Pennsy, John Heimann summoned top officials of First Chicago, a much bigger but equally troubled bank, to Washington. First Chicago was exposed for over $200 million when the silver market crashed. For a major bank in good condition, $200 million in commodity speculation may not be a lot of money, but it is dangerous business for a bank whose earnings were as weak as First Chicago's. First Chicago's net income fell from $138 million in 1978 to $115 million in 1979 and plunged to only $66 million in 1980. There were times when the bank's survival was in question. What was a bank wracked by falling profits and internal dissension doing lending to support speculation in the silver market? John Heimann called top management in to find out.

No sooner had silver prices stabilized than the whole situation started to unravel all over again.

While Heimann was trying to ward off bank failures, Volcker received a crushing piece of news. On the following Monday the Hunts were scheduled to make a large payment to the global metals giant, Englehard Minerals, for a large silver purchase agreed to back in January. The Hunts had no money to pay Englehard. If the Hunts didn't pay, the Fed reasoned, Englehard might sue them. Faced with bankruptcy, the Hunts would unload more silver, igniting a new slide in the market. In no uncertain terms, Volcker later told Congressman Benjamin Rosenthal's committee that he was worried about a financial crisis:

Englehard might be forced with a decision on Monday to sue the Hunts for payment forcing possible bankruptcy and possibly triggering massive liquidation of silver positions to the peril of all creditor institutions and indirectly placing in jeopardy the customers and creditors of those institutions in a financial chain reaction.

That weekend, leading bankers flocked to a conference in Boca Raton, Florida, where Volcker was scheduled to make a major speech. The Hunts went to Boca Raton to meet with the bankers and look for money to pay Englehard. On Sunday evening, March 30, the Hunts met with the bankers to request new financing for their debts to Englehard. The meeting ended at 4 A.M. Monday morning when the banks refused to provide the Hunts with any more credit. Volcker then met with the banks about how to minimize the damage from the silver market crash. While Volcker huddled with the bankers, the Hunts gave in to Englehard. To lower their debts they handed over oil, gas and silver properties worth over half a billion dollars.

Even with Englehard out of the way, the Hunts still had huge debts and no cash with which to pay them. The banks wanted their money back, but were in no mood to lend the Hunts any more.

While Congressman Benjamin Rosenthal pilloried Volcker and the CFTC, the banks were privately scrambling for a way out of their silver mess. Once again, it was Paul Volcker to the rescue. On Saturday, April 5, a top official of one of the Hunts' big creditors called Volcker and sought his approval for a huge new loan to the Hunts. The new credit would consolidate the Hunts' vast debts into one manageable package while beefing up the collateral. Volcker later told Rosenthal that he voiced no objections to the loan, the largest loan to a single family in the history of the United States, provided the Hunts were prohibited from doing any more speculating.

In all likelihood, the bankers approached Volcker because they knew that politically it would be difficult to justify the loan. They needed Volcker's backing. The Hunts, as may be imagined, did not have a lot of friends at that point. By then, at least two congressional committees were investigating the Hunt silver caper. The Hunts didn't help matters when they defied a subpoena to explain matters to Rosenthal's subcommittee of the Government Operations Committee. The subcommittee immediately voted to cite them for contempt of Congress. Moreover, the loans the banks had already extended to the Hunts and brokerage firms between October and March were in blatant violation of the Fed's October guidelines. At a time when most Americans were being asked to do with less credit, it seemed absurd to be giving the billionaire Hunts a new loan. Representative Reuss, the chairman of the House Banking Committee, wanted the Fed to let the banks "take a bath" in the silver losses to "teach them a lesson." Had Volcker disapproved of the loan, the banks and the Hunts would have been in a very difficult position. Both the Hunts and their brokers might have been forced to sell even more silver in an already depressed market, perhaps driving the price to $5 or below. The banks also stood to lose money on Conti-Commodities. The CFTC reported that Conti's huge parent firm, Continental Grain, injected over $80 million into Conti to insure its solvency. The big banks, in turn, were major lenders to Continental.

By itself, a Hunt bankruptcy might have been harmless. But in an integrated global banking system, large-scale defaults are dangerous business. At the bottom was a huge black pit of uncertainty. Nobody really knew how one bank failure would affect other banks and countries. In *Beyond Greed,* Stephen Fay puts the point succinctly:

> ... their [the Hunts] fate had become inextricably linked with that of the financial system of the United States, which was itself linked with that of the City of London, Paris, Frankfurt, and Zurich. In Europe, too, bankers waited anxiously for the latest news from New York and Washington. Looking back, only twenty-four hours after Silver Thursday, Swiss bankers—especially those of the Banque Populaire Suisse and the Swiss Bank Corporation—had decided that the international banking system was experiencing the most severe strain since the collapse of the Herstatt Bank of Cologne in 1974, which led to an international rescue operation. They were afraid that they might have to repeat that operation, on a larger scale, but what made the suspense difficult to bear was that they did not know. No one knew.

Volcker gave the go-ahead for a bail-out of the Hunts in order to protect the fabric of the financial system. Mainly what he did was to sell the concept of the loan to a skeptical Congress. It has been suggested that the huge loan restructuring was primarily a bail-out of the Hunts or their Saudi partners. While both had a strong interest in securing the credit, that was hardly the primary purpose of the loan. The purpose was to prevent further damage to the banking system, which had been rocked by turmoil and uncertainty in the previous six months. On this point Volcker was very candid:

> The new bank loans would be to and secured by the assets and earning power of perhaps the strongest of the Hunt-related companies, the Placid Oil Co. . . . *The immediate purpose would be to protect more securely the interests of existing Hunt silver creditors, bank and non-bank.* . . . I recognize that the outcome, while plainly desirable in the interests of the creditors themselves and financial stability generally, could have as a by-product some stabilization of the financial position of the Hunts themselves . . . the creditors and others have a legitimate interest in not forcing liquidation of silver in an unreceptive market at the expense of their own stability, that of other institutions and the market itself. [emphasis added]

The banks had gone to the brink and their trusted ally, Paul Volcker, had bailed them out. However, it was a thankless job for the Fed chairman. With the Hunts incommunicado, Volcker was the recipient of most of the congressional outrage over the grotesque bail-out of the Hunts. At a particularly tense moment in the hearings, Volcker finally lost his patience when Rosenthal peppered him with questions about how he would prevent the Hunts from doing any more speculating in the silver market. "I'm not running a police force to follow the Hunts around," he exploded.

The Hunts certainly benefited from the huge loan. As Bunker admitted when he finally appeared before Rosenthal's committee, the loan made life "more comfortable" for him and Herbert. They managed to pay off their silver debts without massive liquidation of the family's assets. They still have most of their silver, more bank credit than many countries and plenty of money to dabble in right-wing politics. Senator Stephen Symms and Representative Larry MacDonald, both staunch conservatives, have sponsored pro-Hunt silver legislation and been showered with Hunt largesse.

While the conditions of the loan had stipulated that neither the

Hunts nor "related entities" would be involved in more silver speculation, in May, Bunker's daughter bought a 4 percent interest in a
silver mine. Yet who could be more related, commented Henry
Reuss, "than your own darling daughter?"

For all but the Hunts and their bankers and brokers, the fallout
from the silver joy ride was most unpleasant. While the Hunts got
$1 billion to pay off their debts, interest rates soared and the Fed's
credit controls destroyed the housing market and auto sales. To the
people jamming the unemployment lines in Detroit and Manhattan, the increased financial stability that Paul Volcker offered in return for the Hunt loan must have seemed rather unimportant. If
you had an operation or got your teeth filled in 1980, you also paid
higher prices thanks to the Hunts. According to the CFTC chairman Stone, the price of medical x-ray film rose 93 percent because
of the increase in silver prices.

Meanwhile, Bunker took his silver losses in stride. "Money never
meant anything to us," he said, "it was just sort of how we kept
score."

CHAPTER 7

MR. WONDERFUL

When Paul Volcker approached the podium to address the 1980 convention of the American Bankers Association in Chicago, the Federal Reserve Board chairman was greeted by the tune "Mr. Wonderful." Volcker, a towering 6'7" man who chomps cheap cigars, has been close to the center of the action in international finance for a generation. The bankers know him and understand him. He is one of them. After working as an economist at the Federal Reserve Bank of New York and Chase Manhattan in the 1950s, he became Robert Roosa's assistant in the Treasury Department. When Volcker left government, he returned to Chase, where he stayed until he was given Roosa's old job by Nixon. In 1975, he became president of the New York Fed and, as such, gained a seat on the Federal Reserve Board's powerful Open Market Committee, which sets U.S. monetary policy. When Jimmy Carter was looking for a new Fed chairman in the summer of 1979, Volcker was the chosen candidate of New York bankers. They were delighted, as were foreign bankers, when he got the job.

As far as leading bankers were concerned, this was not just a routine appointment. The U.S. economy was in a severe economic crisis. The financial markets had been pummeled for over a decade by rising inflation, speculation, slow economic growth and a paralyzing lack of leadership from Washington. Something had to be done to reverse the American economic decline, and it would take a strong figure to do it. Significantly, when Volcker was appointed, Carter also asked David Rockefeller to become Secretary of the Treasury, a post that he declined. In an interview published after he retired from the Chase, Rockefeller reveals the seriousness with which he viewed the situation.

... I saw the country headed for an economic crisis. And for me, a Republican, a banker, coming from a wealthy family—to do the things I felt had to be done, I would have just been the fall guy. I couldn't have done an effective job and would have been destroyed.

Volcker, less controversial and considerably poorer, was the logical candidate to do the hard things bankers "felt had to be done" to turn the U.S. economy around.

With Paul Volcker at the helm of the world's most powerful central bank, the banks were relieved. They were also in charge.

When Paul Volcker announced the Federal Reserve's dramatic policy shift on the evening of October 6, 1979, he launched a transformation of U.S. domestic and international economic policy more profound than Nixon's New Economic Policy of August 15, 1971. The principal significance of the October 6 measures were not the technical changes in the Fed's operating procedures.* Rather, the principal meaning was that significant internal policy changes were forced upon the United States by international developments, specifically the near-collapse of the dollar on the foreign exchange markets. For a generation, the United States had the luxury of formulating economic policy in accordance with domestic goals while letting the international situation take care of itself. Such was the nature of the Bretton Woods monetary order and the dominant position of the United States. When international constraints on domestic policy began to appear in the late 1960s and early 1970s, the

* Most economists agree that the October 6 policy changes signaled that the Fed had adopted a "monetarist" strategy, so-called because it focuses on controlling the money supply rather than interest rates. Essentially what the Fed does is determine yearly targets for monetary growth and supply funds to the banking system to meet the targets. However, Volcker is more of a pragmatist than are strict monetarists. Thus, despite his implementation of monetarist policies at the Fed, Volcker continues to be viewed with suspicion by monetarist theologians, particularly Milton Friedman and Treasury Under Secretary Beryl Sprinkel.

United States backed away from international commitments rather than adjust domestic policy to suit them.

By the end of the decade, this was no longer possible.

The global credit crunch launched by Paul Volcker was primarily a response to the growing chaos in the international money markets rather than the problem of domestic inflation, though the two were obviously interrelated. The problem of domestic inflation was, however, of secondary importance to Paul Volcker on October 6. Volcker did not have to travel all the way to Belgrade to learn how bad the U.S. inflation rate was: the figures sit on his desk every day.

What Volcker did learn in Europe was that once again the dollar-based monetary system was about to collapse. The core of the problem was that for the second time in a year corporations, banks, central banks and other investors (including moneyed Arab interests) had stopped accepting dollars as the universal currency.* Instead, there was heavy dollar selling on a global scale and the proceeds were going into gold, silver, deutsche marks, Swiss francs and even art and real estate. In Belgrade, as it had in meetings in western Europe the previous weekend, it became obvious to Volcker that a collapse of the dollar was a very real possibility, perhaps leading to a financial crisis and pressure to remonetize gold, which the United States had fought doggedly for over a decade. To forestall this, there was only one possible course of action: do whatever was necessary to strengthen the dollar. The strategy was simple: in order to lure funds into denominated assets, dollar interest rates would have to be raised. On October 6, Paul Volcker did exactly that.

The effects of the Fed's change of course were felt almost immediately through a dramatic and unprecedented increase in interest rates in the United States. Usury was institutionalized. Mafia loan sharks used to get ten to twenty years in prison for charging rates that now became standard at the country's biggest banks and finance companies. Since the fall of 1979, except for a brief period

* The dollar continued to function as a transactions medium, in that oil was still priced in dollars. But the dollar was used less and less as a reserve currency by the capital surplus OPEC countries—and other countries as well. This was reflected in the substantial diversification in the composition of reserves that took place during this period.

when the economy was sunk in the 1980 recession, the prime rate has been in double digits. Twice since Paul Volcker took over at the Fed, interest rates have hit 20 percent or more. Interest rates have not only increased in nominal terms, but in real terms as well. Real interest rates used to hover at around 1 percent to 2 percent. Since late 1979, real interest rates have climbed as high as 10 percent. The following tables depict the dramatic increase in real interest rates since 1979. Despite the fluctuations, real interest rates have tended sharply upward. In other words, there has been a dramatic change in the price of the one commodity that is more indispensable than oil: money. Even with the well-publicized declines of the summer of 1982, real interest rates remain at extraordinarily high levels of 6–7 percent for corporations and well over 10 percent for consumers and home buyers.

For Volcker, success was not long in coming. As a result of higher interest rates, the dollar strengthened and money rushed out of gold and silver and into dollar-denominated assets. The dollar, one of the sickest currencies of the 1970s, became the world's strongest. The dollar has soared by 20 percent against other major currencies and shot up by between 30 and 40 percent against the mark and the yen. The main reason for this is the higher real rate of return investors can obtain on dollar-denominated assets. Unlike academic economists, analysts close to the currency markets have no illusions about what was behind the dramatic recovery of the dollar. "U.S. [interest] rates are up again," writes Anne Parker Mills, a foreign exchange analyst at New York's Irving Trust Company, "and so— as surely as springtime follows winter—is the dollar." Mills cautions that exchange rate/interest rate relationships are not mathematically precise, but she provides more than enough evidence of the relationship between the two. Note that in the most important currency market of all, the dollar/D-mark market, during every period when the spread between dollar and deutsche mark interest rates increased, the dollar strengthened. When the spread declined, it weakened.

The second major effect of high real interest rates in the United States has been a horrendous economic slump. After the long expansion of 1975–79, the economy was due for a normal recession, but a slump of this magnitude has been unprecedented since the

Table 10
REAL INTEREST RATES IN THE UNITED STATES

Three-Month Treasury Bill Rate

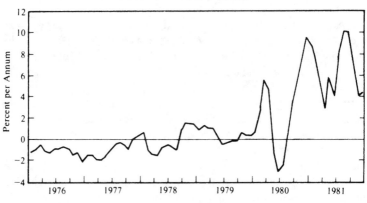

AAA Corporate Bond Rate

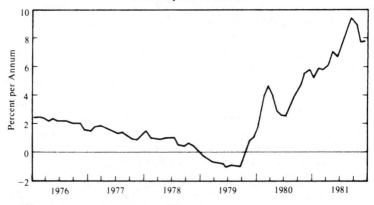

SOURCE: Congressional Budget Office

1930s. Since 1979, when interest rates began their steep climb, the
U.S. economy has been essentially flat. The United States sank into
a sharp recession in early 1980, hobbled through a twelve-month
"recovery," the briefest of the postwar period, and in July 1981 slid
again into recession. The Reagan administration program for recovery, which called for tax cuts for the affluent, smaller checks for

Table 11

| | Exchange Rates | | Interest Rates | | | | % Change Dollar Per 100 Basis Pt. Change in Interest Rate Spread (Dollar Declines in Parentheses) |
| | DM/US$ | % Change $ vs. DM | 3-Month Euro$ | 3-Month Euro-DM | Spread-Basis Points Points | Change in Period | |
			— Percent —				
Jan 3 '80	1.7118		14.00	8.13	588		
Apr 1 '80	1.9766	+15.5	19.44	10.13	931	+343	4.52
Jul 17 '80	1.7367	−12.1	9.06	9.00	6	−925	(1.31)
Feb 17 '81	2.1950	+26.4	18.31	10.62	769	+763	3.46
Mar 24 '81	2.0475	− 6.7	14.38	12.38	200	−569	(1.18)
Aug 10 '81	2.5710	+25.6	18.63	12.56	607	+407	6.28
Nov 9 '81	2.1978	−14.5	13.69	10.69	300	−307	(4.72)
Feb 18 '82	2.3830	+ 8.4	16.25	10.19	606	+306	2.75

SOURCE: Irving Trust Co., *Foreign Exchange Market Trends*. February 18, 1982. Reprinted with permission

those on welfare and other forms of assistance and massive military spending, fell flat on its face in the climate of tight money.

At the end of 1982, U.S. industrial production was *lower* than it was in early 1979. The nation's factories were producing at less than 70 percent capacity. Corporations were going bankrupt at the highest rate since the Great Depression. According to official government statistics, unemployment had risen to over 10 percent and for blacks, other minorities and young people the rates were much higher. The nationwide unemployment rate for blacks was 20 percent or double that for whites. For young blacks, unemployment stood at a staggering 50 percent. In industrial centers like Michigan and Ohio, unemployment was nearing depression levels.

The automobile and housing industries, both crucially dependent on affordable credit, have been prostrate since 1979. U.S. car manufacturers had losses of over $5 billion in 1980 and 1981. In 1981 sales of U.S.-made autos fell to 6.2 million, the lowest since 1961. Dealers have been losing money hand over fist, forcing over 3,200 dealerships out of business since 1979. In the face of declining sales, the high cost of financing inventories has forced dealers to slash their purchases, thereby further depressing production. The auto industry's woes have given Michigan the dubious distinction of having the highest unemployment rate in the nation, 16 percent. The housing industry is in even worse shape. In 1981, new housing starts plunged to their lowest level since 1946 and resales are also down dramatically. Construction of new homes has not increased since 1978. Housing starts in 1981 were only about 60 percent of the 1978 figure. The sad state of the housing industry is reflected in an 18 percent national unemployment rate for construction workers.

The advent of high interest rates has punctured the symbol of the great American Dream—the single family home—as interest rates have pushed housing mortgage costs out of the reach of many families. Price inflation as such is not the problem. The real problem is the cost of money. In 1981, according to *International Currency Review*, a leading financial journal, the median price of houses in the United States was $68,200 and a median family income was $23,-500. With mortgage interest rates of approximately 14 percent, a 30-year mortgage with a 25 percent down payment yields annual interest payments of $7,400 or about 32 percent of gross income, a huge amount even by American standards. "Thus," concludes *International Currency Review,* "the average American family can no longer afford the average American house."

There is no denying that inflation has come down sharply since Volcker embarked on his new strategy. After increasing by more than 13 percent in 1979, inflation in the United States dropped to less than 9 percent in 1981 and down to about 7 percent in 1982. While not even Volcker would claim that the Fed deserves all the credit for reducing inflation, tight money and the recession have played a major role. Still, the strategy involves a major gamble. As Volcker himself admits, if monetary policy is too tight for too long, although helping on the inflation front, it runs the risk of "killing the economy in the process."

Some business critics of the Fed's policies think this policy has already done so. Although business initially supported the Volcker moves, no one is more unhappy with the results than businessmen whose industries have been paralyzed by high interest rates. In fullpage advertisements in the *Wall Street Journal, New York Times* and *Washington Post,* James Stewart, chairman of the Lone Star Cement Co., the largest cement producer in the United States, castigated the Fed. "Congratulations, Doctor," the ad began, "it was a good operation . . . on inflation . . . *too bad the patient died.* Maybe the high interest rate policy of the Federal Reserve will cure inflation—but the rates are killing the economy."

Many leaders in Europe agree. The effects of the Fed's tight money policies have not been limited to the United States. With banks and other financial institutions linked closely together through a global money market, it is virtually impossible for countries to pursue divergent economic policies. Thus, high interest rates in the United States were quickly transmitted to other countries. Most industrialized countries have been forced to raise interest rates in tandem with increases in U.S. rates. Otherwise, they would face the same kind of run on their currencies that plagued the dollar during 1978 and 1979.* The result was a global interest-rate war. In

---

* The implications of this are sometimes not fully appreciated. The strong dollar raised the real cost of Europe's oil imports at a time when falling oil

country after country, the Fed's policies have led, as former German Chancellor Helmut Schmidt commented, to "the highest rates of interest since the birth of Jesus Christ, at least as far as real interest rates are concerned."

The Federal Reserve has become an engine of global deflation. When the Fed dragged the U.S. economy into a prolonged slump in order to rescue the dollar, they carried most of the world along with it. The result has been a deepening world economic contraction. In the leading industrialized countries there are 30 million unemployed. For Europe, the results have been catastrophic. Like the U.S. economy, the rest of the industrialized economies have been essentially flat since mid-1979. Industrial production in the European Economic Community was substantially lower at the end of 1981 than it was in 1979. Industrial production has even declined in West Germany, the community's most powerful member. Unemployment in West Germany, which never exceeded 3.5 percent during the steep 1974–75 slump, stood at more than 7 percent at year-end 1981. France's unemployment soared to more than 8 percent and Britain's to 13 percent. Business failures all over Europe are at startling levels, claiming among its victims firms like Germany's AEG Telefunken.

The global economic slump has also aggravated international trade and balance of payments problems. In 1981, the value of world trade contracted for the first time since 1958. In volume terms, after growing only 1 percent in 1980, world trade fell in 1981 and 1982. U.S. exports have been damaged by the effects of a rising dollar and slow world economic growth. The paralysis in the industrialized countries has depressed Third World exports, leading to a slew of defaults throughout the underdeveloped world. Thus far, the result has been a widening and deepening of the global deflationary spiral with the global outlook growing more pessimistic by the month.

---

prices were one of the few bright signs in the economic outlook. Depressing European currencies even more would worsen this problem. Moreover, as the French socialists have learned, a declining currency is not only inflationary but saps confidence in the economy, each of which reinforces the other.

II

The severity of the global slump begs the question of why an experienced economic policy maker like Paul Volcker would flirt with the risk of a new depression by applying such draconian measures. Unlike Milton Friedman, Volcker is not a rigid monetarist. He is not getting rich on tight money, having taken a $50,000 salary cut to become head of the Federal Reserve. Certainly, he is not winning any popularity contests for his role as the nation's number one Scrooge. Hardly a day goes by when Volcker is not crucified by some congressional committee or reviled by a Reagan administration official for the pain caused by high interest rates. Representative Jack Kemp, an ardent conservative, and liberal Democrat Representative Henry Gonzalez have both called for Volcker's resignation. Hate mail flows regularly to his Constitution Avenue office.

One plausible explanation of Volcker's behavior is that from his vantage point, given the chaotic situation he inherited, there is no other way to undo the tangled web of inflation and speculation. Inflation and speculation are like Siamese twins. In the postwar period, as Professor Hyman Minsky of Washington University has pointed out, the U.S. government has generally opted for greater inflation rather than risk the collapse of economic activity. From close range Volcker observed how Nixon and Arthur Burns legitimized ignoring inflation rather than meeting it head-on. During the 1970s, inflation became firmly embedded in the fabric of the U.S. economy. Volcker also viewed the development of so-called "inflationary expectations," the notion that inflation would continue indefinitely, as exceedingly dangerous. From Volcker's perspective, inflation had become a game that people were doing everything they could to stay ahead of. This led investors, corporations and banks to engage in outlandish financial speculation in order to profit from inflation. The dollar was under heavy pressure in the currency markets for three years. The banks knew Carter's dollar defense program was hopeless and they proved it by outspending the Federal Reserve in the currency markets. Then they started dabbling in gold and silver and lending large amounts of money to people who were dabbling in gold and silver. The question arises as to why Volcker did not take any direct action to control the banks, which were fueling the spiral of inflation and speculation. The answer is that the head of a central bank cannot be expected to take on his main constituents. He is there to protect their interests, not prosecute them. So instead of disciplining the banks, he was forced to deal with the speculative fever by throwing the economy into a deep slump.

Speculation had become not only extremely profitable, but was not very risky. A central element of a government policy designed to prevent deep depressions is that any potential crisis in a major bank must be met with swift government intervention to prevent the crisis from spreading to others. The lesson that banks drew from this—particularly during the Franklin-Herstatt failures of 1974—is that no matter what they did the Fed would always bail them out. One result was to encourage speculation. As Albert M. Wojnilower, chief economist of the First Boston Corporation, observes:

> . . . central banks and the public . . . paid a fearful price for these lender-of-last-resort operations, which encouraged banks to become more reckless lenders than ever. Once the dust had settled, both central banks and market participants came to regard such issues as reliably institutionalized responsibilities. It is now everywhere taken for granted that no monetary authority will allow any key financial actor to fail.

Without a doubt, the inability of governments to control inflation combined with bail-out operations to prevent major financial crises contributed to the growth of destabilizing speculation. However, inflation and speculation were aided and abetted by two key developments in the global financial system. One was the adoption of floating exchange rates in 1973. The other was the rapid growth of the Eurocurrency markets.

Since the adoption of floating exchange rates in 1973, the foreign exchange markets have become the world's biggest gambling casino. Floating rates, which were adopted in desperation when governments gave up trying to control financial flows, have produced wild swings in exchange rates. Balance of payments problems, which floating exchange rates were supposed to minimize, have also been larger under floating rates. Speculation has been a far greater problem than it was under the old Bretton Woods fixed rate system. As Charles Ramond, chairman of New York's Predex Corporation told the *Wall Street Journal*, the widely propagated notion that floating exchange rates would stabilize currencies was "surely the dumbest forecast ever made." Today's massive exchange rate swings result mainly from speculation in the currency markets. In 1977, according to Citibank's own estimates, there was about $50 trillion in foreign currency trading compared to about $2 trillion in world trade. The only explanation for this massive discrepancy is the scope of speculative activity. No constructive purpose is served by wild exchange rate swings induced by large-scale speculative flows.* They distort rather than aid economic policy. Since the early 1970s, when the American economy has been growing and creating jobs and investments, the dollar has been weak. Today the economy is flat on its back and the dollar is stronger than it has been in over a decade. Paul Volcker's tight money policies have rescued the U.S. dollar, but they are killing the U.S. economy.

Leading Eurobanker Geoffrey Bell sums up the experience of floating exchange rates when he says: "This is no way to run the world."

Most bankers, predictably, protest that exchange rate instability results from divergent national economic policies and government ineffectiveness in controlling inflation. Bankers like to masquerade as staunch opponents of inflation, but the evidence shows that they are among its principal promoters. The huge pool of vagabond Eurodollars, for instance, is a major source of global inflation. Obviously, the Euromarket did not create global inflation. Money matters, to paraphrase the Nobel Prize-winning economist James Tobin, but not that much. The roots of inflation lie in the real economy—not the monetary system, but the rapid growth of the Euromarket makes inflation more difficult to control. At key stages in the anti-inflation fight, the global banks have undermined U.S. govern-

---

* In the economics profession, the latest jargon to describe this phenomenon is the tendency of the markets to "overshoot." It is interesting that after a decade of floating exchange rates, some former enthusiasts of floating, such as Fred Bergsten, have concluded that overshooting is endemic to the system and are now calling for greater government intervention in the currency markets.

ment policies to control inflation. Their access to the huge pool of dollars in the Euromarket allows them to expand credit despite Federal Reserve policies to slow credit creation.

Ever since the credit crunch of 1966, U.S. banks have resorted to the Euromarket as a source of funds whenever the Fed tightened monetary policy at home. In 1966, banks tapped the fledgling Euromarket when the Fed clamped Regulation Q ceilings on domestic interest rates. When the Federal Reserve refused to lift ceilings on the interest rates banks could pay on the certificates of deposit, the large banks that had operations in London issued Euro-CDs as an alternative source of funds. The banks' Euromarket branches loaned these funds to New York, which used them to sustain credit expansion at home. In 1969, when Federal Reserve policy turned restrictive in a belated attempt to combat Vietnam-related inflation, the banks played the Eurocard again. By then more banks were involved and they were more experienced at it. In 1969, U.S. banks borrowed about $15 billion from their Euromarket branches in order to maintain credit expansion at home.

Probably the greatest example of how banks use their global reach to undercut U.S. monetary policy came in 1979. Prior to the announcement of the October 6 measures, U.S. banks had been borrowing heavily in the Euromarket (particularly from their own subsidiaries) to expand credit in the United States. Domestic loan demand was strong (in part because low real interest rates encouraged borrowing) and with the proceeds of new OPEC price increases pouring into the Euromarket, it made sense for banks to borrow in the Euromarket to relend at home. The Federal Reserve Board calculated that "U.S. banks borrowed $30 billion from their foreign branch offices during the first three quarters of 1979." The Fed had been tightening monetary policy and interest rates were rising, but the huge flow of Eurodollars into the U.S. economy was fueling credit expansion. In the summer and early fall of 1979, according to the Fed, imported Eurodollars and other exotic bank liabilities financed about "half the increase in bank credit over that period." Volcker correctly perceived that to control inflation, it was necessary to get a handle on bank credit expansion. Thus, on October 6, he did take some steps to reduce the flow of Eurodollars to the

U.S. economy, placing reserve requirements on U.S. banks' Eurodollar borrowings.

While bankers universally supported Volcker's October 6 initiatives, in the ensuing months they flaunted their extraterritoriality and directly undermined the effectiveness of the October 6 measures. Less than a month after the October 6 package, Rimmer de Vries of Morgan Guaranty told the Joint Economic Committee how U.S. banks could get around the new reserve requirements by lending directly to the foreign subsidiaries of U.S.-based companies. The multinationals, over which the Fed has no control, could then bring back the funds to the United States with no questions asked. Chase Manhattan's London branch, for example, could lend to an Exxon subsidiary in Europe which could transfer the funds to New York for use in the United States. Other forms of financial innovation were also used. According to de Vries, blue-chip borrowers could tap nonbank channels of credit, such as the commercial paper markets in New York and London. Finally, foreign banks could lend directly to U.S. companies and Volcker could only protest. As Litton Corporation's treasurer, Charles Black, observes, "There are so many ways to borrow that big, sophisticated companies can use. It's awfully hard to control this kind of thing. There are too many things you can't plug up."

Despite the Fed's October 6 measures, bank lending to their corporate customers remained high. Albert M. Wojnilower of First Boston Corporation points out that loan commitments by banks to their corporate clients actually increased after the October 6 policy change, as corporations moved to insulate themselves from the potential imposition of credit controls. The banks reduced the availability of credit to noncorporate borrowers in order to maintain credit commitments to their top corporate customers. As for the effectiveness of the Fed's new monetarist policies, Wojnilower concludes that they "exerted no perceptible retarding influence" on bank lending.

The multinationals not only ran rings around the Fed's reserve requirements, but the banks completely ignored an explicit Fed request to "avoid loan activity that supports speculative activity in gold, commodity and foreign exchange markets." Though higher interest rates on dollar-denominated assets eventually did stem the flow of funds into gold and silver, it took time. Thus heavy speculation continued until January, when the prices of both metals hit all-time highs. Undaunted by the Fed's directive, leading U.S. banks such as First Chicago and foreign banks such as the Swiss Bancorp continued to lend vast sums to the Hunts and other international speculators. In this way, as demonstrated in Chapter 6, the banks contributed to the speculative frenzy—and to the dangers it posed to the fabric of the financial system. Their lending policies also fueled inflation, particularly in precious metals, ultimately forcing the Fed and the Carter administration to resort to direct credit controls in March of 1980. Still, the credit controls had no lasting impact on the banks. The credit controls imposed a target range of 6–9 percent on the growth of bank loans, but the banks' access to the Euromarket insured that lending to top corporations remained high. The banks merely shifted their corporate loans to the Euromarket and the corporations brought the funds home. In the U.S. balance of payments, as the Federal Reserve itself observed, "this shifting of loans to offshore branches results in a capital outflow from U.S. banks and an inflow through corporations." In the second and third quarters of 1980, over $37 billion flowed out of the United States through bank channels and nearly $26 billion flowed back in through the statistical discrepancy. According to Salomon Brothers, there was a $24 billion reduction in net new corporate borrowing in domestic credit markets in 1980. But this decline was fully offset by the billions the corporations brought back from the Euromarket.

The use of the Euromarket as a way around tight money at home seems to have become a permanent part of multinationals' financial strategies. In 1981, a large outflow of private capital ($27 billion) was accompanied by a similarly large inflow ($24.6 billion) which shows up in the "statistical discrepancy." The Fed staff notes sheepishly in the *Federal Reserve Bulletin* that the large statistical discrepancy reflects "greater use of nontraditional channels of international financial intermediation, particularly those that bypass U.S. banks and in principle should be reported by nonbanks." This explanation is another way of saying the multinationals are using their global reach to gain access to additional credit and bring it home, but not reporting it. There is no evidence Volcker has tried to do anything about it.

The multinationals' access to the Euromarket has clearly complicated the execution of monetary policy in the United States. As Jeffrey Nichols of New York's Argus Research Corporation remarks, the Euromarket "can be considered analytically as a 51st State outside the Federal Reserve System—and not subject to its reserve requirements—but still an integral part of the nation's financial system." The growth of the Euromarket has forced the Federal Reserve into an even tighter monetary posture. Basically, the Fed squeezes the domestic economy harder to offset the flow of funds from the Euromarket. This has worsened unemployment and domestic economic performance. Fed Governor Henry Wallich, one of the few central bankers who openly acknowledges the problems posed by the growth of the Euromarket, describes the problem this way:

> By taking into account this monetary expansion in the Euromarket in setting its domestic money supply targets, the Federal Reserve could, of course, adjust the domestic targets so as to keep the combined amount of domestic and Euromoney on the right track. But as the Eurodollar market grows, *the Federal Reserve would have to bear down increasingly hard on the domestic supply of money and credit in order to offset the expansion of Eurodollars. This would work a hardship on our domestic economy and particularly on U.S. borrowers who did not have access to the Euromarket.* [emphasis added]

In the three years since the adoption of the October 6 measures, that is exactly what has happened. The multinationals have had access to all the credit they need, whereas small businesses, homebuyers and consumers have been clobbered. Despite the astronomical rise in interest rates, new corporate borrowing has continued at high levels. Moreover, a large share of the funds raised by U.S. firms in the Euromarket in 1981 consisted of mammoth loan syndications by corporate giants like Mobil, U.S. Steel and DuPont to finance mergers and acquisitions, such as the fabled Conoco and Marathon Oil takeovers. The surge of borrowing to support M&A, as it is known on Wall Street, was particularly strong in the summer of 1981. Though only half of the credit lines were actually drawn down, this large-scale borrowing increased the demand for credit, keeping interest rates high and draining credit from more productive uses. For the economy as a whole, it was a high price to pay to ease summer boredom on Wall Street.

III

Despite the Fed's so-called credit crunch, there has been no interruption in the supply of credit to the multinationals. When they cannot borrow at home, they can borrow in the Euromarket. Even at home, however, the Fed's tight money policies have resulted in a marked redistribution of credit away from consumers, small businesses and would-be homebuyers to big business. As former Federal Reserve Governor Andrew F. Brimmer observes, when money is tight, banks lend primarily to their top corporate customers. Unless the Federal Reserve loosens monetary policy, there will be a corresponding reduction in credit availability to other customers. Relations with large corporate customers are the core of modern banking and the banks naturally cater first and foremost to corporate needs when things are tight. Corporate wholesale accounts provide huge amounts of business with much less overhead than do traditional "brick and mortar" consumer and small business banking.

The leading victims of the Fed's credit crunch are, not surprisingly, the automobile and housing industries. Both industries have been in the doldrums since 1979. Money is expensive and it has priced new autos and houses out of the reach of many families. The squeeze on housing has been particularly acute.* In 1976, according to Salomon Brothers, home mortgages consumed about 25 percent of all new funds raised in domestic credit markets. In 1981 they accounted for only about 15 percent of the total. New commercial bank lending for mortgages fell from $35 billion in 1978 to $19 billion in 1980 before recovering to $27 billion in 1981, but much of this increase was in commercial rather than home mortgages. Even

---

* Henry Kaufman points out that were it not for the increasing participation of government agencies in home financing, housing's decline would have been more acute.

in nominal terms new mortgage lending in 1981 by commercial banks was less than it was in 1977. Net new consumer credit fell from $26 billion in 1978 to a net contraction in 1980. In 1981, it recovered to about $2 billion but this was far lower than any yearly increase since 1976. Given the drastic decline in consumer and mortgage credit, it is not hard to see why consumers have been unable to lead the U.S. economy out of recession.

This fundamental shift in the credit markets suits the banks, for increasingly they prefer to concentrate on corporate and government lending. This—and not merely risk premiums—explains why large companies are getting back credit at significantly lower interest rates than everybody else. One of the durable myths of banking is that the published "prime rate" is the interest rate banks charge their best business customers. Today, any big corporation that pays the published prime rate is either in deep trouble or has a fool in charge of corporate finances. Competition among banks for corporate business and the proliferation of alternative credit instruments, such as commercial paper, have forced banks to lower the interest rates charged to their top corporate clients. For them, the decline in interest rates began long before it did for everybody else. This practice of lending below the prime originated before the interest rate crunch, but it has now become the accepted way of doing business. In 1981, according to the Federal Reserve, over 61 percent of commercial and industrial loans made by 48 large banks were made at interest rates below the prime. The larger the loans, the greater the likelihood of borrowing below the prime. Meanwhile, small businesses are paying the prime, plus stiff markups. The big banks give preferential treatment to their top customers but, as former Representative Henry Reuss remarks, they wear "prime rate falsies" for everybody else.

The advent of high interest rates combined with changing commercial bank-lending priorities has nearly sounded the death knell of the housing industry in the United States.* The decline of the savings and loan institutions, which is directly attributable to high

---

* Part of this was intentional. One of the tenets of conservative economics is that in recent years Americans have consumed too much and invested too little. While conservatives view housing as a drain on capital needed for industry, they

interest rates, has contributed mightily to the problems of the housing industry. Despite recent financial innovations, such as money market certificates, the S&Ls have been plagued by a massive loss of funds, a process known as disintermediation. In 1981, withdrawals at mutual savings banks and S&Ls exceeded new deposits by almost $40 billion. Operating losses rose over $5 billion. Approximately 85 percent of all S&Ls lost money. For the first quarter of 1982, S&Ls lost $2 billion. (So many S&Ls are on the verge of bankruptcy that the Federal Home Loan Bank Board recently lowered the S&L's capital to assets requirements from 4 percent to 3 percent. This regulatory sleight-of-hand was apparently designed to allow some of the S&Ls to survive a little longer.) A shrinking deposit base means that the S&Ls are less able to supply mortgage money on the scale that they did in the 1970s. In 1977, total new lending by thrift institutions reached $82 billion, but by 1981 this had fallen to under $40 billion. The chronic ills of the S&Ls mean that less credit will be available for housing. The industry will suffer accordingly.

The problem is compounded because deposits are increasingly flowing from domestic financial institutions to the Euromarket. In recent years, funds have flowed out of the domestic thrifts into high-yielding money market funds. The large institutions that dominate the money market funds are depositing them directly in London, effectively draining them out of domestic financial markets. In 1981, assets of money market mutual funds rose by over $100 billion and according to the Federal Reserve, at least $11 billion of this was invested in Euromarket certificates of deposit. (There are billions more in "Euromarket holdings of nonbanks" of which the Fed claims it does not know the origin.) These deposits become part of the huge pool of Eurodollars available for corporate and government lending, but not housing.

The commercial banks, which are in a position to take up the slack created by the demise of the thrifts, have shown little inclination to do so. Instead, they are pressing the government to eliminate

---

are unable to see that businesses only invest to serve future consumption and that an increase in investment is impossible without an increase in consumption.

remaining ceilings on interest rates. The inevitable result of this would be the end of the national commitment to broad-based home ownership. Since the New Deal, housing has been accorded a privileged position in U.S. financial markets because it plays a large role in maintaining economic growth and business investment. From a commercial banker's standpoint, however, the inability of many families to afford higher interest rates has increased risks. In other words, home mortgages are becoming increasingly unbankable. The upshot will be permanent damage to the housing industry. As First Boston's Albert M. Wojnilower states:

... freeing the financial markets—which in the United States is tantamount to shrinking the housing subsidy by withdrawing preferences hitherto accorded mortgage-lending institutions—will reduce home building. Freeing the thrift and mortgage markets from government subsidy and guaranty is like freeing the family pets by abandoning them in a jungle.

CHAPTER 8

THE PAPER ECONOMY

The situation is certainly more risky. Twenty years ago, I would have said the odds were 1,000 to 1 against another depression; 10 years ago, 100 to 1 against it; today, the odds are maybe 8 or 10 to 1. That is still substantially against it, but the odds are coming down.

HENRY KAUFMAN
Chief economist
Salomon Brothers

I

This book began with the Bretton Woods conference of 1944 because that important event marked the beginning of the recovery from the global economic wreckage of the 1920s and 1930s. Two men, John Maynard Keynes and Harry D. White, put their heads together to hammer out a blueprint for a liberal and internationalist postwar economy. The Bretton Woods world did not quite work out as planned, but it worked. For a generation that had known two world wars, fascism, depression and financial ruin, that was all that mattered.

Whatever their shortcomings, the Bretton Woods accords contributed immeasurably to the restoration of world economic confidence, without which global recovery might never have taken place. For a decade or so, the gold/dollar system worked reasonably well. Like Britain before it, the United States became the world's banker. New York became the clearinghouse for settling international transactions. Wall Street provided long-term capital to the rest of the world to propel economic recovery. With recovery underway, the United States maintained open markets, insuring the growth of world trade and production. Prices were stable and there was a welcome absence of financial panics. Consumption levels in the industrialized countries rose to unprecedented heights. Even poor Third World countries, such as Mexico and Brazil, began the transition from backwardness to the status of industrial powers. By the late 1950s, it seemed, the international economic order established at Bretton Woods had come to rest at what economists like to call equilibrium.

Subsequent events showed that the economists had it all wrong. In the late 1950s, the global system was not resting at a point of equilibrium. In retrospect, the brief stability provided by the Bretton Woods arrangements proved to be temporary. It turned out to be a short transition period from one state of disequilibrium to another. Robert Triffin saw it coming as early as 1959. He predicted that the Bretton Woods monetary system was not sustainable and called for urgent negotiations to replace it. But as the Vietnam War intensified, the United States became more wedded to the dollar system than ever. Robert Roosa and Charles Coombs kept the system going for a few more years, but it finally collapsed. In 1971, under prodding from the speculators, Nixon closed the gold window. Two years later, the speculators wrecked the old fixed rate relationships. In the face of mounting exchange rate instability, governments largely opted out of the international monetary arena in hopes that returning decision making to the market would lead to the best of all possible worlds. Instead, things have gone from bad to worse.

The breakdown of international order contributed mightily to making the 1970s the decade of global stagflation. The disease was particularly serious in the United States. A quick glance at the so-called "misery index," the sum of the annual rates of unemployment and inflation, shows that since the mid-1960s, the performance of the biggest and richest economy in history has grown steadily worse.

Change a few numbers around and the U.S. misery index describes the fate of the other industrialized countries as well. Of the major economies, only Japan has fared reasonably well. Still, Japan's economic performance is much less impressive than it was during the 1960s and 1970s. In the Third World, Saudi Arabia and Kuwait aside, the problems of stagflation are infinitely worse. For the Soviet bloc, economic performance has been dismal, leaving eastern Europe deeply in hock to Western banks. In an interdependent world economy, the ills of one country are quickly transmitted to others. As the growth of production slows down, world trade suffers. Falling export earnings bring defaults and bankruptcies from Poland to Mexico. Festering protectionism has been spawned by

Table 12

	(1) Average Annual Consumer Price Rise	(2) Average Annual Unemployment Rate	(1 + 2) Misery Index
Harry S. Truman (1948–1952)	3.9	4.5	8.4
Dwight D. Eisenhower (1953–1960)	1.4	4.9	6.3
John F. Kennedy (1961–1963)	1.1	6.0	7.1
Lyndon B. Johnson (1964–1968)	2.6	4.1	6.7
Richard M. Nixon (1969–1974)	6.0	5.0	11.0
Gerald Ford (1975–1976)	7.5	8.1	15.6
Jimmy Carter (1977–1980)	9.8	6.5	16.3
Ronald Reagan (1981–)	8.7	8.5	17.2

SOURCE: *Economic Report of the President 1982.*

massive unemployment and industrial disorder in the industrialized countries. The price of Japan's extraordinary success in some industries, for instance, has been a massive upsurge in anti-Japanese protectionism.

The picture, then, is one of a global economy coming apart at the seams.

The worsening global economic performance has been accompanied by an unprecedented boom in global banking. The foundations of the global money market were laid in the 1960s, but the edifice grew to staggering proportions during the decade of stagflation. One of the great growth industries of the 1970s was Eurobanking. In a little over a decade, international banking was transformed from a small appendage of the Wall Street bond market to history's first global money market.

A century ago, Walter Bagehot, the father of modern central banking, called the City of London "by far the greatest combination of economical power and economical delicacy that the world has ever seen." Bagehot would faint if he could see the City today. The London-based global money market has become a 24-hour-a-day financial supermarket where anyone who is creditworthy can swap dollars for marks, yen or Kuwaiti dinars with a short phone call. Lunch or dinner with a banker of any significance can get you overnight money denominated in scores of currencies, five to ten-year Eurodollar loans or long-term funds, through an infinite variety of securities. If you so desire, you can even swap all your paper for gold or silver. In London, Chicago and New York, you can bet on the future course of interest rates on certificates of deposits, Treasury securities and Eurodollars in the burgeoning financial futures markets. As Citibank's Walter Wriston, banking's preeminent globalist, puts it, "mankind now has a completely integrated, international financial and informational marketplace capable of moving money and ideas to anyplace on this earth in minutes."

Throughout the 1970s, international banking expanded at a rate of more than 25 percent per year, much faster than world production and world trade. Currency trading, commodity speculation, financial futures and bank lending have swelled to unprecedented proportions over the past decade. The outstanding size of the Euromarket is now nearly $2 trillion, while trillions more in foreign currencies change hands every year. The oil-importing Third World countries have debts estimated at more than $600 billion. Mexico and Brazil owe $160 billion together. Novel financial instruments, such as money market funds, have grown from virtually nothing to hundreds of billions in a few short years. Despite the recent declines, interest rates are bringing investors record returns on short-term paper. These days, when corporate executives and their investment bankers have lunch or dinner, generally the topic is not financing industrial expansion but mergers and acquisitions. The individuals and companies making money today are not doing it by building ships, steel plants and houses. They are making it by trading paper.

The world economy has contracted a quintessentially British disease. In Britain the real economy is dying, but the City is flourishing as never before. The City's ancient pubs and private restaurants are jammed with hearty spirits and rowdy laughter. But beyond the square-mile City, depression and bitterness dominate the landscape. Increasingly, the same is true of the world at large.

In one important sense, it is no accident that banking and finance flourish in an atmosphere of economic decline. The business of banks is making loans. For individuals, corporations and governments weaned on the postwar ideology of never-ending growth, declining incomes generally lead to a greater reliance on credit to maintain expenditures. In the United States alone, the growth of the credit business has been staggering. The total borrowing of business consumers and governments has exploded from $700 billion in 1960 to $1.6 trillion in 1970 to over $4.5 trillion in 1982. Though conservative ideologues point to the growth of government debt, in recent years businesses have piled up debt at the fastest rate. Henry Kaufman of Salomon Brothers estimates that from the start of 1976 to the end of 1981 the debt of nonfinancial corporations doubled from $600 billion to $1.2 trillion.

The borrowing binge is fueled by stagflation. Confronted with steadily rising prices, businesses and consumers buy now on credit rather than pay higher prices tomorrow. When sagging markets depress corporate earnings, companies borrow to finance current operations and takeovers of profitable concerns. Governments, pressed to increase jobs and economic growth, borrow to finance programs they hope will stimulate their economies. In order to keep lending, the banks borrow from each other. A more important reason for the explosion of global banking is the nature of banking in the postwar period. Competition has led to the debasement of credit standards and increasingly imprudential levels of borrowing and lending. A bank is afraid to deny a loan to a valued customer for fear that a disgruntled corporation will take its business elsewhere. In global banking, conservatism and great discretion in lending are generally equated with slow growth and obscurity. (Rare is a bank like S. G. Warburg that is content to remain small and still commands great respect in the market.)

Bankers' aggressive impulses and the deterioration of the world economy feed upon each other. Together they lead inexorably to overextension of the banking system. Take the example of Chicago's Continental Illinois, the sixth largest bank in the United States. In the late 1970s, while Continental's neighbor, First Chicago, was floundering in internal dissent and bad loans, Continental Illinois was aggressively expanding its loans to corporate America. By 1982, Continental had become the number one lender to American industry and surpassed First Chicago as the industrial belt's leading bank. As the *Wall Street Journal* explained:

> Continental has drawn special attention because of its eager lending strategy of the last half-decade. The bank sought to spur loan growth by courting companies in profitable but high risk markets—for example, in real estate, energy, and the middle range of businesses with between $25 million and $100 million in annual sales. Continental consequently became the fastest growing of the nation's big banks, and its profits soared.

Ironically, just as Continental's chairman, Roger Anderson, was overcoming obscurity among top U.S. bankers, his aggressive strategy turned sour. The prolonged world slump brought major business failures and with them came massive problem loans for the sixth largest bank in the United States. A list of the bank's problem borrowers soon turned up on the front page of the *Wall Street Journal.* They included Braniff, Wickes Cos., and AM Interna-

Table 13

	(*in millions*)
International Harvester	$200
Alfa of Mexico	$100
American Invsco Corp.	
and Gouletas family interests	$100
McLean Gardens, Ltd.	$ 40
Wickes Cos.	$ 41
Braniff International Corp.	$ 25
AM International Inc.	$ 12

tional, which have all gone bankrupt. A major Continental borrower, International Harvester, is on the ropes, surviving on the largesse of its creditors. The Mexican conglomerate Grupo Industrial Alfa has suspended payments on its debts of $2 billion to foreign banks. American Invsco, the family firm of Evangeline Gouletas, the socialite married to former New York Governor Hugh Carey, fell on hard times in a housing market clobbered by tight money and high interest rates. The same fate met McLean Gardens, a Washington, D.C., condo-conversion project.

Continental's problems were bad enough even before the bank was rocked last summer by the failure of the Penn Square Bank of Oklahoma. The small bank was an aggressive lender to oil and gas companies. Unable to swallow all the loans it could market, Penn Square began "selling" many of its energy loans to major banks. Penn Square sold over $1 billion in energy loans to Continental and another $200 million to Chase Manhattan. (Penn Square's chief energy man, 34-year-old Bill Patterson, was apparently quite a loan salesman. At an Oklahoma City watering hole, according to *Fortune*, Patterson used to entertain visiting bankers by drinking beer out of his boot.) However, when oil and gas profits crumbled under the pressure of a weak economy, Penn Square went belly-up. Penn Square's collapse plus Continental's other problems left the bank with a $61-million second-quarter loss, the largest by a U.S. bank in years. Chase slipped by with only a $16 million second-quarter loss, due mainly to Penn Square and the earlier failure of Drysdale Securities, a Chase client.

Careerism and competition to please top management encourage the tendency to overlend. Many bankers who came out of business school as conservatives quickly abandoned such pristine notions in order to get somewhere in the business. Careerism comes first, prudence and the underlying security of loans later. Certainly these attitudes played a large role in Chase's Penn Square losses. In the aftermath of Chase's big crisis in the mid-1970s, management turned on the pressure to improve profitability and restore Chase's reputation. This led, among other things, to intense competition between two of Chase's domestic banking departments, the corporate banking department and the institutional department. According to a detailed account in the *New York Times*, Chase's institutional people were envious of the corporate department's monopoly over the bank's large domestic loans, while the institutional department remained largely a processing center for interbank relationships. The institutional department, on the lookout for ways to generate more profits, began to buy chunks of Penn Square's loans and finance Drysdale Securities. When the little Oklahoma bank collapsed, Chase was left holding around $200 million in bad loans. The driving force behind Chase's institutional department, William R. Hinchman, was sacked along with eight of his colleagues. To be sure, large loan losses inevitably raise important questions about the competence of the officers who approve them, but top management's attitude didn't help. As one Chase officer told the *New York Times*, "there was pressure from the top to produce profits and growth." To do so, he said, "you would have to stretch."

II

The Continental and Chase examples show that aggressive lending in the midst of economic decline is a recipe for disaster. For a time, banks can thrive in a declining economy, but it is foolhardy to think this can go on forever. Sooner or later, as mounting loan losses indicate, the day of reckoning must come for the banks themselves.

The severe global slump, painfully high interest rates and unprecedented volatility in financial markets are beginning to create real problems for the banks. That many of the banks' international borrowers are in difficult straits is well known. Third World and eastern European debt has risen rapidly relative to their GNP, exports and available cash. Many of these borrowers can't even pay the interest on foreign debts let alone the principal. Bankers generally counter that since banks are prohibited from lending more than the value of 10 percent of their capital to one borrower,* their international portfolios are diversified enough to prevent any default from endangering the health of a well-managed bank. In reality, the banks' portfolios are less diversified than they would have you believe. Many large banks have much more than 10 percent of their capital in each of dozens of countries. The banks have sold federal regulators on the idea that their exposure to different borrowers in countries like Mexico should not be aggregated because independent entities will be able to service their debts regardless of what happens to other borrowers. Yet this claim is belied by the experience of Poland, Mexico, Costa Rica and other countries. This is what the concept of "country risk" is all about. When countries experience severe foreign exchange shortages, it may be virtually impossible for any company to obtain foreign currency. In this instance even a solvent borrower might be forced to suspend debt payments. The banks' total global exposure makes them extremely vulnerable to such problems.

What is happening to the banks' major corporate clients is equally startling. American industry is in financial trouble. Twenty years ago, according to Salomon Brothers' Henry Kaufman, corporations had more than one dollar of cash for each dollar of short-term debt. Today they have 40 cents. Short-term debt has soared relative to long-term debt, which means that companies have a lot less time to work off the debt. Interest payments are consuming a record 16 percent of corporate profits. The only solution to the problem is a vigorous economic recovery that will boost profits significantly. Yet such a recovery is unlikely with interest rates remaining at present levels. In the meantime, as a result of mounting debt problems, many firms once considered top credit risks are so no longer.

Sooner or later, their bankers wind up sharing the losses. Even before the Chase and Continental balance sheet carnage, the major

---

* Recently, the Office of the Comptroller of the Currency raised this limit to 15 percent and to 25 percent for secured loans.

banks' loan losses were climbing back toward their highs of 1975–76. For ten major U.S. banks, according to Morgan Guaranty, bad loans, called nonperforming assets in the jargon, peaked at 5.2 percent of total loans in 1976. After dropping to 1.5 percent in 1980, they rose to 1.8 percent in 1981 and promise to be much higher in 1982. Morgan cites the extraordinarily bad loan ratios of 1975–76 as evidence that current fears about the stability of the financial system are exaggerated. At present, it is true, the banks' bad loans as a percentage of total loans are still below the levels of 1975–76. However, the source of the banks' current troubles is much more frightening. As Morgan acknowledges, the bank debacles resulting from the severe 1974–75 recession were concentrated in real estate. Today, one major source of the banks' problem loans is the heart of corporate America. The losses are coming from major companies, such as International Harvester, energy firms, the airlines and financial firms. (The real estate losses have been passed on to the battered savings and loan institutions, which are going under at an alarming rate.)

Moreover, the problem of bad loans is probably more extensive than is generally realized. This is because banks are less than candid about reporting them to federal regulators and the regulators have yet to force the issue. Banks have their own internal standards for treatment of problem loans, but management retains a great deal of discretion about what goes into that category on the balance sheet. Moreover, management has an interest in concealing the true extent of potential problem loans, particularly when they are large. When banks place loans in "nonaccrual" or "nonperforming" status, prudence would suggest that the banks set aside loan-loss reserves to cover potential losses of income. Since loan-loss reserves damage profits and therefore the bank's image, management has a direct stake in minimizing potential problems.

Theoretically, bank examinations carried out by the Comptroller of the Currency should compel the banks to be up-front about potential losses. However, the bank examination process is inherently flawed. The people who examine the banks' balance sheets for the comptroller are accountants, not bankers. Even if they receive the relevant information, they are in a poor position to evaluate the problem loans. Moreover, there is a good deal of evidence that bank

examiners don't receive adequate information from the banks.
(When Penn Square realized that some of its loans were going sour,
it concealed this by making interest payments on its clients' behalf.)
The bigger a bank is, the harder it may be to get information out of
it. Most senior bankers can stare down a bank examiner unless the
examiner appeals to his superiors to force a recalcitrant bank to cooperate. Unless the comptroller forces the issue with the bank's
management, it is likely that the bank will be able to cover up potential problems just as, for instance, they cover up foreign exchange dealings. It all depends on how tough the comptroller is. As
one corporate executive observes, "John Heimann could stare down
a banker, this new guy (Reagan appointee C. T. Conover) you don't
know." Thus it is likely that the banks are probably carrying a lot
more potentially bad loans on their books than they admit. Citing
the example of banks' loans to Poland, one securities analyst told
the *Wall Street Journal* that "not one dime is classified as bad debt."
He adds that "federal bank examiners are letting the banks get
away with it."

The banks themselves are highly leveraged. They have large financial exposure relative to their ability to weather financial difficulties. For each outstanding dollar of loans, America's biggest
banks have between three and five cents of capital and reserves.
Such low capital/asset ratios, as they are known, are unprecedented
in the history of American banking. During the greatest period of
bank failures in history, the 1920s and 1930s, the capital/asset ratios
of American commercial banks averaged 10 percent or more, or two
to three times as great as they are now. At present, Citibank, Chase
Manhattan, Bank of America, First Chicago and Continental Illinois each have less than four cents of capital for each dollar of
loans. Of the major banks, Morgan is the "well-capitalized" one
with a little more than four cents. The reason why banks have such
thin safety margins is not hard to figure out. The more conservative
a bank is, the harder it is to grow. Significantly, a list compiled by
The Banker of the 100 best-capitalized banks in the world does not
include one of the major New York, Chicago or California banks.
Nor are there many top non-American banks on the list. Among
major global banks, the undercapitalization disease is almost universal.

The precariousness of the banking system not only shows up in thin capital structures. A major point of vulnerability is the banks' heavy reliance on *borrowed* funds. Chase and Citicorp don't rely on checking account deposits to finance their loans to Poland and General Motors. Banks fund their loans primarily by borrowing from each other. In 1981, these borrowings funded more than half of the assets of major American commercial banks, up from 45 percent five years ago. For banks' international operations, the percentages of bought money in total liabilities are much higher. In the Euromarket, about two-thirds of all loans are interbank loans. While bankers see the interbank market as a perpetual source of funds, the extent to which the banks are large lenders to one another increases the potential exposure of each to the other's problems. In normal times, the interbank market is a reliable source of funds. The banks leverage themselves to the hilt and hope that the interbank market never closes down. If it ever does, they will be in big trouble.

III

Every book that deals with banking and finance must inevitably confront the issue of financial crises. This includes not only isolated crises resulting from speculation, but the prospects of a real crash, leading to a paralysis of the financial system. History is littered with financial panics and crashes. Can it happen again?

No predictions will be made here about the likelihood of a financial collapse. This is not a novel. No one can or should try to predict a banking crisis. As Charles Kindleberger writes, "Our profession of economics does not know the dynamics of the system well enough to do so." We just don't know whether or not the system is going to collapse. Let me hasten to add that this is not an endorsement of bankers' condescending attitudes toward those who take the threat of a crisis seriously. It is as irresponsible for bankers to issue cavalier assurances that a crisis is impossible as it is to imply that it is inevitable. To wit, the views of leading commercial bankers, such as Citibank's Walter Wriston, can safely be dismissed. As Warburg's Eric Roll puts it, a commercial banker must have "a moderately optimistic view of the world . . . because otherwise he would go out of business." With twice as much sunk in Mexico and

Brazil as his capital and reserves, Wriston is in so deep that if he questioned the stability of the system, he might precipitate the crisis he is hoping to avoid.

Leaving predictions to the novelists, it is still worth noting that a growing number of mainstream observers are reaching the conclusion that something is seriously wrong with the banking system. It is significant, for instance, that Charles Kindleberger takes a moderately pessimistic view of the situation. Long considered a mainstream Keynesian, Kindleberger finds the standard Keynesian view of monetary problems as deficient and misleading as the monetarist view. Kindleberger is concerned about a financial crisis that could lead to a global depression. Like Wharton's Guttentag and Herring, Kindleberger concludes that international banking is more susceptible to "panics, manias and crashes" than domestic banking. He views foreign exchange speculation as particularly dangerous and destabilizing. Kindleberger is not an alarmist, but he is concerned enough about the prospects for trouble to advocate a strong international "lender of last resort" with the authority to act swiftly to stop a banking crisis in its tracks.

Another Keynesian, Professor Hyman Minsky, goes further. He asserts that the basic structure of the financial system is inherently fragile. The key to Minsky's explanation is the postwar economy's growing dependence on credit and debt outlined above. To prevent a classic "debt deflation crisis," businesses (and by implication, foreign countries) must have adequate cash flow to service debts as they fall due. Even if they do not, as long as the banks don't cut them off, they can keep borrowing to maintain debt payments. The banks' willingness to lend is virtually unlimited during periods of economic expansion. When recession comes, the rules of the game change. As falling sales depress profits, there comes a point where even the most reckless bankers conclude that more lending to troubled concerns is foolhardy. Faced with this situation, the banks are tempted to cut off delinquent debtors. Yet if the banks stop lending, the financial position of the debtors worsens, threatening existing debts with default.

Each time a crunch comes, the whole debt structure threatens to collapse.

This is where the government comes into the picture. Like Kindleberger, Herring and Guttentag, Minsky has no illusions that "the market" provides an automatic stabilizer for the banking system. The stabilizer is and must be government. Government has a dual role. Since the 1930s, government spending has propped up the real economy while central bank rescue operations have stabilized the financial system. Traditionally, when recession hits, deficit spending and Federal Reserve monetary policy have "leaned against the wind" in order to prevent the kind of dramatic fall in prices and production that triggered the Great Depression. Basically what is involved is shooting money into the economy to keep the chain of payments going. In times of stress, the banks need clear indications from the Federal Reserve that it will try to prevent isolated financial failures from destroying the financial system.*

Minsky acknowledges that in recent times the government and Federal Reserve did the job. Will they be able to do so in the future? In 1979 Minsky predicted they would not, for reasons that have been a principal theme of this book.

> Given the fragility of our financial system we will soon experience another brink reminiscent of those of 1966, 1969–70 and 1974–75. This time, however, big government will not be as quick or as able (*because of international financial relations*) to throw money at the problem, as in 1974–75. In addition, the Federal Reserve will be more reluctant to intervene by increasing the monetary base and extending broad guarantees than it was in 1974–75. The subsequent recession will be both longer and deeper. [emphasis added]

The key phrase is "because of international financial relations." The Federal Reserve was forced out of its traditional stance of "leaning against the wind" because the international monetary system was about to collapse. Since the Fed's change of course in the fall of 1979, there has been virtually no economic growth in the United States or in Europe. The global integration of national fi-

---

* One of the treasured anecdotes of central banking reportedly took place in the men's room at the Harvard Club of New York. A commercial banker found himself at an adjoining stall with Arthur Burns and asked the Fed chairman if he would defend the banking system in a crisis. While Burns' response of "maybe" sent the banker reeling, he always said the right thing in more traditional settings.

nancial markets has made it impossible even for powerhouses like West Germany to lower interest rates enough to stimulate their economies. (Mitterrand's France, the only major country that has tried to change course, has faced a massive run on the franc that forced two major devaluations in less than a year. Not surprisingly, the policy objectives of M. Mitterrand have since been changed.*) It was not until the emergence of a major Third World debt crisis in the summer of 1982 that the Fed made any concerted effort to ease monetary policy. When it did, interest rates dropped, the dollar fell and a severe financial crisis was averted. This change in monetary policy enabled the Federal Reserve to discharge one of its responsibilities, preventing a collapse of the banking system. However, the relaxing of monetary policy has been insufficient to stimulate an economic recovery. Nor is it likely to be able to do so. A prolonged campaign to bring down interest rates would simply lead to a flight from the dollar and eventually a new dollar crisis.

While most bankers supported the move toward higher interest rates, the spiral of global deflation that has resulted has brought pressures in the financial system to the boiling point. Corporations, Third World countries and some banks have been having severe financial difficulties. Many have been surviving mainly by "distress borrowing." Nothing displeases a troubled company or country more than borrowing money at record interest rates but when the alternative is bankruptcy they don't have a choice. Meanwhile, the

---

* The run on the franc was motivated by both economic and political factors. Initially, Mitterrand was trying to speed up economic growth while the rest of Europe seemed content to await the future course of U.S. interest rates. This divergence of policies led to predictions of higher inflation, thereby exerting pressure on the franc. However, bankers were also appalled by the rash of bank nationalizations and the harsh treatment accorded Chairman Pierre Moussa of Paribas. In an editorial entitled "Revenge and the French Franc," *Euromoney* castigated Mitterrand and warned that his actions "may badly damage the franc." The message was: mistreat international bankers and they will mistreat the franc. After the two realignments of the European Monetary System forced by speculation against the franc, Mitterrand turned decidedly conservative in an attempt to save the franc. In the fall of 1982, when new pressures on the franc emerged, France arranged a massive $4 billion syndicated loan to defend the franc in the markets.

banks have to keep on lending to the Mexicos and Polands. The alternative is to call in their loans, declare the borrowers bankrupt and swallow huge loan losses. Since more red ink is the last thing they want on their books, the banks keep lending while hoping that somehow things will get better.

The banks and the Federal Reserve are playing a very dangerous game. An ever larger accumulation of paper claims is being piled on top of an economic base that is not growing. The financial system looks like an inverted pyramid that is tottering in the wind. This game can go on for a time, maybe a long time, but not forever. Ultimately all this paper represents claims on real goods and services. Production must go up or the paper is no good. Yet as long as real interest rates remain high the global slump will persist and bad debts will pile up. In a speech entitled "Flying at Minimum Speed," First Boston's Albert Wojnilower goes to the heart of the problem:

> ... the economic airliner on which we are all traveling together has for four years been flying at no more than the minimum speed needed to stay aloft. If one flies at minimum speed indefinitely, only through great luck can disaster be avoided.*

IV

If the financial system ever snaps, all that stands in the way of major financial failures is the Federal Reserve, the Comptroller of the currency and assorted lesser agencies. In the international arena, the backstop consists of the Federal Reserve, the Bundesbank, the Bank of England and a few of the other major central banks. If a crunch comes, will the regulators be able to save the banking system? One thing is clear: if they don't, there is nobody else.

Since the mid-1960s, the track record for central bank rescue operations has been reasonably good. Bank regulators maintain that

---

* Wojnilower and Salomon's Kaufman, known respectively on Wall Street as Dr. Death and Dr. Doom, were widely—and unjustly in my view—criticized for their August 1982 reversals of earlier pessimistic forecasts that interest rates would rise throughout 1982. In retrospect, their main error was in assuming that the economy would be stronger than it turned out to be.

the key to such operations is keeping the chain of payments going by pumping money into the system and liquidating or merging insolvent institutions in orderly fashion. The ability of salvage operations to postpone disaster should not be underestimated. If central bankers can get to the troubled institutions quickly enough, firm action can calm the markets. "Even Citibank could disappear," says John Heimann, if it was done in a way that prevented panic from spreading throughout the markets.

Still, there is no guarantee that ad hoc rescue operations will always be successful. There is a widely held notion that a handful of bankers and central bankers can manipulate the financial system at will. This is a myth. Typically in a crisis, the regulatory authorities get involved rather late in the game. Often they do not have enough information to evaluate the scope of the problem, let alone do something about it. Nor are central bankers infallible. If they make mistakes of a certain magnitude, such mistakes can lead to a global financial catastrophe. It is to John Heimann's credit that while he was juggling the fate of First Pennsylvania, he also managed to examine First Chicago's exposure to the Hunt family. But even competent bank regulators are only human. What would Volcker do if five or ten major financial institutions tottered at the same time?

Cross-border rescue operations are infinitely more complex and therefore more difficult. In the international arena, the key to avoiding a major crisis is to keep the interbank market functioning. After the Herstatt-Franklin debacles, Gordon Richardson, governor of the Bank of England, stated unequivocally that henceforth the major central banks would "support the markets in any way which may prove necessary." With government support, the banks can band together and shore up the interbank market. But although bankers argue that funds are always available to reputable banks at a price, on closer inspection, the interbank market is also a device that can rapidly transmit the troubles of one bank to others. As Wharton's Professors Guttentag and Herring argue, the international interbank market is a pretty shaky arrangement because the "potential for contagion" is great.

At least two-thirds of all Euro-currency deposits are inter-bank deposits, but detailed information on who owes what to whom is not available to the market. This means that a run on an international bank, even if it originates in developments unique to that bank, can lead to a run on other international banks which are suspected of holding claims against the first bank.

In the aftermath of the Franklin and Herstatt failures, contagion did spread, virtually closing down the interbank and foreign exchange markets to all but the top banks. What could prevent a similar crisis of confidence or contagion from developing today?*

The proliferation of Euromarket centers around the world has led some bankers to wonder if the system is adequately policed. A leading Eurobanker, Geoffrey Bell, worries that an interbank crisis in some obscure Euromarket outpost might overwhelm the ability of governments to cope with it.

Do we have sufficient safety nets in the interbank market if a crisis arises in, say, Bahrain? After Drysdale and Penn Square, you don't know the chain. I find a sense that governments and central banks have lost control. They realize now that the Euromarkets are so big that they are beyond their control; they're at the mercy of events.

The main reason why governments and central banks have "lost control" over events is that the rapid international expansion of the world's biggest banks has sapped the effectiveness of national regulations. For bankers, one of the prime attractions of going global is that it allows them to slip between the cracks of national regulations. Controlling the Euromarket, as the investment banker Richard Weinert says, is "like trying to hold on to a wet bar of soap." National regulations are inadequate and global regulation is virtually nonexistent. As the *Economist* has written: "One of the regulators' biggest problems is that the international banking market is a global market but that there is no global regulator. There is no certainty that all banks' operations around the world are being brought into the watchers' field of vision."

* On the technical side, one improvement has been the evolution of what is known as "same day settlement" through the New York Clearing House for International payments. In the past, it took two days or more to sort out international interbank transactions. Same day settlement of international transactions speeds up the process of identifying banks that can't make payments, but it does nothing to alleviate the problems that might cause a bank to fail.

The closest thing to an overseer of the global financial system is the Bank for International Settlements in Basel. The BIS, known as the central bank of central bankers, was created in 1930 to consolidate and facilitate German reparations payments. Most of the shares of the BIS are held by European central banks and the current president is Fritz Leutweiler, former head of the Swiss National Bank. The Federal Reserve is not a shareholder in the BIS, but participates in the monthly meetings of central bankers convened by the BIS.* The BIS collects data on international bank lending, which is analyzed and published by its acclaimed research staff. It handles the accounts of central banks around the world (including the Russians), so it knows quickly who is going broke. Its location in Switzerland places it in one of the world's most important financial centers. The BIS is active in the markets, which means it is privy to market gossip that can pinpoint potential problems. The central bankers of the ten major industrial countries meet at the BIS on the second Tuesday of every month to discuss the problem of the month in international banking. (Henry Wallich attends on behalf of the Fed.) The meetings are highly valued because the BIS is virtually the only forum where the major central bankers can get to know each other and discuss problems in the financial system without provoking a panic. (Owing to the so-called Basel rule, reports Richard Janssen of the *Wall Street Journal*, there are no press briefings during or after the meetings. Central bankers are expected to avoid all contact with journalists while in Basel.)

The BIS has evolved into a de facto international lender of last resort for the banking system because there is no one else. The BIS has survived and grows more powerful as the financial crisis deepens. Its clout results primarily from its prestige among central bankers. In the aftermath of the Franklin and Herstatt failures, the BIS took the lead in devising measures to deal with future Euromarket

---

* During the Bretton Woods negotiations, Harry White wanted to abolish the BIS and transfer its functions to the IMF. Treasury officials believed that the BIS was close to the Nazi government, though the BIS maintained that it channeled Jewish money out of Germany and concealed it from the German authorities. White decided to try to kill the BIS when it refused to turn over some confidential information Treasury wanted. The Europeans resisted, however, and once Fred Vinson replaced Henry Morgenthau at Treasury, he dropped the issue.

crises. Specifically the central bankers of the major industrialized countries authorized the BIS to create a Standing Committee on Banking Regulations and Supervisory Practices, which functions like a subcommittee of the panel of central bankers. The committee, sometimes known as the Cooke Committee, is chaired by the Bank of England's Peter Cooke. In August 1975, the Cooke Committee issued a set of principles on international bank supervision known as the Concordat. According to the principles of the Concordat, responsibility for supervising banks that operate across national borders is to be shared by the authorities in the bank's home country and those of the countries in which it operates. Basically, the issue of the parent bank's solvency, the quality of its assets, is delegated to the home central bank while the liquidity needs of foreign branches are the responsibility of the host country. The Concordat was designed to bolster confidence in the international financial system by increasing cooperation among national monetary authorities and bank supervisors. The central bankers tried to achieve a balance between convincing the banks that government cooperation could prevent bank failures and taking all the risks out of international banking and thereby encouraging recklessness. Undoubtedly, the Concordat was a step forward. "As long as one keeps an eye on it," says Henry Wallich, "the kettle is less likely to boil over." Prior to the 1975 Concordat, literally no one knew what would happen in the event of the Euromarket crisis.

Still, important problems remain. The Concordat is not and was not designed to serve as a blueprint for action in the event of a financial crisis. Central banks are not bound to any specific course of action because they are signatories to the Concordat. One can imagine a whole host of circumstances in which a central bank might be unwilling or unable to provide liquidity to a foreign bank operating within its borders. Pumping large amounts of money into the banking system to salvage a large bank might offend an inflation-fighting central banker. A rescue operation might be politically unpopular if a bank failed because it was involved in nefarious or illegal activities. A central bank willing to intervene might not have access to the foreign currency needed to do the job. Sometimes it may be hard to distinguish between an unnecessary bail-out and a potential crisis situation.

Recently, the limitations of the Basel Concordat were revealed during the crisis of the Italian bank Banco Ambrosiano. When it was discovered that Banco Ambrosiano had a billion dollars in unidentified loans to Panamian borrowers from a Luxembourg subsidiary, a panic that endangered not only the subsidiary but the Italian parent ensued. (The problem was complicated because the bank had close ties to the Vatican, and its chairman, Roberto Calvi, had been found hanging from Blackfriars Bridge in London.) Although the Bank of Italy assembled a steering committee of banks to save the parent, it refused to assume responsibility for the loans made by Ambrosiano's Luxembourg subsidiary, arguing that this was beyond the scope of its responsibilities. Yet the authorities in Luxembourg also refused to stand behind the loans. They argued that the subsidiary was not really a bank and therefore not entitled to be bailed out.

Bankers were angered and accused the Bank of Italy of "wrecking the fabric of the Euromarket" by refusing to act as a lender of last resort. Although 200 banks stood to lose only about $400 million on Ambrosiano, the lack of cooperation between international authorities creates a dangerous margin of uncertainty about what would happen if a big bank tottered. In part, some degree of uncertainty is desirable. Otherwise, the banks would have no reason to exercise prudence in their borrowing and lending. Yet, lack of cooperation among central banks could also paralyze effective action in a major crisis when timeliness would be the key to success.

Another unanswered question is which monetary authorities would be responsible for bailing out banks from nontraditional banking centers. Banks from the Middle East, Latin America and Asia have flocked to the international markets in recent years. Banks from India, Israel, Brazil, Mexico, Venezuela and Argentina operate in the international arena. Yet they have no credible lender of last resort that could intervene in the event of a crisis. One banker just laughed at the suggestion that their national monetary authorities could do the job.

The persistence of these uncertainties casts serious doubts on the assumption that adequate machinery is in place to cope with a major international banking crisis. Still, one should not underestimate the ability of the world's most powerful bankers to get out of a jam. Get Walter Wriston, Wilfried Guth, Fritz Leutweiler, Paul Volcker and Peter Cooke in one room and they can call in a lot of favors from around the world. It is clear that in a crunch, if the leading bankers and central bankers do not hang together, they will surely hang separately. This realization is undoubtedly what led Deutschebank's Wilfried Guth to propose that the banks create their own private international "safety net" to cope with potential bank failures. The head of Germany's largest bank knows that if a crisis occurs, there will be no time to discuss the appropriate course of action.

V

A dramatic transformation of global banking has occurred over the past decade. Changes over the next ten years may be more far-reaching. The changes bankers want to see involve abolishing most of the major regulatory constraints on U.S. banks. Many bankers say that if this happens, it may revolutionize America's financial institutions. Barring a major financial panic or a resurgence of protectionism, banking in the 1980s will be dominated by a few financial conglomerates that offer a full range of financial services on a global scale. Some bankers believe that if enough regulations are abolished the Eurobanking base will move from London to New York.

In a sense, globalization made changes in many U.S. banking laws inevitable. The globalization process has weakened the effectiveness of national regulations. What banks cannot do at home, they do abroad. Domestic banking laws prohibit commercial banks from engaging in investment banking activities in the United States, so banks such as Manufacturers Hanover moved to London and established new investment banks. For years, the Federal Reserve maintained interest rate ceilings to hold down the cost of money. The banks promptly moved deposit taking abroad where the controls did not apply. When the Federal Reserve imposed direct curbs on bank lending to reduce credit expansion, the banks booked their corporate loans in London and Nassau. The corporations brought the funds home with no questions asked.

The growth of the Euromarket has made national controls over the banks so ineffective that bankers argue that controls should be eliminated altogether. Addressing themselves to the probusiness, antigovernment sentiment that dominates official thinking in the Reagan administration, the banks are aggressively marketing a laundry list of changes in the banking laws that would transform the nature of banking in the United States. In essence, the banks are pushing federal regulators to allow them to become "universal banks" in the German and Swiss tradition. Basically, this would involve abolishing the distinction between investment banks and commercial banks and the thrifts, forcing all to compete in one integrated financial market. In this campaign, the banks have discovered allies in bank regulators who fear that they are overextended internationally. Former Comptroller John Heimann, among others, argues that the escape route from the banks' global difficulties lies in changing government regulations so they can do more domestic business. To encourage banks to trim their global activities, in other words, they should be offered incentives to redeploy at home.

The banks have set their sights on three legal changes in particular. With the expansion of international branches virtually completed, the banks want to strike down the McFadden Act of 1927, which prohibits interstate branch banking. Many banks already do business in dozens of states, but they have thus far been prevented from opening full-scale branches that would allow Citibank, for instance, to compete on an equal footing with Bank of America in the huge California consumer banking market.* (Meanwhile, Bank of America, which is fighting to keep Walter Wriston out of California, has erected a 28-story tower on Madison Avenue to serve as the base for its New York operations.) Bankers argue that technological advances alone have made McFadden obsolete. In this sense, they say, banking legislation would merely catch up with technology. As Walter Wriston writes:

> Communications satellites simply go around these barriers, just as the blitzkrieg went around the Maginot Line. A toll free telephone call can

---

* Citibank won a major victory in September 1982 when the Fed approved its acquisition of the Fidelity Savings & Loan of San Francisco. This appears to pave the way for branching across state lines plus further blurring of the distinction between commercial banks and the S&Ls.

transfer 5¼% savings into a 17% money fund without regard to geography, or line up a mortgage where the rate is best. It's done every day.

Other major targets of deregulation are the legal constraints imposed by the Glass-Steagall Act, which separates commercial banking from investment banking. Under Glass-Steagall, enacted in 1933 to curb the abuses spawned by the banks' activities as both underwriters of securities and commercial lending institutions, investment banking and commercial banking were divorced from one another. Thus the old House of Morgan became two independent companies, J.P. Morgan & Co. (The Morgan Bank) and Morgan Stanley. The huge commercial banks want a crack at the lucrative underwriting and mergers and acquisitions advisory fees that flow to investment banks such as First Boston, Lehman Brothers Kuhn Loeb, Morgan Stanley and Goldman Sachs. The commercial banks argue that since they already have proven expertise in investment banking in London, it is silly to prohibit them from employing it at home.

The final goal of the current lobbying effort is to end government controls on interest rates. Pressure to end the controls comes mainly from the big commercial banks, which feel squeezed by the rapid growth of money market mutual funds in recent years. Wriston and others argue that competition from existing financial conglomerates, such as Merrill Lynch, Shearson/American Express and Sears/Dean Witter/Coldwell Barker threatens the survival of commercial banks. There is some merit to Wriston's complaints about the Shearsons and Merrills of the financial world. If you are one of the affluent few who maintains a cash management account, you can run a checking account off your money market fund that will pay you higher interest on your short-term funds than the paltry 5.25 percent mandated by the Fed, which regulates the nation's commercial banks. (Wriston's argument is exaggerated because commercial banks offer this service to their corporate clients through "sweep accounts," which channel idle checking balances into high-yielding accounts.) A major step toward decontrol was taken in the Monetary Control Act of 1980, which created the Depository Institutions Deregulation Committee to phase out interest rate ceilings by 1986.

Added together, the various proposals for deregulation aim to create a new kind of financial conglomerate. This one-stop "Bank 'n' Burger," as Wriston calls it, would offer loans, stocks, bonds, currency trading, credit cards, money market funds plus all corporate banking services. Citibank's Wriston has become the ideological chieftain of the move toward deregulation. (At one point, Wriston even threatened to sell Citibank so that its parent Citicorp could do business that banks cannot.) While the Fed has some reservations about deregulation, the Reagan administration is supportive. The secretary of the treasury, Donald Regan, built one of the biggest financial conglomerates around, Merrill Lynch. The banks' campaign, which is well organized and well financed, is probably too advanced to be reversed. When deregulation comes it will be a classic case of what Professor Edward S. Herman of the Wharton School calls "legislation by *fait accompli.*"

Yet there is little evidence that repealing the nation's banking laws, which were designed to prevent speculative abuses and undue concentration of financial power, will improve the performance of the banks or the U.S. financial system over the long run. It would do little to correct the precariousness of the financial system and may have the opposite effect.

Permitting commercial banks to branch across state lines will not solve their international problems. Domestic versus international expansions is not an either/or proposition. Bankers talk a lot about reducing the growth of their global activities, but in truth they must stay in with both feet or get out completely. Take foreign currency trading as an example. Massive daily fluctuations in currency values and international interest rates have made aggressive dealing essential to the profitability of the big banks and their clients. No reputable bank could conceivably downgrade its trading activities for fear of losing corporate business. In fact, for the banks, currency trading is becoming more important than ever. According to Citibank's Heinz Riehl, currency trading is particularly attractive as a profit center because it generates quick income without saddling the bank with long-term loan exposure in the Mexicos and Polands of the world. For the ten biggest U.S. banks, according to Salomon Brothers analyst Thomas Hanley, foreign exchange trading profits grew from about $200 million in 1977 to nearly $800 million in

1981, a fourfold increase. Clearly, no serious global bank can walk away from foreign exchange trading.

Whatever its merits, letting Citibank open branches in California or Morgan Guaranty underwrite General Motors securities offerings will not dampen their desires to expand abroad. A rapid expansion of domestic business might encourage them to lend even *more* abroad. This is because an increase in domestic business would diversify bank loan portfolios and make room for additional foreign lending. To be sure, there is evidence that the banks would like to scale down the number of countries they get involved with. (Yet, judging from the stampede to get into Africa, virgin territory as far as American banks are concerned, it would appear that competition is as intense as ever.) The banks cannot, however, chop their lending to the biggest Third World and COMECON debtors. With large amounts of interest and principal due over the next two years, cutting Mexico, Brazil, Argentina and Poland off would only result in more red ink for the banks. In fact, it might even encourage countries to default because they would have less to lose if they did. The basic leverage banks have over large debtors is their need to borrow more money. Finally, at most big banks, the international departments form large and powerful constituencies. They will resist changing the focus of their careers from London and Paris to Cleveland and Anaheim.

Ultimately, the campaign for deregulation grows out of an age-old problem of capitalism: the inherent instability of competition.* The emergence of new markets attracts large numbers of market participants, which results in destructive competition and low profits. At the end of World War II, a few large banks based in the United States and Britain dominated international banking. As the global marketplace expanded, waves of new competitors came from the United States, the Continent, Japan and the Arab world. In general, the result has been "overbanking" and intense price competition. By encouraging the banks to market loans aggressively, competition has also led to the debasement of credit standards. Risks in

---

* While banking is not competitive in the textbook sense of the term, judging from the ease with which banks can enter the market and the price warfare that has traditionally characterized the syndicated loan market, global banking is clearly more competitive than many other mature industries.

international banking have grown accordingly. In a remarkably candid observation, one of the leading Eurobankers, Michael Sandberg of the Hong Kong and Shanghai Bank, calls the modus operandi of the highly competitive Euromarket "bad banking."

> Viewed objectively, it could be said that Eurolending, particularly when syndicated, is sometimes bad banking. If this seems extreme, one should ask if it is good banking to borrow short to lend long at a fine spread someone else has assessed.

In recent years, U.S. commercial banks have also been facing increasing competition in the domestic market. Hordes of foreign banks have set up offices in the United States. At the end of 1981, there were 255 foreign banks with offices in New York, most of them established in the last few years. According to the Federal Reserve, foreign banks in the United States have nearly $200 billion in assets. The new entrants to the U.S. market are primarily large banks that compete directly with major U.S. banks for prime corporate business. Intense competition among the banks plus the emergence of cheaper sources of money, such as the commercial paper market, has increased corporate bargaining power vis-à-vis the banks, making it increasingly difficult for banks to squeeze profits out of traditional corporate relationships. Top companies often spur their bankers to raise funds directly in commercial paper. In the elite consumer market, the competition that banks face from the Shearsons and Merrills is real, though it has damaged and beleaguered savings and loan institutions more than commercial banks.

The traditional solution to the problem of excess competition is increasing concentration through bankruptcies and mergers. While the stated aim of deregulation is to increase competition, one inevitable result will be a greater concentration of financial power.* This is already happening as a natural outgrowth of high interest rates and a dismal economic climate. The plight of the S&Ls is the most obvious example. Leading bankers recognize that more financial

---

* This does not rule out the possibility that deregulation will bring greater competition in certain regional markets. There would be greater competition for banking business in California, for instance, if the large New York banks gain access to the market through regulatory changes.

institutions are going to disappear and they want bank regulators to turn them loose to expedite the process. As Willard Butcher, David Rockefeller's successor at Chase Manhattan, has written:

> Under present conditions, it will be difficult for all 42.000 different American depository institutions to thrive. The question is, do we want orderly or disruptive change? Allowing mergers would be the most constructive way for a fragmented industry with too many entities. . . .

Butcher and other bankers maintain that greater concentration in the financial marketplace would benefit "depositors, shareholders and the general public." The evidence presented in this book suggests a different conclusion. Deregulation would not only increase the concentration of financial power, but further distort the distribution of banking services in the United States. Not long ago, community activists used to denounce banks for "redlining" poor neighborhoods. Today, the banks are essentially redlining the whole average-income housing market. In recent years, the banks have shown a declining interest in traditional "brick and mortar" banking, shifting their attention to wholesale or corporate banking. Some banks, like New York's Bankers Trust, emulating the Morgan style, have dumped their retail branches, while others are gradually getting out of housing and consumer finance. The demise of smaller financial institutions through deregulation will exacerbate this problem. Allowing commercial banks to invade every area of financial life is a good way to ensure that more money will flow into Mexico, megamergers and skyscrapers in Manhattan, but it sounds like a poor way to build more houses and get the U.S. economy back on its feet. Corporations and the affluent will receive better banking services than ever. Average and lower income Americans will get less.

Increasing the concentration of financial power will do little to make the banking system more sound. Glass-Steagall was designed to prevent some of the speculative abuses that led to the crash and the Great Depression. Yet no advocate of deregulation has demonstrated why the repeal of Glass-Steagall would not lead to the same abuses today. Some weak institutions might disappear, but the giants that remain would feel the same pressures to compete with other large institutions. Commercial banks would be encouraged to increase their exposure to individual clients. If a company failed, the bank would be in trouble, because it would be stuffed with the firm's stocks and bonds as well as loans. There is no evidence to suggest that the banks would police themselves anymore than their ancestors did. Chase Manhattan's recent Drysdale Securities debacle illustrates how careless leading banks can be. New York's second-largest bank was engaged in extensive securities dealings with a maverick firm that had leveraged $6.5 billion in speculative bond positions on a tiny capital base of some $20 million. (That is leverage that makes Chase and Citibank look well capitalized.) When Drysdale couldn't pay, Chase swallowed a $135 million loss and set off a major turmoil in the government bond market. Chase should have expanded powers to underwrite corporate securities and take positions in the highly volatile bond market?

Moveover, a crisis in a highly concentrated financial system would be more serious than in a decentralized system. Liberal economist Robert L. Heilbroner of the New School for Social Research argues that one of the reasons why the slump that followed the Great Crash was more severe than its predecessors was that government regulation lagged behind the growth of huge financial entities. "When adversity struck," Heilbroner observes, "it was capable of spreading fearful wreckage throughout the system. The Great Crash triggered a self-feeding, self-worsening collapse of interconnected but unsupported scaffolding." Financial concentration would be even more dangerous today because both the banks and their customers are leveraged to the hilt. In a highly concentrated financial system, a crisis could easily bring down the whole banking system. The losers would not only be those officers who were sacked, but depositors, shareholders and the public at large.

Deregulation is dangerous business in a banking industry imbued with what Albert Wojnilower calls the "narcotic addiction of borrowing and the related phenomena of gambling and asset-price speculation." With the proliferation of speculative instruments, such as financial futures, foreign exchange, new leveraging techniques and megamergers, the U.S. economy is increasingly becoming a paper economy without a foundation. The money that is sorely needed to rebuild the foundation is being used for other things. As financial markets are deregulated, their behavior becomes more outlandish. This worsens the prospects for a genuine economic recovery and points directly to a major financial crisis. One cannot improve on Wojnilower's words:

> The freeing of financial markets to pursue their casino instincts heightens the odds of such crises. With few bounds left on short-term price changes, floating rates in the key banking sector, new futures markets, large international crowds of participants—and with a much more unstable "outside" world providing continual reminders of the futility of longer-range plans—bizarre financial behavior is to be expected. Because, unlike a casino, the financial markets are inextricably linked with the world outside, the real economy pays the price.

Wojnilower is one of the few on Wall Street who believes the answer is greater government regulation. To restore some prudence to the financial system, Wojnilower has proposed greater capital requirements on banks, stiff margin payments to discourage speculation in futures markets, and the banning of floating interest rates. Henry Kaufman, Wall Street's other perennial bear, advocates abandoning the Fed's monetarist shock treatment and replacing it with controls on the growth of credit and debt. In the international arena, Robert Roosa, Geoffrey Bell and John Heimann have formed a blue-chip panel called the Group of 30 that advocates scaling down the role of the dollar and replacing it with some acceptable international currency unit. One could add a host of others, including a ban on bank credit for certain corporate mergers, reserve requirements on money market mutual funds, federal guidelines to channel adequate credit to the housing industry and increasing government participation in the exchange markets.

Would it be too much to expect some of the saner voices on Wall Street, the Wojnilowers, Kaufmans and Roosas, to be heeded in time to avoid disaster? Probably, yes. There is too much money in the global gambling casino for the banks to pass up. Wojnilower ventures a candid assessment of the prospects for reform: "How impractical!" Gambling in the financial markets will go on, probably increase, until eventually it stops, not because of greater government intervention, but because of some wicked financial failures.

In this sense, we have come full circle. The world economy recovered from the wreckage of depression and war because government intervened to save the system from its own excesses. Harry White and John Maynard Keynes were friends of business enterprise, not enemies. Today, the lessons of history have been largely forgotten. The props of the system are crumbling under the raw political power of business. In time, no doubt, the safeguards enacted to prevent another great crash will also be dismantled.

In the midst of a frightening economic decline, the biggest game on earth plays on. It has been going on for 40 years, since it collapsed the last time. How long it will go on is anyone's guess. Governments may be more adept at containing crises today than they used to be, but history shows that eventually the game will end. It will end, not because the players will have been shackled by government regulations, but because they will have abused their vast freedom.

None of this is likely to influence the high rollers of Wall Street, the City or Hong Kong. They will deny that trouble is brewing right up until the time it splashes onto the front pages. They are addicted to the game and getting out would mean the end of life as they know it. Instead, they keep the game going by making it bigger and riskier. No one ever got rich making it smaller. If the present players get squeamish, they know there are always others ready to take over. For this reason alone, the bankers cannot police themselves. As in the past, it may take a major financial crisis before the regulators decide to discipline the bankers for their own good. By then, it will be too late. When the game ends, the bankers will be among the losers.

NOTES

1. FROM BRETTON WOODS TO CAMP DAVID

PAGE 13

There are a number of useful volumes on the background to Bretton Woods and the accords. These include Seymour E. Harris, ed., *The New Economics* (New York: Augustus M. Kelly, 1965), chaps. 24–29; Alfred E. Eckes, Jr., *A Search for Solvency* (Austin: University of Texas Press, 1975); Benjamin M. Rowland, "Preparing the American Ascendency: The Transfer of Economic Power from Britain to the United States, 1933–1944," in Rowland, *Balance of Power or Hegemony: The Interwar Monetary System* (New York: New York University Press, 1976); John Morton Blum, *From the Morgenthau Diaries: Years of War, 1941–45* (Boston: Houghton Mifflin, 1967), chaps. 5, 9; Robert Triffin, *Europe and the Monetary Muddle* (New Haven: Yale University Press, 1957), chap. 3; Eric Roll, *The World After Keynes* (London: Pall Mall Press, 1968), chap. 8. See also the articles by Morgenthau and White in *Foreign Affairs,* January 1945.

PAGE 14

The Roll quote is from *The World after Keynes,* p. 91.

On Harry White, see David Rees, *Harry Dexter White: A Study in Paradox* (New York: Coward, McCann and Geoghegan, 1973); Nathan I. White, *Harry Dexter White, Loyal American* (Waban, Mass.: Bessie White Bloom, 1956); and David Caute, *The Great Fear* (New York: Simon & Schuster, 1978), pp. 57–83.

PAGE 15

On European economic performance in the 1920s and 1930s, see Fred Hirsch and Peter Oppenheimer, "The Trial of Managed Money: Currency, Credit and Prices, 1920–1970," in *The Fontana Economic History of Europe,* vol. 5, part II, chap. 11; and John Kenneth Galbraith, *Money* (Boston: Houghton Mifflin, 1975), chaps. 12–14.

PAGE 16

World exports from Edward M. Bernstein, "The Nature and Causes of Deep Depressions," August 1962, mimeo.

The Keynes quote is from John Maynard Keynes, *Essays in Persuasion* (New York: Norton, 1963), pp. 293–94.

The Coombs quote is from *The Arena of International Finance* (New York: John Wiley, 1976), p. 3. Coombs' book is a superb account of the Bretton Woods years.

"Aequilibrium Britannicum" is from Eric Roll, "International Capital Movements: Past, Present, Future," Per Jacobssen Lecture, September 26, 1971. This is a short and invaluable guide to international financial developments in the twentieth century. Skidelsky quote is from "Retreat from Leadership: The Evolution of British Economic Foreign Policy, 1870–1939," in Rowland, *Balance of Power or Hegemony.*

PAGE 17

Keynes quote is from Harris, *The New Economics,* p. 392.

On London's financial role, see J. B. Condliffe, *The Commerce of Nations* (New York: Norton, 1950), pp. 347–48. See also the essays in Rowland, *Balance of Power or Hegemony.* For a critical view, see Harry Magdoff, *The Age of Imperialism* (New York: Monthly Review Press, 1968), chap. 5.

PAGE 18

On U.S. economic policy in the 1920s, see Charles P. Kindleberger, *The World in Depression, 1929–1939* (Berkeley: University of California Press, 1973). For years a controversy has raged concerning the nature of U.S. foreign economic policy after 1929. Kindleberger rejects the views of revisionist historian William Appleman Williams and others that the U.S. sought global hegemony from the early 1930s. Kindleberger asserts that the U.S. took no steps in this direction until the exchange of the White and Keynes plans in the early 1940s. In my view, both viewpoints need modifying. The U.S. wanted the benefits accruing to a leading power, like expanded foreign markets, but did not want to bear the costs of managing the global economy, specifically putting aside its immediate interests in order to halt the global deflation. At best it discharged these responsibilities very badly. Implicit in Kindleberger's position, however, is that better U.S. policies could have prevented the great depression. That seems doubtful. See Kindleberger, *The World in Depression,* pp. 297–98.

On U.S. monetary policy, see Charles R. Whittlesey, Arthur M. Freedman and Edward S. Herman, *Money and Banking: Analysis and Policy* (New York: Macmillan, 1963), pp. 456–57.

PAGE 19

The Bernstein quote is from "The Nature and Causes of Deep Depression."

The Kindleberger quote is from *The World in Depression,* p. 305.

Morgenthau quoted in Gabriel Kolko, *The Politics of War* (New York: Random House, 1968), p. 257.

PAGE 20

The quote "dictated the essential terms" is from Rowland, *Balance of Power or Hegemony,* p. 215.

On the gold standard, see Keynes' brilliant polemics in *Essays in Persuasion,* part III, from which the quotes are taken.

On gold production, see Anna J. Schwartz, memoranda to the U.S. Gold Commission, September 10, 1981.

PAGE 22

Keynes' "essential concern" is from Hirsch and Oppenheimer, "The Trial of Managed Money," p. 623.

White's views on the IMF are from *Foreign Affairs,* January 1945.

PAGE 23

On bankers' opposition to the Bretton Woods accords, see Blum, *From the Morgenthau Diaries.*

The Morgenthau quotes are from *Foreign Affairs,* January 1945.

PAGE 26

U.S. trade surplus is from *Economic Report of the President,* 1982.

The Block quote is from *The Origins of International Economic Disorder* (Berkeley: University of California Press, 1977), p. 83.

PAGE 27

On the Marshall Plan and Bretton Woods, see Thomas Balogh, *Fact and Fancy in International Economic Relations* (New York: Pergamon Press, 1973).

The Roll quote is from *The World After Keynes,* p. 101.

PAGE 28

The Solomon quote is from *The International Monetary System: 1945-1976* (New York: Harper and Row, 1977), p. 31.

PAGE 29

The Galbraith quote is from *Money,* p. 316.

On the Triffin dilemma, see his *Gold and the Dollar Crisis* (New Haven: Yale University Press, 1969), introduction and pp. 162-91; *Europe and the Money Muddle* (New Haven: Yale University Press, 1957), chap. 3; "The International Role and Fate of the Dollar," *Foreign Affairs,* Winter 1978-79; and "The Evolution of the International Monetary System: Historical Re-appraisal and Future Perspectives," *Princeton Studies in International Finance,* No. 12, 1964.

On the 1960 gold speculation, see Coombs, *The Arena of International Finance,* pp. 13-14.

PAGE 30

Figures on the U.S. gold supply and foreign dollar liabilities are taken from *International Financial Statistics,* May 1978, pp. 396-97. See also Triffin, "The International Role" in *Foreign Affairs.*

The U.S. balance of payments is from the *Federal Reserve Bulletin*, April 1973, p. 327.

U.S. inflation figures are the annual changes in the consumer price index. See the *Economic Report of the President, 1982*, p. 295.

PAGE 31

The Lekachman quote is from *Economists at Bay* (New York: McGraw-Hill, 1976).

For Magdoff's views, see *The Age of Imperialism*, chap. 5.

PAGE 32

On the dollar and German inflation, see the Karel Holbik, ed., *Monetary Policy in Twelve Industrial Countries* (Boston: Federal Reserve Bank of Boston, 1973), p. 207.

De Gaulle's views on the dollar and gold are well known. For a critical view, see Gordon Weil and Ian Davidson, *The Gold War* (New York: Holt Rinehart Winston, 1970), chap. 4. De Gaulle's "exorbitant privilege" comment is mentioned by Robert Triffin, "The International Role," in *Foreign Affairs*.

On the dollar support measures, see Coombs, *The Arena of International Finance*, chaps. 3, 4, 5 and 11.

PAGE 33

On the creation of the SDR, see Hirsch and Oppenheimer, "The Trial of Managed Money," pp. 635–36; and Coombs, *The Arena of International Finance*, chap. 11.

On Keynes' "bancor," see Joan Robinson, "The International Currency Proposals," in Harris, *The New Economics*.

The Mendelsohn quote is from *Money on the Move: The Modern International Capital Market* (New York: McGraw-Hill, 1980), p. 10.

PAGE 34

Roosa quote is from Robert V. Roosa and Fred Hirsch, "Reserves, Reserve Currencies and Vehicle Currencies: An Argument," *Princeton Essays in International Finance*, No. 54, 1966, p. 6.

On the monetary events of 1971, see Geoffrey Bell, "The International Financial System: Collapse and Reconstruction?" *International Currency Review*, October 1971; *The Eurodollar Market and the International Financial System* (London: John Wiley, 1973). For an excellent journalistic account, see William Safire, *Before the Fall* (Garden City: Doubleday, 1975). See also Martin Mayer's *Fate of the Dollar* (New York: Times Books, 1980), chap. 6.

The Stein quote is from Safire's *Before the Fall*, p. 510.

PAGE 35

The Kissinger quote is from his *White House Years* (Boston: Little, Brown, 1980), p. 962.

On Nixon and Burns, see Coombs, *The Arena of International Finance,* chap. 12, p. 207. In personal conversations, Coombs' views on their policies were even stronger.

PAGE 36
The Coombs quote is from *The Arena of International Finance,* p. 207. Foreign dollar holdings are from *International Financial Statistics,* p. 397.

On the Nixon-Connally-Burns nexus, see Kissinger, *The White House Years;* and Martin Mayer, *The Fate of the Dollar.* An excellent treatment of the whole period can be found in Robert Z. Aliber, *The International Money Game* (New York: Basic Books, 1979), pp. 101–4.

PAGE 37
The Houthakker quote is from Coombs, *The Arena of International Finance,* p. 208.

On Connally and Schweitzer, see John Brooks, *The Games Players* (New York: Times Books, 1980), pp. 287–91.

PAGE 38
The Bernstein quote is from a memorandum to clients, May 1971. On the August 1971 developments, I have benefited from conversations with Charles Coombs, Edward Bernstein and Fred Bergsten. The Volcker-Connally controversy is discussed by Mayer, *The Fate of the Dollar.*

PAGE 39
On the Camp David meeting, the best source is Safire's *Before the Fall.* Nixon quote is from Galbraith, *Money,* p. 349.

PAGE 40
Aliber's observation is from *The International Money Game,* p. 104.

2. THE GLOBAL MONEY MARKET

PAGE 41
The Mendelsohn quote is from *Money on the Move,* p. 35.

A convenient discussion of the IET and other measures can be found in *Money on the Move.* I have also benefited from a personal conversation with Robert Roosa. For a critical analysis, see Fred Hirsch and Peter Oppenheimer, "The Trial of Managed Money," pp. 629–31.

PAGE 42
On the depression and its effects on international lending see Hirsch and Oppenheimer, "The Trial of Managed Money"; Herbert Feis, *Europe, The World's Banker* (New York: Norton, 1965), preface; Kindleberger, *The World in Depression*; and Kindleberger, *Manias, Panics and Crashes* (New York: Basic Books, 1978), pp. 72–74 and 135–37.

On multinationalization, see Raymond Vernon, *Sovereignty at Bay* (New York: Basic Books, 1971); Richard J. Barnet and Ronald E. Müller, *Global*

Reach: The Power of the Multinational Corporations (New York: Simon and Schuster, 1974); C. Fred Bergsten, Thomas Horst and Theodore Moran, *American Multinationals and American Interests* (Washington, D.C.: Brookings Institution, 1978); and Myra Wilkins, *The Maturing of Multinational Enterprise* (Harvard University Press, 1971); and the sources cited in these four volumes.

PAGE 43

The Citibank quote is from *Global Financial Intermediation* (New York: Citibank, 1980), p. 7.

The Wriston quote is from the *New York Times*, July 7, 1982.

The Gay quote is from *Business Week*, August 21, 1978.

The Abely quote is from *Business Week*, August 21, 1978.

PAGE 44

The Chase advertisement is from *Institutional Investor*, International Edition, July 1982. Unless specified, all quotes from *Institutional Investor* are taken from the international edition of the magazine.

Figures on early overseas expansion by U.S. banks are from Frank M. Tamagna and Parker B. Willis, "United States Banking Organization Abroad," *Federal Reserve Bulletin*, December 1956. Figures on postwar foreign branches are from Andrew F. Brimmer and Frederick Dahl, "The Growth of American International Banking: Implications for Public Policy," *Journal of Finance*, May 1975.

Figures on London branches are from Brimmer and Dahl, "American International Banking"; and Jane D'Arista, "International Banking," in *Financial Institutions and the Nation's Economy*, a compendium published by the House of Representatives Committee on Banking and Currency, 1976, part 4.

PAGE 45

The Weinert quote is from "Why the Banks Lent to LDCs." Unpublished manuscript.

Figures on the bond market are from Mendelsohn, *Money on the Move*, p. 211.

On Siegmund Warburg, see "The Confessions of Siegmund Warburg," *Institutional Investor*, April 1980; and Joseph Wechsberg, *The Merchant Bankers* (New York: Pocket Books, 1966), chap. 4.

PAGE 46

The Mendelsohn quote is from *Money on the Move*, pp. 18–19.

PAGE 47

On the Glass-Steagall Act, see Charles R. Whittlesey, *Banking and the New Deal* (Chicago: University of Chicago Press, 1935); and Helen Marie Burns, *The American Banking Community and the New Deal Banking Reforms* (Westport, Conn.: Greenwood Press, 1974).

Information on the VFCR and other programs is from Brimmer and Dahl, "American International Banking." I am also grateful for background information provided in a personal interview with Dr. Brimmer.

Figures on overseas branches are from Brimmer and Dahl, "American International Banking."

PAGE 48

On the multinational consortium bank, see Michael von Clemm, "The Rise of Consortium Banking," *Harvard Business Review*, May–June 1971; and Jane S. Little, *Eurodollars* (New York: Harper and Row, 1975), pp. 85–91. A generally useful volume is Stephen I. Davis, *The Euro-Bank* (London: John Wiley, 1976).

PAGE 49

On the growth of shell branches, see Brimmer and Dahl, "American International Banking"; Jane D'Arista, "International Banking"; Richard B. Miller, "The Caymans—Offshore Banking Paradise," *The Bankers Magazine*, January–February 1981; Miller, "Why Bankers Love the Cayman Islands," *Business and Society Review*, Spring 1981; and Federal Reserve Bank of Atlanta, *Economic Review*, July–August, 1980, p. 22.

PAGE 50

The lawyer's quote is from Sampson's *The Money Lenders* (New York: Viking, 1981), p. 228.

Data on overseas assets of U.S. banks are from Brimmer and Dahl, "American International Banking."

Data on foreign deposits of U.S. banks are from Thomas Hanley, et al., *Multinational Banking: Semi-annual Statistics,* Salomon Brothers, various issues; Group of 30 data on this subject was also made available to me by John Heimann.

PAGE 51

Data on profits of U.S. banks are from Norman Fieleke.

The Brimmer quote is from Brimmer and Dahl, "American International Banking."

PAGE 52

Table 1 is from Fieleke. "The Growth of U.S. Banking Abroad: An Analytical Survey," in *Key Issues in International Banking* (Boston: Federal Reserve Bank of Boston, 1977).

PAGE 53

Table 2 is from Hanley, *Multinational Banking,* various issues.

PAGE 54

On increasing competition in international lending, see Dwight B. Crane and Samuel Hayes III, "The New Competition in World Banking," *Harvard Business Review*, July–August 1982; *The Banker, Euromoney,* and *In-*

stitutional Investor each publish an annual list of the world's 500 largest banks.

Data on number and assets of foreign banks in the U.S. is from the *Federal Reserve Bank of New York Quarterly Review*, Summer 1982. See also Peter Merrill Associates, *The Future Development of Foreign Banking Organizations in the United States* (Washington, D.C.: American Bankers Association, 1981), chap. 3.

PAGE 55

The Yassukovitch quote is from Cary Reich, "Michael Von Clemm Strikes Back," *Institutional Investor,* December 1980.

On Morgan, see Andrew Sinclair, *Corsair: The Life of J. Pierpont Morgan* (Boston: Little, Brown, 1981); on Giannini, see Matthew Josephson, *The Money Lords* (New York: Weybright and Talley, 1972); and Martin Mayer, *The Bankers* (New York: Ballantine, 1974); on Meyer, see Cary Reich, "The Legacy of André Meyer," *Institutional Investor,* April 1979.

PAGE 56

The Giannini quote is from Josephson, *The Money Lords.*

On Wriston, see Mayer, *The Bankers;* "The Money Men," *New York,* December 1, 1980; and Anthony Sampson, *The Money Lenders.*

PAGE 57

On the negotiable certificate of deposit, see Mayer, *The Bankers;* and Albert M. Wojnilower, "The Central Role of Credit Crunches in Recent Financial History," *Brookings Papers on Economic Activity,* 1980: 2.

On Michael von Clemm, see Cary Reich, "Michael von Clemm Strikes Back." For background information on the Euro-CD I am grateful to Michael von Clemm.

PAGE 58

On Crédit Suisse First Boston Ltd., see "The Heady Days of the Bought Deal," *Euromoney,* August 1980.

The von Clemm quote is from *Institutional Investor,* March 1982.

PAGE 59

On the 1966 credit crunch, see Wojnilower, "The Central Role of Credit Crunches"; Robert Solomon, *International Monetary Systems;* and Brimmer and Dahl, "American International Banking."

PAGE 60

Data on OPEC deposits in the Euromarket are from a letter by Assistant Treasury Secretary Marc Leland to Representative Benjamin Rosenthal, July 15, 1981.

Data on deposits in U.S. banks by OPEC countries are from a letter from Federal Reserve Board Chairman Paul Volcker to Representative Benjamin Rosenthal, July 10, 1981.

PAGE 61

On Minos Zombanakis, see Cary Reich, "Can Zombanakis Really Deliver on His Promises?" *Institutional Investor,* August 1978.

PAGE 62

SAMA's AT&T deal is from *Institutional Investor,* October 1978.

On the size of the Euromarket, see Morgan Guaranty, *World Financial Markets,* September 1982, p. 11.

On Third World debt, see Thomas Hanley, *Multinational Banking,* June 30, 1982, p. 10.

PAGE 63

Wall Street Journal quote is from the issue of August 5, 1981. On East-West trade, see Richard J. Barnet, *The Giants* (New York: Simon & Schuster, 1977), chap. 6; and Marshall I. Goldman, *Dollars and Détente* (New York: Basic Books, 1975), chap. 2 and pp. 34-35, 71-75.

PAGE 64

Banker's views are quoted by Mark Deverell of Barclay's International at "The Euromarkets 1982," a conference sponsored by the *Financial Times,* London, February 9-10, 1982.

The McDonough quote is from *Euromoney,* January 1973.

PAGE 65

On Chase in Russia and China, see "David's Connections," *Institutional Investor,* May 1981. On banks in the USSR, see Goldman, *Dollars and Détente,* pp. 34-35, 1982.

"Stateless Money" is from *Business Week,* August 21, 1978. "The Geobankers" is from *Institutional Investor,* May 1981.

PAGE 66

Morgan figures are from *World Financial Markets,* various issues. For a different viewpoint on the size of the Euromarket, see Henry Wallich, "Euromarkets and U.S. Monetary Growth," *Journal of Commerce,* May 1-2, 1979.

PAGE 67

I have avoided a lengthy discussion of the so-called credit multiplier effect because in my view it misses the main point. The Euromarket, as critics of the multiplier thesis point out, is not an autonomous money market but an extension of the money markets of the major money center countries. There is substantial leakage from the Euromarket into national money markets, and therefore the academic question of whether or not an infinite expansion of credit within the market is possible is beside the point. What matters is that the creation of the Euromarket facilitated a general increase in the global supply of credit, if only because it freed U.S. banks from reserve requirements. To the extent that the Euromarket facilitated currency speculation it also resulted in additional monetary expansion in countries which fought speculation through exchange market intervention, especially Germany and Switzerland. Similarly, debates on whether interbank funds constitute "money" are superficial because they overlook the crucial role of the interbank market in generating additional bank loans to nonbank entities. For a clear exposition of the issues, see Geoffrey Bell, *The Eurodollar Market and the International Financial System*, pp. 49–53.

Citibank figures are from *Global Financial Intermediation*.

PAGE 68

Table 3 is from the Federal Reserve Bank of New York *Quarterly Review*, Spring 1982.

PAGE 69

The Citibank quote is from *Global Financial Intermediation*, p. 19.

Morgan estimates are from *World Financial Markets*, various issues.

On the interbank market, see Group of 30, *Risks in International Bank Lending* (New York, May 1982), pp. 16–21; see also Group of 30, *How Bankers See the World Financial Market* (May 1982), pp. 15–17 and 56–57.

PAGE 70

Figures on banks' interbank deposits are from Hanley, *Multinational Banking*, various issues.

3. THE TRIUMPH OF HAUTE FINANCE

PAGE 72

The discussion of the period from August 15, 1971, to the Smithsonian Agreement in December relies on Kissinger's *White House Years*. Given his self-professed limitations in economic matters, I was initially skeptical of Kissinger's account. But Fred Bergsten, who worked for Kissinger at the National Security Council and later became one of his more vocal critics, has vouched for the general accuracy of Kissinger's version of these events.

PAGE 73

On the Smithsonian Agreement see Aliber, *The International Money Game;* and Solomon, *The International Money System.*

The revaluation of the yen is from the IMF *Annual Report*, 1972.

PAGE 74

On the British pound, see Aliber, *The International Money Game*, p. 46.

The Mendelsohn quote is from *Euromoney*, March 1973, p. 20. For Volcker mission, see *Business Week*, February 17, 1973.

PAGE 75

The devaluation of the dollar is discussed in IMF *Annual Report*, 1973, p. 66.

The Senate Subcommittee quote is from *Multinational Corporations in the Dollar Devaluation Crisis:* Report on a Questionnaire, Subcommittee on Multinational Corporations, U.S. Senate Committee on Foreign Relations, June 1975, p. 6.

The Pompidou quote is from Solomon's *The International Monetary System,* p. 277.

PAGE 76

The Aliber reference is from *The International Money Game,* chap. 4. Sterling devaluation is discussed in Coombs, *Arena of International Finance.*

In the early years of the Euromarket, business was conducted almost exclusively in dollars. By 1973, according to data from Morgan Guaranty, the dollar's share of total Euromarket transactions had fallen to 73 percent of the total, a substantial shift for a market of that size. On diversification out of the dollar, see also David Kern, "The Non-Dollar Sector of the Euromarket," *Euromoney,* September 1972.

PAGE 77

The Vernon quote is from *Storm Over the Multinationals* (Cambridge, Mass.: Harvard University Press, 1977), p. 121; see also Thomas G. Evans, ed., *The Monetary Muddle* (New York: Dow Jones, 1973), pp. 136–44.

"Betting Against the Dollar" is from the *Wall Street Journal,* April 3, 1973.

The quote is from Evans, *The Monetary Muddle,* p. 150. See also *Business Week,* February 17, 1973, p. 22.

For Gulf Oil's foreign exchange losses, see *The Monetary Muddle,* p. 147.

PAGE 78

Rockefeller is quoted by Martin Mayer in *The Bankers,* p. 442.

The Harry Browne quote is from *New Profits from the Monetary Crisis* (New York: Morrow, 1978), p. 124.

The Nicholas Kaldor quote is from *Essays on Economic Growth and Stability* (London: Duckworth, 1960), p. 17.

PAGE 79

Citibank's Brussels losses provided by Citibank's Heinz Riehl.

Citibank's foreign exchange profits from Hanley, *Multinational Banking,* various issues.

Citibank foreign exchange market share is from *Euromoney,* August 1982, p. 65.

PAGE 80

German controls are discussed in David F. Lomax and P. T. G. Guttman, *The Euromarkets and International Financial Policies* (New York: John Wiley, 1981), pp. 46–8, 52.

The Bartels memo is dated January 1971 and was forwarded to Vice-President Donald Cameron in New York on January 28, 1971.

PAGE 81

The Cameron memo was dated February 22, 1972, and was entitled "German Branch Funding–Swiss Pool."

PAGE 82

The Bartels quote is from the January 1971 memo.

Timmeny comments forwarded to Bloomquist in a letter dated August 23, 1973.

Timmeny resignation letter to the Board of Directors dated December 31, 1973.

The Aronson quote is from *Money and Power* (Beverly Hills: Sage Publications, 1977).

The Giddy figures are from "Measuring the World's Foreign Exchange Market," *Columbia Journal of World Business,* Winter 1979, p. 38.

Capital flows from the United States are from the *Federal Reserve Bulletin,* April 1972; see also Geoffrey Bell, *The Eurodollar Market and the International Financial System,* chap. 6. See also IMF *Annual Report,* 1972, pp. 15–16 and 29.

PAGE 84

U.S. bank outflow is from *Federal Reserve Bulletin,* April 1972.

On the bank outflows and weakening of the dollar, see Geoffrey Bell, "The International Financial System: Collapse and Reconstruction?" *International Currency Review,* October 1971; see also Eric Roll, "International Capital Movements," pp. 18–22 and p. 30.

The Kriz quote is from *Euromoney,* December 1971, p. 22.

IMF figures are from the International Monetary Reform Documents of the Committee of Twenty (Washington, D.C.: IMF, 1974), pp. 78–84.

PAGE 85

The Coombs quote is from *The Arena of International Finance,* p. 212.

That it was the May crisis that led to the closing of the gold window is confirmed by William Safire, who reports that on the way back from Camp David, Nixon informed him that he and Connally had been planning the August 15 measures for two months. See *Before the Fall,* p. 527.

On U.S. capital outflows, see the *Federal Reserve Bulletin,* April 1974, p. 24.

The David Kern quote is from "The Non-Dollar Sector of the Euromarkets," *Euromoney,* September 1972.

PAGE 86

D'Arista quotes are from *Financial Institutions and the Nation's Economy,* pp. 924–25. First quarter 1973 loans are from *Federal Reserve Bulletin,* April 1974, p. A-78. See Kern, "The Non-Dollar Sector"; and Morgan Guaranty, *World Financial Markets,* various issues.

Official holdings of U.S. government securities from IMF, *International Financial Statistics,* May 1977, p. 401.

PAGE 87

C. Fred Bergsten, Thomas Horst and Theodore Moran, *American Multinationals and American Interests* (Washington: Brookings Institution, 1978), pp. 273–83.

Church Committee study is called *Multinational Corporations in the Dollar Devaluation Crisis.* Hearings which accompanied the study are published in part 13 of *Multinational Corporations and U.S. Foreign Policy,* July 21 and December 9–10, 1975.

PAGE 88

The Church quote is from *Multinational Corporations in the Dollar Devaluation Crisis,* p. v.

PAGE 89

The German surplus is from *IMF Annual Report,* pp. 14–15. Only a part of this large increase can be accounted for by an increase in the dollar value of mark-denominated exports.

PAGE 90

For the Spero findings, see Joan Spero, *The Failure of the Franklin National Bank* (New York: Council on Foreign Relations, 1980).

PAGE 91

Henry Kaufman is quoted in Edward I. Altman and Arnold W. Sametz, eds., *Financial Crises: Institutions and Markets in a Fragile Environment* (New York: John Wiley, 1977), p. vii.

For post–Franklin-Herstatt trading volumes see Giddy, "World's Foreign Exchange Markets"; and Stephen I. Davis, *The Euro-bank,* pp. 81–82 and 133–34.

PAGE 92

On hot money in the Euromarket, see chaps. 5 and 6.

4. THE ECONOMICS AND POLITICS OF GLOBAL DEBT

PAGE 93

On Morgan's foreign lending, see Andrew Sinclair, *Corsair,* pp. 170–73 and 232–33.

PAGE 94

This banker quoted Mark Deverell at a conference on "The Euromarkets in 1982," sponsored by the *Financial Times,* London, February 9–10, 1982.

For sources on Third World and COMECON debt see notes for pp. 153–54 below.

PAGE 95

On bank lending in the nineteenth and early twentieth centuries, see Stephen Davis, *The Euro-Bank*, pp. 13–25.

PAGE 96

The Feis quote is from *Europe, the World's Banker*, p. xiii.

PAGE 97

On relations between the corporations and banks, see Richard Weinert "Why the Banks Lent to LDCs," and "The First Real International Bankers," *Fortune*, December 1967.

The Friedman quote is from *The Emerging Role of Private Banks in the Developing World* (New York: Citibank, 1977).

PAGE 98

The Weinert quote is from "Why the Banks Did It," *Foreign Policy*, No. 30, Spring 1978.

Private bank involvement in the Third World in the early 1970s is from Brimmer and Dahl, "American International Banking"; D'Arista, *Financial Institutions;* and Mendelsohn, *Money on the Move*.

PAGE 99

On the economic shocks of the 1970s, see Sidney Dell et al., *The Balance of Payments Adjustment Process in Developing Countries: A Report to the Group of 24* (United Nations: UNDP 1979), chap. I.

On Third World exports and imports, see Dell, *Balance of Payments;* and IMF, *Annual Report*, 1975, pp. 20–22; on the terms of trade, see the IMF *Annual Report*, 1981, p. 17; and IMF, *World Economic Outlook 1982*, pp. 137–39, 149.

On the effects of higher oil prices see IMF, *World Economic Outlook 1982*, pp. 58, 163; and Morgan Guaranty, *World Financial Markets*, March 1982.

PAGE 100

On the effects of the slowdown in economic growth, see IMF, *World Economic Outlook 1982*, p. 58.

The Brandt Commission quote is from the International Commission on International Development Issues, *North-South: A Program for Survival*.

On the impacts of higher interest rates, see IMF *Annual Report*, 1981, pp. 52–53; Morgan Guaranty, *World Financial Markets*, March 1982, p. 7; *World Financial Markets*, May 1981, pp. 10–11; *Amex Bank Review*, April 26, 1982, pp. 2–3; *Amex Bank Review*, January 25, 1982, p. 5; and J. de Larosière, speech to the Chambre Nationale de Conseillers Financiers, Paris, April 1, 1982.

PAGE 101

Long-term debt of Third World countries is from *IMF World Economic Outlook 1982*, p. 170; for the private banks' share of the debt, see Morgan

Guaranty, *World Financial Markets*, August 1982; and Thomas Hanley, *Multinational Banking*, various issues; and IMF, *External Indebtedness of Developing Countries*, May 1981, pp. 3–12.

PAGE 102

Wall Street Journal quote is from the issue of February 4, 1980.

On the Third World's debts to private banks, see IMF, Morgan Guaranty and Amex Bank sources referred to above.

The Brazilian economist's quote is from the *Wall Street Journal*, February 4, 1980.

PAGE 103

Third World debt service payments are from IMF, *World Economic Outlook 1982*, p. 173; see also Larosière, speech to Chambre Nationale.

On the foreign currency reserves of Third World countries see *Amex Bank Review*, February 22, 1982.

PAGE 104

Wallich figures and a discussion of the 10 percent rule are from "LDC Debt: To Worry or Not to Worry," a speech to the Bankers Association for Foreign Trade, June 2, 1981.

For the market share of U.S. and non-U.S. banks, see Hanley, *Multinational Banking*, various issues; and Rodney Mills, "U.S. Banks Are Losing Their Share of the Market," *Euromoney*, February 1980.

On increasing competition in international banking, see Group of 30, *Risks in International Bank Lending* (New York: Group of 30, 1982). The Group of 30 calculates that in recent years, on the average of 66 new banks per year have been entering the international syndicated loan market. On Arab banks see Richard O'Brien, *Private Bank Lending to Developing Countries*, World Bank Staff Working Paper No. 482, August 1981, pp. 45–46.

PAGE 105

Eastern European lending is from Hanley, *Multinational Banking*, various issues.

PAGE 106

On Eastern European debt service ratios, see Wharton Econometric Forecasting Associates, various releases.

The Herring and Guttentag quote is from *Financial Disorder and International Bank Lending*, Wharton School, March 1981, pp. 2–24.

On Oil Shock II, see Walter J. Levy, "Oil and the Decline of the West," *Foreign Affairs*, Summer 1980.

PAGE 107

On inflation during the Carter administration, see chap. 5.

On the impacts of higher interest rates, see the sources listed in the notes for pages 151–52 above.

The Rockefeller quote is from "Rough Seas Ahead: The LDCs and the Credit Squeeze," Remarks at the Chase Econometrics Luncheon, New York, January 10, 1980.

The Volcker quote is from "The Recycling Problem Revisited." Remarks before the Graduate School of Business, New York University, March 1, 1980.

PAGE 108

On the terms of lending in 1979, see Hanley, *Multinational Banking*, various issues.

The Wriston quote is from his speech at the International Monetary Conference, Lausanne, Switzerland, June 1981.

The Roll quote is from his speech at the International Monetary Conference, Lausanne, Switzerland, June 1981.

PAGE 109

The Weinert quote is from a personal interview with the author.

The Morgan data are from *World Financial Markets*, May 1981.

PAGE 110

On spreads and fees, see O'Brien, *Private Bank Lending*, p. 8; and Larry Gurwin, "Playing the Cosmetics Game," *Institutional Investor*, August 1982.

The facts of the Polish debt crisis are well known. For convenient summaries, see "The Secrets of the Polish Memorandum," *Euromoney*, August 1981; see also the special issue devoted to Eastern European debt in *Institutional Investor*, January 1982.

PAGE 111

On the roots of the crisis, see Daniel Singer, *The Road to Gdansk* (New York: Monthly Review Press, 1981).

The August loan is detailed in the *Wall Street Journal*, August 21, 1980.

The October loan is from the *Wall Street Journal*, October 13, 1980.

PAGE 112

The Minkiewicz quote is from the *Wall Street Journal*, October 13, 1980.

On German banks' Polish loans, see the *Wall Street Journal*, December 24, 1981.

PAGE 113

The McCarthy quote is from *The Washington Post*, May 11, 1982. The banker's quote is from *Institutional Investor*, January 1982, p. 60.

PAGE 114

Poland's debt rescheduling reported in the *Wall Street Journal*, April 7, 1982 and September 16, 1982.

Woloszyn quoted by Felix Rohatyn in "The Case for Putting Poland in Default," *Wall Street Journal*, April 19, 1982; see also the *Wall Street Journal*, March 15, 1982.

Page 115

Figures on the Mexican debt crisis are from "Mexico: Economic and Financial Statistics," a memorandum distributed by the Ministry of Finance of the United Mexican States, September 20, 1982. On U.S. banks' exposure in Mexico, see Hanley, *Multinational Banking,* various issues.

The Bank of America acceptance facility for Pemex is from *Institutional Investor,* September 1981, pp. 144–45.

Page 116

Basil Caplan figures are from "Mexico—The World's New Biggest Debtor," *The Banker,* July 1982.

Morgan figures are from *World Financial Markets,* various issues.

The Alfa debt problem is discussed in Alan Robinson, "The Position of Alfa is Delicate, Delicate, Delicate," *Euromoney,* June 1982; and the *Wall Street Journal,* June 10, 1982.

On Mexico's economic crisis, see Alan Riding, "Taming the Mexican Passion for More," *New York Times,* September 12, 1982; Susan Kaufman Purcell, "Banking on Mexico—Badly," *New York Times,* August 24, 1982; and the *New York Times,* August 17, 1982.

On the meeting at the New York Federal Reserve, see Riding, "Taming the Mexican Passion"; and Robert Bennett, "Bankers Pressured to Assist Mexico," *New York Times,* August 21, 1982.

Page 117

For the suspension of Mexico's principal payments until the end of 1983, see Alan Riding, "New Debt Plans Set by Mexico," *New York Times,* September 7, 1982.

For Wallich's views, see his speech to "The Euromarkets in 1982," a conference sponsored by the *Financial Times,* London, February 9, 1982; and his speech to the Conference of International Banking Supervisors, Washington, September 1981.

Page 118

On the SEC's new rules, see SAB 49, October 26, 1982, and the *Wall Street Journal,* November 5, 1982.

For the effects of reschedulings on the banks, see Felix Rohatyn, "The Case for Putting Poland in Default."

Page 119

On the inevitability of government bail-outs see Albert M. Wojnilower, "The Central Role of Credit Crunches."

On the U.S. government's payments of Poland's debts to U.S. banks, see the *Wall Street Journal,* September 16, 1982; *The Washington Post,* May 11, 1982.

Page 120

On the Mexican bail-out, see Alan Riding, "Taming the Mexican Passion"; and the *Wall Street Journal*, August 24, 1982 and December 29, 1982.

For the amounts of Third World debts due in the next year, see Morgan Guaranty, *World Financial Markets*, August 1982.

PAGE 121

On the Ditchley group, see the *New York Times*, October 28, 1982; the *Financial Times*, October 27, 28, 1982; and the *Journal of Commerce*, October 29, 1982.

PAGE 122

Friedman quotes are from a personal interview with the author and from *Institutional Investor*, September 1980.

PAGE 123

The Hauge quote is from *Euromoney*, October 1977.

The IMF financial contribution to the recycling process is from *IMF Survey*, January 25, 1982; and IMF Memorandum, Department of External Relations, March 1, 1982.

PAGE 124

For a case study of Peru, the banks and the IMF, see Michael Moffitt, testimony before the House of Representatives Subcommittee on International Financial Institutions, Committee on Banking, Housing and Urban Affairs, February 6, 1980; see also Karen DeYoung, "Peru Appears on the Verge of Defaulting on Foreign Loans," *Washington Post*, March 14, 1978. For an extended discussion of the relationship between the IMF and the banks, see Howard Wachtel, *The New Gnomes* (Washington: Institute for Policy Studies, 1977).

PAGE 126

The Butcher quote is from *Euromoney*, October 1980, p. 53.

Burns is quoted by Howard Wachtel in *The New Gnomes*.

On the IMF's role after Oil Shock II, see *IMF Survey*, January 25, 1982. It should be kept in mind that commitments of resources by the IMF are often much larger than actual disbursements. However, the dramatic increase in commitments after Oil Shock II does illustrate the banks' increasing reliance on the presence of the Fund.

The Banker quote is from the September 1980 issue.

PAGE 128

For the Williamson quote, see his testimony before the House of Representatives Subcommittee on International Financial Institutions, Committee on Banking, Housing and Urban Affairs, February 6, 1980.

For a critique of IMF stabilization programs, see Norman Girvan, "Swallowing the IMF Medicine in the 1970s," *Development Dialogue*, 1980:2, and Moffitt, testimony before the House; see also Sidney Dell, *Balance of Payments Adjustment*, chap. 3.

PAGE 129

On U.S. assistance for Jamaica, see *Business Week*, October 18, 1982, pp. 162–63.

PAGE 130

For the Fund's analyses of the success of stabilization programs, see Thomas Reichmann and Richard Stillson, "How Successful Are Programs Supported by Stand-by Arrangements?" *Finance and Development*, March 1977; Reichmann, "The Fund's Conditional Assistance and the Problems of Adjustment 1973–75," *Finance and Development*, December 1978; and J. de Larosière, March 4, 1982, Minneapolis.

PAGE 132

The Jamal speech is from the chairman's address to the Annual Meetings of the IMF and World Bank, Washington, D.C., 1980.

The Cockburn quote is from a personal conversation with the author.

5. THE DECLINE OF THE DOLLAR

PAGE 134

On the Carter administration's foreign economic policy, see the *Wall Street Journal*, January 17, 1977; and the *Washington Post*, March 14, 1977. I have also benefited from conversations with C. Fred Bergsten, assistant secretary of the treasury for international affairs, and the *Washington Post*'s Hobart Rowen, who has written excellent articles on this period.

For Carter's notion of the "dirty float," which was promulgated even before he took office, see *Business Week*, November 22, 1976; for a later version, see *Business Week*, November 14, 1977.

For Germany's attitude, see the London *Times*, November 22, 1977.

PAGE 135

On foreign exchange markets and currency trading, see Roger M. Kubarych, 1977; *Foreign Exchange Markets in the United States* (New York: Federal Reserve Bank of New York, 1978); Heinz Riehl and Rita M. Rodriguez, *Foreign Exchange Markets* (New York: McGraw-Hill, 1977); and Ian Giddy, "Measuring the World's Foreign Exchange Market," *Columbia Journal of World Business*, Winter 1979. There is no academic source that can substitute for visiting foreign exchange trading rooms and talking with currency traders. This chapter relies heavily on their insights. A number of these interviews were conducted with writer Jeffry Stein in 1979 for a magazine article which was never published.

PAGE 136

The $50 trillion figure is from a survey of Citibank's foreign exchange dealing practices performed by its principal outside counsel, Shearman and Sterling, done at the request of the Audit Committee Board of Directors. For a different set of estimates, see Giddy, "Measuring the World's Foreign Exchange Market."

The $2 trillion figure is from the IMF External Relations Department. It includes total world exports and imports.

On the relationship between floating exchange rates and foreign currency trading, see Group of 30, *Foreign Exchange Markets Under Floating Rates* (New York, 1980).

PAGE 137

The Volcker quote is from the foreword to Kubarych, *Foreign Exchange Markets*. The growth of foreign exchange trading was also encouraged by the adoption of the so-called FAS-8 by the Financial Accounting Standards Board, requiring foreign subsidiaries of U.S. companies to translate current foreign exchange gains and losses. However, this was less of a factor than the move to floating exchange rates and the resulting growth of the markets themselves.

The Kubarych quote is from *Foreign Exchange Markets*, p. 10.

PAGE 139

On Dow, see Laura White Dillon, "Dow's Controversial Currency Strategy," *Institutional Investor*, July 1979; see also *Business Week*, August 14, 1978, particularly the comments of Geoffrey Bell and Robert Triffin.

PAGE 140

The executive's quote is from Laura White Dillon, "The Education of U.S. Multinationals," *Institutional Investor*, January 1980; see also M. A. Ferrara, "The Rise of Foreign Exchange Clubs," *Institutional Investor*, October 1980.

PAGE 141

On the mechanics of foreign currency trading, I benefited immeasurably from a series of conversations with the late Charles Coombs.

PAGE 143

On U.S. economic policy and the dollar in the early 1970s, see chap. 3 above.

PAGE 145

On Treasury's concern, see *Business Week*, January 9, 1978, p. 92.

PAGE 146

On the decline of the dollar, see *Business Week*, March 20, 1978. On Blumenthal, see *Business Week*, April 24, 1978, pp. 32–34.

PAGE 147

The Zijlstra quote is from Martin Mayer, *The Fate of the Dollar*, p. 192. Mayer's book draws interesting parallels between the Carter and Nixon years.

The Volcker quote is from a speech at Adelphi University, October 24, 1978; see also his "Political Economy of the Dollar," Federal Reserve Bank of New York *Quarterly Review*, Winter 1978–79.

Page 148

Bank foreign exchange profits are from annual reports; *Euromoney,* April 1979; and Hanley, *Multinational Banking,* various issues.

On Citibank, see *Euromoney,* April 1979 and August 1982.

Page 148

For the material on the Edwards case, I have relied primarily on two documents (and supporting documentation) from the enforcement division of the Securities and Exchange Commission. They are *In Re Citicorp,* written by SEC attorney Thomson von Stein, February 1981; and a memorandum to the commission written by von Stein, David P. Doherty and Robert Ryan, December 1981. I have also relied on the minutes of the commission's hearing on the Citibank case, held December 22, 1981. I am also grateful to David Edwards and his attorney, Jonathan Lubell, for background information. Citibank's Heinz Riehl refused to discuss the case with me. Wriston's office never responded to requests for an interview. At various times during the case, informative articles were written by Larry Kramer of the *Washington Post* and Jeff Gerth of the *New York Times.*

Page 156

The Fouraker quote is from the *Wall Street Journal,* November 27, 1978. The Costanzo quote, which according to the SEC he subsequently disclaimed responsibility for, is from a Citibank press release dated November 24, 1978.

The quote is from von Stein, the *Wall Street Journal,* September 14, 1982.

Page 159

For Wallich's and Leach's views, see *The Eurocurrency Market Control Act of 1979,* Hearings before the Subcommittee on International Financial Institutions, House of Representatives Committee on Banking, Housing and Urban Affairs, July 1979.

Page 160

The comptroller's letter was dated December 8, 1980, and was written by Billy C. Wood, deputy comptroller for multinational banking.

Page 163

The Taylor quote is from *Euromoney.*

The Group of 30 survey is from *Foreign Exchange Markets Under Floating Rates,* p. 37.

Figures on the dollar's decline are from Charles C. Coombs' speech to the National Committee for Monetary Reform, New Orleans, November 3, 1978; his speech to the International Financial Seminar, London, May 8, 1980; his speech to the annual *Institutional Investor* Conference, New York, April 25–27, 1980; and his speech to the Lombard Association, London, October 11, 1978.

For Treasury's attitude in mid-October, see the *Wall Street Journal,* October 20, 1978.

Figures on the dollar's decline in October are from W. Michael Blumenthal, testimony before the Joint Economic Committee, December 14, 1978.

Wall Street Journal quote is from November 6, 1978.

PAGE 164

On the November 1 dollar defense package, see the cluster of articles in the *Washington Post,* November 2, 1978; and the account in the *Wall Street Journal,* November 6, 1978.

6. THE GREATEST HIGH

PAGE 165

The Sinclair quote is from the *Wall Street Journal,* January 22, 1980. The Bunker Hunt quote is from an excellent series on the Hunt brothers' foray into the silver market by Ralph Soda of the Gannett News Service.

PAGE 166

London *Times* editorial, November 2, 1978.

On U.S. intervention in the foreign currency markets, see the Federal Reserve Bank of New York *Quarterly Review,* various issues; and the *Washington Post,* March 8, 1979.

PAGE 167

On the dollar's decline in 1979, see the *Wall Street Journal,* September 6, 1979.

The Greenspan quotes are from his testimony before the Joint Economic Committee, November 5, 1979.

PAGE 169

On gold prices, see *Newsweek,* October 1, 1979; *Business Week,* October 1, 1979; and *Business Week,* February 11, 1980. On silver prices, see *The Silver Crisis of 1980,* a report by the staff of the Securities and Exchange Commission, October 1982, pp. 3–8.

PAGE 170

The anecdote about "small groups of Arabs" is from the *New York Times,* October 4, 1979.

On the recycling process, see Chase Manhattan, *Arab Investors: Who They Are, What They Buy and Where* (New York, 1980), pp. 6–7.

Simon's arrangement with the Saudis is detailed in *Federal Response to OPEC Country Investments in the United States,* Part I—Overview, Hearings before the Subcommittee on Commerce, Consumer and Monetary Affairs, Committee on Government Operations, House of Representatives, September 22, 23, 1981, pp. 451–55.

On interest rates see the statistical appendix of Morgan Guaranty's *World Financial Markets*, various issues. According to the Treasury Department, the Middle Eastern oil exporters liquidated about $1 billion in Treasury bonds in 1979 and acquired only about $2 billion in Treasury bills. See *Federal Response to OPEC Country Investments in the United States*, p. 160. In the next 18 months, after interest rates rose, they acquired about $13 billion in Treasury bonds.

PAGE 171

The Keynes quotes are from *Essays in Persuasion*, pp. 182, 208. As polemics against the gold standard, these essays have no equals.

PAGE 172

On gold prices, see the sources listed for page 169 above.

PAGE 173

On Volcker, see John Dizard, "Is Volcker Tough Enough to Defend the Dollar?" *Institutional Investor*, October 1979.

On the demonetization of gold, see *Business Week*, October 1, 1979; and Martin Mayer, "The Message from the Gold Markets," *Fortune*, November 5, 1979.

PAGE 174

Teeters and Partee quotes from the *Wall Street Journal*, November 20, 1979.

The gold panic quote is from *Business Week*, October 1, 1979.

PAGE 175

The October 6 package is described in the Federal Reserve's press release, October 6, 1979, p. 1.

Figures on banks' borrowings and financing speculation are from the Federal Reserve's October 6 press release, pp. 3–5.

PAGE 176

The Jones quote is from hearings before the Joint Economic Committee, November 5, 1979.

The *Wall Street Journal*, October 8, 1979.

The Partee quote is from the *Wall Street Journal*, November 20, 1979.

On inflation and gold prices, see *Business Week*, February 11, 1980.

PAGE 177

On bank lending for gold and silver speculation, see pp. 290–93.

On the effectiveness of the Fed's reserve requirements, see chap. 7; see also Rimmer de Vries, testimony before the Congressional Joint Economic Committee, November 5, 1979.

On the Iranian freeze, see *Euromoney*, January 1980; and Anthony Sampson, *The Money Lenders*, chap. 17.

PAGE 178

On Arab involvement in the gold and silver markets, see Stephen Fay,

Beyond Greed (New York: Viking, 1982), chap. 5; and *Business Week,* February 11, 1980.

PAGE 179

The *Wall Street Journal* and Reuss quotes are from the *Wall Street Journal,* February 6, 1980.

PAGE 180

On bank lending and the Fed's credit controls, see Albert M. Wojnilower, "The Central Role of Credit Crunches"; on Eurodollar borrowings see the *Federal Reserve Bulletin,* April 1980, pp. 288–89; and April 1981, pp. 269, 273–75; see also the *Wall Street Journal,* March 13, 1980.

The Fed's announcement of credit controls was reprinted in the *Financial Times,* March 17, 1980.

For the decline in the U.S. economy in the second quarter of 1980, see the *Economic Report of the President,* 1981.

The soybean caper is from the series by Ralph Soda of the Gannett News Service.

PAGE 181

For background on the Hunts, see Stephen Fay, *Beyond Greed;* and Roy Rowan, "A Hunt Crony Tells All," *Fortune,* June 30, 1980.

On silver production and prices, see *Wolff's Guide to the London Metal Exchange* (London, 1979), p. 206.

Herbert Hunt quote is from *Silver Prices and the Adequacy of Federal Actions in the Marketplace,* Hearings before the Subcommittee on Commerce, Consumer and Monetary Affairs, House of Representatives Committee on Government Operations, April–May 1980.

PAGE 182

On the Hunts' silver purchases, see the *Washington Post,* April 18, 1980.

PAGE 185

For estimates of the Hunts' silver holdings, see the SEC, *The Silver Crisis of 1980;* Commodity Futures Trading Commission, *Report on Recent Developments in the Silver Futures Markets,* submitted to the Committee on Agriculture, Nutrition and Forestry, U.S. Senate, May 1980; Alan Trustman, "The Silver Scam: How the Hunts Were Outfoxed," *Atlantic Monthly,* October 1980; and Fay, *Beyond Greed.* The consensus: no one knows how much silver the Hunts owned.

On the Hunts and the banks, see Federal Reserve, "Interim Report on Financial Aspects of the Silver Market Situation," in *Silver Prices and the Adequacy of Federal Actions in the Marketplace.*

PAGE 187

The First Chicago episode is reported by Fay, *Beyond Greed,* chap. 11; I have also benefited from a conversation with former Comptroller John Heimann.

PAGE 188

The Stone quote is from his testimony in *Silver Prices and the Adequacy of Federal Actions in the Marketplace*, p. 11.

PAGE 189

The Volcker quote is from his testimony before the Rosenthal Committee, April 30, 1980.

PAGE 191

The Fay quote is from *Beyond Greed*, p. 223.

PAGE 192

The Volcker quote is from his testimony before the Rosenthal Committee, April 30, 1980.

The Hunt political contributions are from the *Wall Street Journal*, October 2, 1980; and Jack Anderson's column in the *Washington Post*, January 16, 1981.

PAGE 193

The Reuss comment is from a personal conversation with the author. Silver prices and inflation are from Stone's testimony before the Committee on Banking, Housing and Urban Affairs, U.S. Senate, May 29, 1980.

Bunker's comment is from *Fortune*, June 30, 1980, p. 55.

7. MR. WONDERFUL

PAGE 195

The Rockefeller quote is from "David's Connections," *Institutional Investor*, May 1981.

PAGE 196

The falling use of the U.S. dollar in international finance is reflected in the large number of nondollar financings in the Euromarket in 1979. As a result, according to Morgan Guaranty, Eurodollars as a percentage of all Eurocurrencies fell to an all-time low of 72 percent in 1979.

PAGE 197

The Mills quote is from *Foreign Exchange Market Trends*, February 18, 1982. No doubt, other factors, such as political instability in Europe and the U.S. stock market boom, have worked in the dollar's favor. Yet high real interest rates in dollar-denominated paper established the parameters within which the dollar now trades, even as interest rate differentials have narrowed. When the Fed eased monetary policy dramatically in the fall of 1982 in an attempt to head off a monetary crisis, interest rates came down and the dollar weakened against the yen and the mark.

PAGE 200

Statistics on the U.S. economy are from the *Economic Report of the President*, 1982; and the monthly releases of the Bureau of Labor Statistics.

Figures on bankruptcies are from Manufacturers Hanover Trust *Financial Digest*, July 12, 1982.

PAGE 201

International Currency Review quote is from "The Consequences of Permanently Higher U.S. Interest Rates," *International Currency Review*, October 1981.

The Volcker quote is from an interview with Andrew Tobias, in the *New York Times Magazine*, September 19, 1982.

PAGE 202

The Helmut Schmidt quote is from the *New York Times*, July 21, 1981.

On German monetary policy and the dollar, see Chase Manhattan, *International Finance*, September 15, 1980; June 7, 1982.

On the contraction in world trade, see the *Wall Street Journal*, March 30, 1982.

PAGE 203

The Minsky reference is from "Capitalist Financial Processes and the Instability of Capitalism," a paper delivered to the Association for Evolutionary Economics, December 29, 1979. This theme is central to Minsky's work, especially his *John Maynard Keynes* (New York, 1975).

On Arthur Burns, see the brilliant review of Burns' book *Reflections of an Economic Policymaker*, by Professor Leonard Rapping of the University of Massachusetts, in which he calls Burns a "closet inflationist." See *Challenge: The Magazine of Economic Affairs*, November–December 1979; see also Aliber, *The International Money Game*.

PAGE 204

The Wojnilower quote is from "The Central Role of Credit Crunches."

On destabilizing speculation, Professor Nicholas Kaldor adequately disposed of the traditional notion that there can be no such thing as destabilizing speculation, the view that Milton Friedman and other monetarists hold to this day. See his "Speculation and Economic Stability," in *Essays on Economic Stability and Growth* (London: Duckworth 1960), especially pp. 17–19.

PAGE 205

The Ramond quote is from the *Wall Street Journal*, December 29, 1981.

On the so-called "overshooting," which is nothing more than excessive swings in currency values caused by bandwagon trading, see Fred Bergsten, "The Coming Crisis in International Money and Trade," a paper delivered to a conference on "The Euromarkets in 1982," sponsored by the *Financial Times*, London, February 9, 1982. In this paper he concludes that "the repeated overshooting of major exchange rates raises fundamental questions about the stability of the existing international monetary regime." Apparently, it turns out, free-floating is not the "best international monetary system at the present stage of world economic history," which Bergsten asserted in 1978. See chap. 3 above.

PAGE 206

To the best of my recollection, this point about U.S. banks borrowing from their overseas branches was first made by former Federal Reserve Board Governor Andrew Brimmer. Figures on this phenomenon since 1979 are available from the Fed's October 6 press release announcing the new monetary control measures and the *Federal Reserve Bulletin*, April 1980, 1981 and 1982. Federal Reserve economists have confirmed this point on an off-the-record basis. The Treasury Department has also acknowledged that the large and growing problem of the statistical discrepancy in the balance of payments results from Euromarket transactions: "It has generally been concluded by those who have studied the problem that the rapid unrecorded fluctuations in capital flows, often to and from the Euromarkets, lie at the heart of the problem." See the testimony of Assistant Secretary Marc Leland before the Rosenthal Committee, September 23, 1981, annex.

PAGE 207

For an unabashed demolition of the Fed's attempts to control lending by large multinational banks, see Rimmer de Vries' testimony before the Joint Economic Committee, November 5, 1979.

The Black quote is from *Business Week,* March 10, 1980.

The Wojnilower quote is from "The Central Role of Credit Crunches."

The Fed's request was contained in the October 6 press release.

PAGE 208

For a discussion of how the banks ignored the Fed, see *Silver Prices and the Adequacy of Federal Actions in the Marketplace;* and Fay, *Beyond Greed,* chap. 11.

Figures on borrowing and lending are from the *Federal Reserve Bulletin,* April 1981, pp. 273–75; and Salomon Brothers, *Prospects for Financial Markets,* 1982, p. 24. The Salomon figures represent net increases in amounts outstanding of mortgage debt, bank term loans, short-term loans and sales of open market paper.

PAGE 209

The Nichols quote is from his testimony before the Joint Economic Committee, November 5, 1979.

The Wallich quote is from a speech to the *Institutional Investor* Bond Conference, November 1979.

The figures on 1981 merger borrowing are from Morgan Guaranty, *World Financial Markets,* various issues. The ritual was repeated in the summer of 1982 with billions in borrowing to finance the Bendix–Martin Marietta–United Technologies takeover battle.

PAGE 210
The Kaufman reference is from his testimony before the House Budget Committee, March 16, 1982.
Salomon Brothers' figures are from *1982 Prospects for Financial Markets.*
PAGE 211
On the prime rate, see Y. S. Park, "Devaluation of the U.S. Prime Rate," *The Banker*, May 1982.
Figures on the S&Ls are from Salomon Brothers, *1982 Prospects for Financial Markets;* and the *Wall Street Journal*, April 6, 1982.
PAGE 213
The Wojnilower quote is from "The Central Role of Credit Crunches," p. 303.

8. THE PAPER ECONOMY

PAGE 214
The Kaufman quote is from *U.S. News & World Report*, April 12, 1982.
PAGE 216
The misery index is calculated from the *Economic Report of the President*, 1982, pp. 269, 295, though the idea for the chart comes from Sidney Weintraub, *Our Stagflation Malaise* (Westport, Conn.: Quorum Books, 1981).
PAGE 217
Walter Bagehot, *Lombard Street* (London, 1873), p. 2.
The Wriston quote is from the *New York Times*, July 7, 1982.
PAGE 218
The Kaufman figures are from his testimony before the House Budget Committee, March 16, 1982. For an early statement of this view, see Paul M. Sweezy and Harry Magdoff, "Keynesian Chickens Come Home to Roost," in *The End of Prosperity* (New York: Monthly Review Press, 1979).
PAGE 219
On Continental Illinois, see the *Wall Street Journal*, June 1, 1982; and the *New York Times*, August 2, 1982.
PAGE 220
On Penn Square and Bill Patterson, see *Fortune*, August 23, 1982.
PAGE 221
On Chase, Penn Square and Drysdale, see the *New York Times*, July 25, 1982; and *The Banker*, July 1982.
PAGE 222
The Kaufman reference is from testimony before the House Budget Committee, March 16, 1982.

PAGE 223

On banks' loan losses, see the *Morgan Guaranty Survey*, June 1982.

PAGE 224

For the securities analyst quote, see the *Wall Street Journal*, July 30, 1982.

On capital asset ratios in the 1920s and 1930s, see Charles R. Whittlesey, Arthur S. Freedman, Edward S. Herman, *Money and Banking: Analysis and Policy* (New York: Macmillan, 1963), pp. 119, 522.

PAGE 225

On bought money, see Hanley, *Multinational Banking: Semi-Annual Statistics*, June 1982.

Kindleberger's views on financial crises are from his *Manias, Panics and Crashes*, especially chap. 11. This book includes a restatement of Kindleberger's controversial view that the Great Depression was caused by the collapse of the international trading and money systems. In light of this, his criticisms of floating exchange rates and the dangers of excessive foreign currency speculation are particularly significant.

Roll quote is from his "Commentary" on the 1978 Per Jacobsen Lecture at the IMF Annual Meetings.

PAGE 226

The Minsky references are from "Capitalist Financial Processes and the Instability of Capitalism."

PAGE 228

On Mitterrand, see *Euromoney*, December 1981, p. 11.

PAGE 229

The Wojnilower speech was reported in the *Wall Street Journal*, September 22, 1982.

PAGE 230

The Richardson quote is from Citibank, *Global Financial Intermediation*, p. 48.

The Guttentag and Herring quote is from *Financial Distress and International Banking*.

PAGE 231

The Geoffrey Bell quote is from *Business Week*, August 16, 1982; I have also benefited from a conversation with Mr. Bell on this point.

The *Economist* quote is from March 20, 1982.

PAGE 233

The Concordat was reprinted in *Euromoney*, October 1982. For a candid statement of its limitations, see *The Banker*, August 1982, pp. 8–9.

PAGE 234

On the impact of Ambrosiano, see "Can the Cooke Committee Stand the Heat?" *Euromoney*, October 1982.

On the entrance of new banks into the Euromarket, see the Group of 30, *Risks in International Bank Lending* (New York: Group of 30, 1982).

PAGE 235

In a sense, some Eurobanking moved to New York with the establishment of International Banking Facilities in 1981. Essentially, IBFs allow banks to do from New York the business that used to be done offshore free of regulation. Of course the distinction is a bit silly, since business from Nassau and the Cayman islands was always done in New York and London anyway!

PAGE 236

The Wriston quote is from *Euromoney*, October 1981, p. 54.

PAGE 237

For a good summary of deregulation to date, see the 1981 *Annual Report* of the Federal Reserve Bank of Minneapolis.

PAGE 238

Foreign exchange profits are from Hanley, *Multinational Banking,* various issues.

PAGE 239

The Group of 30 calculates that on average 66 new banks per year are entering the Eurocurrency loan business.

PAGE 240

The Sandberg quote is from *Euromoney*, October 1981, p. 58.

On foreign banks in the United States, see the Federal Reserve Bank of New York *Quarterly Review*, Summer 1982, p. 48.

PAGE 241

The Butcher quote is from *Euromoney*, October 1981, p. 71.

PAGE 242

The Heilbroner quote is from the *New York Times Magazine*, August 15, 1982.

PAGE 243

The Wojnilower quote is from "The Central Role of Credit Crunches."

INDEX

Printed in the United States
By Bookmasters